Science and Society
in
Prehistoric Britain

Science and Society
in
Prehistoric Britain

Euan W. MacKie
BA, PhD, FSA

Schau', Mime, du Schmied:
so schneidet Siegfrieds Schwert!

(Watch, Mime, you smith,
how Siegfried's sword can cut!)

RICHARD WAGNER, Siegfried, I, iii

ST. MARTIN'S PRESS
NEW YORK

For Professor Alexander Thom
per ardua ad astra

All rights reserved. For information, write:
St. Martin's Press, Inc., 175 Fifth Avenue, New York, N.Y. 10010

Printed in Great Britain

Library of Congress Catalog Card Number: 76–48755

First published in the United States of America in 1977

Contents

Illustrations

PLATES

(between pages 116 and 117)

FIGURES

Tables

Acknowledgements

I am grateful to Mr Nicholas H. Hawley for preparing figs 3-5, 7, 9, 10, 15-25, 27, 30, 31 and 33 and to Mrs B. Mackenzie for typing the manuscript. I thank Mr J. S. Bibby, of the Macaulay Institute for Soil Research, Aberdeen, for allowing me to reproduce his diagram as fig 15. The Director General of the Ordnance Survey kindly gave permission for the new 6 inch map to be used as a basis for fig 27.

The following people read through the manuscript and made many helpful comments and suggestions: Mr H. A. W. Burl, Dr G. I. Crawford, Mr A. Morrison, Dr A. E. Roy and Professor A. Thom. I am most grateful to them all, particularly to Mr Burl and Mr Morrison for their archaeological opinions and to the others for advice on the mathematical and astronomical sections. I also had the benefit of useful discussions on various aspects of the work with Dr A. S. Thom and Dr J. Williamson, the latter providing me with some very useful leads on the subject of historical metrology. None of these people is of course responsible for any of the more controversial interpretations to be found in the second half of the book, nor for my views on megalithic astronomy, geometry and metrology in the first half. Drs D. V. Clarke and J. N. G. Ritchie very kindly told me about the radiocarbon dates of samples from their own excavations in Orkney in advance of publication and allowed me to make use of them. I should probably also acknowledge the unknowing help of the Apollo space programme of the USA out of which, I understand, came the capacity to make cheap electronic calculators. It is doubtful if some of the mathematical forays in Part One, simple though they really are, would have been attempted without the help of one of these to lighten the work and give confidence to an essentially innumerate mind.

A Note on Measurements

Throughout this book measurements of length are given in yards, feet and inches, and sometimes in feet and tenths of feet. There were two main reasons for the decision to do this, taken in spite of the change to the metric system currently under way in Britain. The first is that, since nearly all the pioneering work on the prehistoric metrology of Britain was done in Imperial units, it seemed appropriate to continue this tradition, at least for the time being. The second stems from the realisation that many non-metric modern units of linear measurement seem likely to be directly descended from very ancient ones and that it therefore did not seem right to translate these into Napoleon's arbitrary system. In a few cases such as that of the brochs, where the measurements in the field were made in metric units, these are also given in brackets. The following conversion factors may be used if necessary: to convert yards to metres, $\times$ 0.9144; feet to metres, $\times$ 0.3048; inches to centimetres, $\times$ 2.5400.

1

New Aspects of Prehistoric Britain

INTRODUCTION

During the past nine years three changes of fundamental importance have taken place in the factual foundations which support the elaborate theoretical picture of prehistoric British society in the latter part of the Neolithic period and in the Early Bronze Age which archaeologists have built up over the years. The first of these changes, which make much of this traditional picture obsolete, has been discussed quite frequently in the past few years and involves the correction backwards of radiocarbon (C-14) dates by the tree-ring calibration. This process has reached a stage of refinement at which it is possible with considerable confidence to 'translate' the carbon dates obtained for archaeological material into calendar years and thus to relate chronologically sites and events in prehistoric Britain more reliably not only to each other but also to the histories of the literate Bronze Age civilisations of the Mediterranean and the Near East. One of the most important effects of this recalibration of radiocarbon dates has concerned some famous and elaborate monuments, for example Stonehenge and Silbury Hill. These had hitherto been thought of as Bronze Age in date and explained as the creations of wealthy chiefs grown rich on the metal trade, but they are now known to belong to the middle and end of the Neolithic period and to the very beginning of the metal age. They are thus now too old for the social and economic explanations originally devised for them. The old theories have to be abandoned, but in my view no picture of Late Neolithic Britain has yet been constructed into which either the incredibly sophisticated temple of the last phase of Stonehenge, or its astronomically sophisticated first stage, or the enormous mound of Silbury Hill, will easily fit. Not only have the sites been pushed backwards in time, but in the process they have lost the *raison d'être* given to them.

The second important addition to that basic archaeological evidence which forms the foundations of the study of Neolithic and Bronze Age Britain has been due to the work of Professor Alexander Thom, known in mathematical and astronomical journals since the early 1950s but available in book form only since 1967. This work has provided a mass of new evidence — reviewed in the first half of this book — which in my opinion leads inescapably to the conclusion that some very advanced astronomical and geometrical knowledge had been accumulated in Britain and Brittany well before the beginning of the Bronze Age, to such an extent that it is hard to believe that there was not at that time a learned and skilled professional order of wise men — perhaps already very old — whose members were able to pursue their studies full time while supported by the rural population, and could command the labour required to erect the hundreds of henge monuments, stone circles and standing stones, some of which were their 'observatories'. Here again the implications of these discoveries have not been integrated into general archaeological theory, although clearly Thom's views, even if only partly correct, must completely alter our picture of the society of the time.

The third important addition to our knowledge of Late Neolithic Britain has been due to the remarkable series of excavations carried out from 1967 to 1971 by Geoffrey Wainwright on the giant henge sites of southern England — Durrington Walls, Mount Pleasant and Marden. This work, by showing that the large henges contained massive wooden roofed buildings accompanied by abundant signs of habitation, has again completely changed our ideas of what these henge sites were for. The smaller henges which had been explored earlier had seemed to be purely 'ritual' sites — temples perhaps — and they lacked any evidence of a domestic function. Now some of the largest seem to have been specially demarcated living areas, and the implications of these discoveries (which are discussed at length in chapter 7) are potentially profound and need to be integrated into our picture of Late Neolithic British society. Hitherto, it seems to me, they have not been so integrated in any satisfactory or comprehensive way.

It is my belief that these revolutions in our knowledge of British prehistory are not random or separate but are fundamentally linked. The basic theme of this book is that these three areas of profound new discoveries — each difficult to assimilate in isolation — will, when combined, explain each other very well and allow us to construct a new and detailed social interpretation of the period. The existence of the powerful and skilled learned order clearly implied by Thom's discoveries provides the explanation for the surprisingly early appearance of the great temple-observatories at Stonehenge, probably for the enormous mound of Silbury Hill, and for the many henge sites, large and small. It may even provide an explanation for the whole vexed problem of the spread and development of the chambered tombs of an earlier epoch. The drastic back-dating of some of the well-known sites hitherto thought to have been built in the great period of the Early Bronze Age — during the time of the Wessex culture in the middle of the second millennium BC — conversely provides that learned order with impressive temples, sanctuaries and observatories, while the discovery of the large, inhabited henge sites gives it the necessary residential and training centres. Previously there had been no trace of such ceremonial centres among the standing stone sites that Thom originally studied and from which the new views stem.

As a result of all this it is now possible, as I hope to show, to construct a well-rounded picture of the hierarchical, stratified society of Late Neolithic

Britain, whose upper echelons lived in special ceremonial centres, evolved a sophisticated system of observational astronomy and field geometry (the remains of the practical applications of which are everywhere to be seen in the highland zone), and commanded the manpower, resources and technical skill to erect some of the largest earthworks in Europe as well as a stone temple whose architectural sophistication is unmatched outside the Bronze Age urban civilisations of the Near East. The evidence for the existence of this powerful and skilled learned order is most plain in Late Neolithic times, but if its existence then is regarded as likely, this conclusion must have a profound effect on our understanding of many other buildings and remains of prehistoric Britain and Europe. The whole problem of the origin and purpose of the Early Neolithic chambered tombs so often aired in the past[1] could be viewed in an entirely different way[2] as also could the vexed question of where the 'megalith builders' came from. There is an increasing tendency now to explain prehistoric European cultural developments in terms of strictly local evolution[3] and to reject the idea of influence from the more advanced city-dwelling societies of the Mediterranean and the Near East, but the assumptions inherent in this non-diffusionist approach have to be looked at very carefully in the light of the interpretations of Late Neolithic British society that will be pursued here.

Motives for writing this book

Since this work represents in effect a singlehanded attempt to stop dead in its tracks one of the massive juggernauts of archaeological theory — built and propelled by many hands, past and present — and to start it moving again in quite a new direction, some words of explanation seem due about the reasons for embarking on this potentially hazardous enterprise. The first reason for attempting the task has already been stated: it is that I believe the new theories to be advocated here integrate very satisfactorily three important new sets of archaeological discoveries about Late Neolithic Britain and are therefore superior to existing theories which do not, in my view, relate them adequately if at all. In particular, the work of Thom has suggested a hitherto unimagined degree of intellectual and technical skill in the Britain of 4,000 years ago, and yet these ideas — controversial and stimulating as they are — have not really been absorbed by the archaeological profession. Indeed it sometimes seems that the old, pre-Thom ideas are being used as reasons for discounting the new evidence.[4] This state of affairs cannot be right, and it is clearly necessary to analyse the new material carefully and, if it then proves necessary, to evolve new explanations which will incorporate *all* the archaeological evidence and not just the familiar part of it. This is the basic aim of this work.

The second reason for this book is that I have the impression that the value and importance to the advancement of archaeology (and indeed to all scientific disciplines) of hypotheses and explanations is not always appreciated as much as it should be. We are accustomed to being warned about jumping to conclusions on inadequate evidence — and rightly so — but judging from results, the belief seems to be common that collecting and classifying the evidence is often enough. Yet in true science and scholarship the controlled framing of hypotheses and theories to explain the data and to test predictions made by these explanations, and *simultaneously to suggest fresh avenues for research*, is of crucial importance. Yet on the whole, integrating social explanations are but rarely attempted for the archaeological evidence of the prehistoric period, though happily the Iron Age is now an exception.[5] Perhaps the decades-long, patient and detailed study of the dating and development of the Early Neolithic chambered cairns — almost the life work of many people — best typifies what must be regarded as the almost deliberate avoidance of basic social theory in British archaeology. The result is that the old explanations tend almost to acquire a life of their own, and for lack of challengers, to last for far too long.

For many years until quite recently the basic outlines of British prehistory had indeed been accepted as settled. The Mesolithic, Neolithic, Bronze and Iron periods succeeded each other in that order. The chambered cairns and long barrows were the collective sepulchres of the earliest Neolithic farmers, and the typological development of the former and the nature of the associated material cultures is becoming ever better understood even if the actual reason for their existence is nothing like as obvious. The ceremonial sites known as henge monuments belong to the later part of the Neolithic period and should be linked in some way with the much more numerous stone circles of the highland zone. The Bronze Age quite clearly began with the invasion of the Beaker people, though there is some doubt about exactly how this influx of foreigners took place and in what numbers. The newcomers introduced the earliest metal tools as well as the new burial rite of single crouched inhumation, usually under a round barrow or cairn. However, this funerary rite had largely died out again by the Middle Bronze Age and was replaced by the universal practice of cremation, the bones being placed in a cinerary urn usually in an unmarked grave. During the Bronze Age the art of metal-working was imported to Britain and steadily improved; the main forms of weapons and tools evolved into more efficient forms so that each phase is defined by distinct artefact types. Finally, in the early part of the first millennium BC, came the Late Bronze and Iron Ages with their hill-forts, almost complete absence of traceable burials, gradual spread of iron-working, large round farmhouses and Celtic-speaking tribes — a period which lasted until the advent of urban civilisation with the Roman conquest from AD 43 onwards.

In general the kind of society which has been envisaged for these three 'ages' of British prehistory was barbarian and tribal (we can exclude for present purposes the earliest, Mesolithic period when there seem to have been only scattered bands of hunters and food gatherers). Occasionally there are suggestions of high kings and other forms of powerful central authority — people who were capable of organising mighty engineering works like Avebury, Stonehenge II and III and Silbury Hill — and there are frequent strong hints of powerful chieftains in the Early Bronze Age in the rich barrows of that period clustered thickly around Stonehenge. By and large, however, the population is thought to have followed simple agricultural and stock-breeding pursuits, though the chiefs certainly enriched themselves by trade in the Bronze Age. Suggestions that there were skilled classes of professional specialists — astronomers, 'scientists' and so on — have usually been received with some scepticism. The last major attempts at explaining what sort of prehistoric societies produced the various archaeological cultures of England and Scotland were probably those of V. G. Childe in the 1930s and 1940s,[6] and even if no startling new evidence was available, it might well be argued that it is high time that a fresh attempt was made and some new explanations put forward for consideration. Indeed there have recently been several notable attempts by Colin Renfrew to re-think the basic assumptions underlying the accepted framework of British and European prehistory by holding that the recalibration of radiocarbon dates through the tree-ring chronologies requires that the old diffusionist explanations be abandoned.[7]

The third reason for writing this book really follows from the last and stems from my own belief that all fields of science and scholarship are never in a really healthy state unless argument and debate are constantly going on over the evidence being amassed. Indeed I would go so far as to say that the existence of at least two alternative explanations for a given set of data is essential if the true scientific spirit of enquiry is to flourish. Moreover, this situation should obtain at all levels in the discipline, not only during the collection of new material but also, if possible, later on when the material is well known and has been absorbed into the general body of knowledge. If only one view is held, at whatever level, the options open to specialists in that field, and perhaps more important, to the research students they guide and train, become progressively narrower. Such a situation is likely to become one in which ever smaller and finer bricks are being added to the existing theoretical edifice and the questioning of the fundamental assumptions forming its foundations becomes progressively more difficult until it finally ceases altogether. This can happen, though a moment's thought should reveal just how insecure some of these foundations are. For research in such a situation the law of diminishing returns can operate and the discipline be in danger of becoming authoritarian and dogmatic, at least over its fundamental assumptions. Because the foundations and basic theories remain unquestioned, success may go mainly to those who accept the *status quo* and will work to support it.

The appearance of a rival theory should completely change this situation, at whatever level it is operating. The alternative explanations should act as incentives to both supporters and opponents for the collecting of fresh evidence and the reassessment of old material to determine which explanation fits the facts best. Moreover, for most people this situation is the only one which provides the real stimulus for the critical reappraisal of past assumptions, for the ruthless separation of fact and theory (even in territory which has become hallowed by the eminence of its defenders) which is the hallmark of the true scientist. Such clashes between alternative explanations occur as a matter of course in the lower levels of a discipline, among the research workers and over new discoveries, but fundamental assumptions and basic theories are rarely questioned even though they are bound to be furthest removed from the actual facts. Thus opportunities for offering good alternative basic theories are correspondingly rare and must usually await an important new discovery or insight. Colin Renfrew believes that the recalibration of C-14 dates has provided one such opportunity, and it is my belief that the work of Professor A. Thom has presented British prehistorians with another; and I propose to take advantage of it.

Yet another reason for this foray into basic archaeological theory may well be that the present climate of British archaeology, contrary to what might be deduced from the previous paragraph, is quite favourable to those who wish to reassess and re-think both the evidence and the methodology used by the profession. We have recently had many articles and a few books which advocate the 'new archaeology', the abandonment of the historical approach, the firm embracing of the new mathematical and scientific techniques of study and analysis, and which question many long-held and cherished assumptions. This might therefore be the right time for a work that stems from a detailed theory based on the most advanced mathematical analyses. Yet at the same time there are dangers in some present trends, of a flight from reality into a deliberately myopic abandonment of the study of the past in terms of evolving human individuals and groups and societies. There seems to be a tendency to want to treat archaeological evidence as a self-contained entity, a mass of data which can be arranged into many patterns and combinations that are somehow supposed spontaneously to generate explanations. In the immortal phrase: 'The entities, processes, aims, procedures and concepts of archaeology have a validity of their own in reference to the archaeological frame and despite their generation by — and partial correlation with — former social and historic entities.'[8] Paradoxically, the Thom theories, founded on astronomy, spherical trigonometry and very precise surveying, illustrate well the limitations of this approach. (In fairness one must note that the same authority later expressed quite a different view. 'The aim of any archaeological classification must always be to define sensible assemblages of traits that will, or should, reflect the pattern of ancient social traditions or groupings.'[9] No one could have anything but praise for these sentiments.)

One final reason for this book — which some might believe the best — is that there have been many works from the wilder fringes of science and scholarship on the general theme that one might describe as 'the wonderful secret knowledge that our ancestors possessed and that we have lost', a version perhaps of the old ideas of the vanished Golden Age and the Fall (from the garden of Eden). Such topics run the whole gamut from Stone Age computers through leys and mysterious power lines across the countryside to Atlantis and even to contact with visitors from other worlds. Unfortunately the idea of sophisticated ancient astronomical practices is much favoured by the devotees of these cults and this has prejudiced many sensible people against reputable work in the field. It may also be that the more uninhibited speculations of astronomers have contributed to this reluctance.[10] The only remedy for such a situation is to take the bull by the horns and to write a bold, yet hopefully sober, assessment of the significance of these new discoveries so that there is something else to read apart from undisciplined works from the unscholarly fringe.

THE NATURE OF ARCHAEOLOGICAL EVIDENCE

It is important to be clear at the outset about the nature of archaeological evidence since this determines all aspects of the archaeologist's discipline, and it is its nature which dictates what the discipline itself must be and sets limits to what it can do. This evidence consists of the broken, fragmentary and often random pieces of the material culture — weapons, tools and constructions of all kinds — and what concrete traces of other activities of vanished human societies have survived. As far as the prehistory of temperate Europe is concerned, evidence from written records is for all practical purposes nonexistent before the Roman conquests even though literate societies existed contemporaneously in the Mediterranean and Near East. Archaeological evidence, like that of the other historical sciences (palaeontology, historical geology, palaeobotany et al), is distinct in one crucially important way. Most other scientific evidence is self-sufficient; in other words the process of collecting, classifying and analysing the data leads directly on to the formulation of explanations and hypotheses which in turn suggest fresh avenues of research and experiments to test their reliability. In a sense the known evidence of the natural sciences is a slowly enlarging fragment of a complete picture which one knows is there, and which, one may assume, will ultimately be revealed.

It is quite otherwise with archaeological evidence. The discovery, collection, classification and analysis of data proceed similarly of course (and it is over the *methods* of best performing these tasks that much of the current debate among the 'new archaeologists' and between them and the others is in fact about) but at this point the process stops. Archaeological data by itself is totally meaningless, and by itself tells us very little. A moment's thought will show that all explanations of what it means in terms of its human originators must come from elsewhere, and not from the facts themselves. Almost without exception, they are derived *by drawing analogies* with functioning living or historically recorded societies; they cannot be generated by the material itself. This is because, as far as the material remains of past human actions (except writing) are concerned, the vital and complex processes of social interaction between individuals and groups which led to their creation have vanished and are forever irrecoverable. These processes were of course the thoughts and actions of men and women now dead, and who (at least in the places and period this book is concerned with) left no written records of their motives.

One or two simple examples should make the truth of this statement apparent. In the case of the bronze objects known as axes we can directly determine from our knowledge of metallurgy and our analyses of the metal implements that they are made of an amalgam of copper and tin and that both metals must have been deliberately melted before they were blended together. We can also directly conclude that the molten bronze was poured into a mould of some kind to have achieved its present shape, and can discover how by experiment. These deductions lead on to a few others, e.g. that because of the rarity of deposits of tin ores a fairly complex organisation must have existed to transport the raw materials or the actual objects to the places of their use. Similarly we might fairly conclude that the use of bronze objects must have conferred considerable advantages on their owners to justify all the effort involved in getting them. Studies of all the various types of comparable bronze tools and their geographical distribution will fill out these deductions considerably, but that is more or less the limit of what can be directly inferred from prehistoric archaeological evidence: the processes of manufacture will be well understood, some knowledge about the use will be gained from microscopic studies of the working ends, and direct evidence of the transport of metal over large distances will be available.

However this is definitely the limit of direct inference. In the absence of written records the objects themselves can tell us nothing of their makers or why they were made, or of who used them and for what purpose. To supply the necessarily tentative answers to questions concerning whether an axe was made by a man or a woman, by a full-time smith or a farmer or herdsman, whether it was used as a battle axe, a wood-working tool or just for display, or whether it was very expensive or cheap — and then go on to make more general inferences about the nature of the society concerned from this and allied evidence — we have to employ a totally different method of reasoning. We decide on the likeliest explanations, or answers to these questions, by drawing *analogies* with what appear to be comparable modern or historically recorded societies and institutions and by using our own knowledge of human behaviour. Such answers will depend essentially on what the archaeologists concerned think was *likely* to have happened, and qualitatively are totally different from the earlier answers which were based on direct inferences from hard evidence. Broadly speaking, the simplest analogies are to be favoured in these interpretations. For example, there is clearly no point in suggesting a more complex function for a chambered mound containing human skeletons than that of a tomb unless there are good reasons to do so.

This gap between direct inference on the one hand and explanation of the data in social terms by analogy on the other becomes even more striking when we consider actual excavated sites — places and structures which prehistoric man used for some purposes and on which a variety of complex debris and traces remains. Here the hard evidence consists *solely* of the structures, features and strata uncovered, of the way these are related to one another horizontally and vertically, and of the objects and specimens found physically associated with these features. After one has directly observed what is present, and what things are associated with what features, one has immediately to resort to analogy to explain the phenomena. When faced with a large mound of stone containing drystone or megalithic chambers in which are deposits of human bones, pottery and so on, we call it a Neolithic 'chambered tomb' because it looks like a tomb to us on the basis of what we know of modern and recorded burial practices. But in fact we do not and cannot *know* that this ancient structure really was built and used as a family tomb in our sense of the word — and was not primarily a temple, or a place of sacrifice, or a war memorial — because the builders and users cannot tell us what it was for. We call the series of massive earthen banks and ditches often found encircling the summits of hills 'hill-forts' because they look like forts to us in the light of our own knowledge of such things, but we are in fact making an assumption by drawing analogies with similar sites of known function. We cannot know for certain that Iron Age people used them in this way, except in a very few cases such as when Julius Caesar describes an attack on an identifiable site.[11] It is very important for the reader to keep in mind these strict limits on what we can really *know* about prehistoric peoples, as opposed to what we can intelligently estimate about them, limits which are firmly imposed by the nature of the evidence. Familiar explanations of sites are challenged many times in this book and new ones suggested, and it is essential to judge the new theories first by their simplicity and secondly by their capacity to explain as much as possible of the available *evidence:* they should not necessarily be judged by how they compare with currently accepted *interpretations.*

This unbridgeable gulf between deductions from direct observation and those from analogy perhaps constitutes the primary difference between the *historical sciences* such as prehistoric archaeology and the *natural sciences* all of whose explanations are, or should be, based on direct observation. The reality of this gulf is perhaps not always appreciated by archaeologists, particularly by those who specialise in prehistoric times and have no choice but to make the most of the non-written evidence they have. It is often assumed that the problem of what can fairly be deduced from evidence is simply one of ever-increasing uncertainty in the hypotheses as they become further removed from the facts. For example Hawkes[12] maintained that there were four main categories of human life in prehistoric times which are increasingly remote from archaeological evidence: they comprise (1) techniques and technology, (2) economy, (3) social and political institutions, and (4) ritual and ideology. However the gulf referred to earlier falls between groups (2) and (3) and theories about the latter are framed on a totally different basis from those about the former. The importance of recognising this gulf in deductive methods, and the narrow limits of what can be *directly* inferred from the hard evidence, becomes very great in situations like that which has produced this book (and also that of Renfew, for example), i.e. when fundamental established theory is challenged and radically different explanations are offered. At such times we are absolutely obliged to recognise just what a small proportion of our picture of the past is solidly based on fact and what a very large one is based on analogy and thus open to complete revision even without the appearance of really important fresh facts.

This book raises questions about the use of the henge monuments — whether they were the sites of barbarian rituals concerned with economic needs or the ceremonial centres of skilled learned orders — and about the nature of British Neolithic and Early Bronze Age society — whether it was predominantly homogeneous, segmented and rural or rather a complex, highly stratified hierarchical organisation with an advanced political structure and many specialised groups, almost a proto-urban society in fact. All answers to such questions will inevitably depend on the analogies a particular writer thinks are most plausible, but in the case of this work they will take account of both the standard archaeological evidence and the new material described in the following chapters. Ultimately, of course, any such answers given must depend on the solid substratum of archaeological facts, and in spite of the narrow limits to what can be directly deduced from this, these hard facts must set broad limits on the kinds of social organisations that can be superimposed on them. Occasionally too, fresh and hitherto unsuspected direct deductions can be made about well-known sites simply by considering a different social analogy and comparing the implications of this with the evidence. Sites like Durrington Walls and Skara Brae will be treated in this way.

Archaeological procedures

In the light of the remarks just made we may now briefly review the nature and scope of archaeological discovery and research — illustrated diagrammatically as a stepped pyramid in fig. 1. The activities are grouped there into two distinct categories, first those in which inferences and deductions are made *directly* from the evidence, and secondly (as the detached summit of the pyramid) those in which they cannot be so directly derived and depend primarily on *analogy*. In the base of the pyramid two levels of activity are distinguished, the upper one a little further removed from the hard facts being recovered in the lower one. This part of the scheme is split into vertical columns to represent the three main classes of archaeological activity, each of which ascends into the upper level. As already explained there is a natural division based on methodology between these two spheres of activity and, as we shall see, much of the modern argument about the so-called 'new' archaeology and the older varieties could be said to revolve round the question of whether part or all of the second, upper sphere is a legitimate part of archaeological activity at all or whether it is only 'counterfeit history' and therefore valueless.

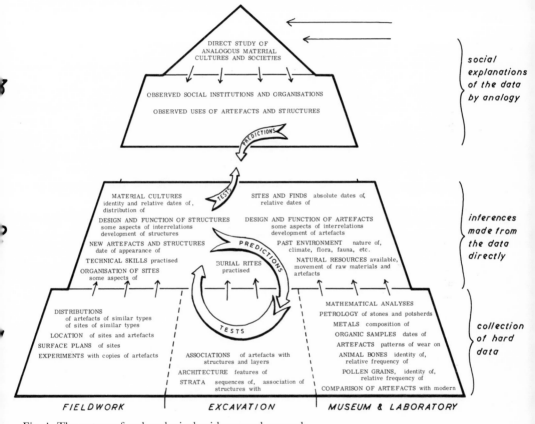

Fig. 1. The nature of archaeological evidence and research

On the primary level of direct inference are the three kinds of activities that collect the hard facts of archaeology: surface fieldwork of all kinds, excavation of ancient sites, and the detailed study of artefacts and related material in the museum and laboratory. Surface fieldwork provides us with an idea of the distribution of sites of certain kinds and establishes the outlines of the geographical extent of potential archaeological cultures. The sophisticated development of surface fieldwork is relatively recent and received a tremendous boost first from aerial photography, later from various electrical methods of below-ground surveying, and most recently from photogrammetric planning of sites from stereoscopic pairs of aerial photographs. In some areas, such as that of the study of hill-forts, surface fieldwork is the only practical method of getting a large amount of knowledge at a reasonably rapid rate, since the sites are numerous and their excavation time-consuming and expensive. In all studies of ancient sites and structures fieldwork is the essential counterpart of the excavation of selected sites, providing for example the only complete way of discovering the relations between these sites and the terrain in which they are found. Occasionally it is possible to get information about the relative dating of sites of different kinds from surface exploration, but excavation is the only decisive way of doing this and must be the essential second stage in a planned programme of archaeological research.

Excavation consists of the careful dissection of the deposits on an archaeological site with the aim (a) of recovering as many artefacts and other evidence of human activity as the skills and techniques available permit, (b) of recovering the layout and organisation of the ancient site, and (c) of reconstructing its history by interpreting the meaning of the superimposed layers or strata which are linked with the ancient structures. Excavation gives the essential knowledge in depth about the nature of prehistoric material cultures and of individual, once living, communities and their evolution.

From excavation detailed knowledge about the technology, economy, domestic and funerary habits of a vanished people is obtained. The reconstruction of actual events on individual sites, if found to be repeated in a sufficient number, will allow us to suggest that certain general processes in the communities concerned were taking place. Hints about vanished beliefs and rituals are obtained from the excavation of burials and other apparently non-functional sites, but here, as with the other practices mentioned above, the amount which is directly deducible becomes smaller and many of the explanations will be derived by analogy and from what the archaeologist concerned thinks, from his own experience and knowledge, is a probable social framework to fit onto his data. We are moving imperceptibly in practice — but suddenly in reality — up into the second major sphere of archaeological work, that of explaining the mass of heterogeneous data and of trying to reconstruct, however tenuously, the vanished societies and individuals which produced it. The list of specialised techniques for recovering detailed evidence from excavations and artefacts is a long one and is well described in several books.[13]

Mathematics and archaeology

Much of the 'new' archaeology is concerned with the application of mathematical and statistical techniques to archaeological data; moreover, the theories about prehistoric astronomy, a discussion of which forms the foundation of this book, are themselves based on precise mathematical analyses. Hence a few words on the basic principles which have to be borne in mind when using such techniques are appropriate. It goes without saying that the use of mathematics is an indispensable aid to any discipline handling large quantities of data, and that every archaeologist should at the very least be aware of what is possible in this field even if he cannot himself perform the more advanced techniques. But it is essential that the limits of mathematics in the understanding of the past must be clearly understood or great errors can result.

An elementary warning should be written with letters of fire on the mind of every archaeologist who makes use of mathematical and statistical techniques, or of the conclusions drawn with their aid by someone else. M. H. Moroney puts the point clearly: 'It is true that it is extremely difficult to interpret figures when they relate to some concrete problem. It is equally true that it is extremely easy to do arithmetic. Herein lies the real difficulty. Averages can be calculated to nineteen places of decimals with astonishing ease. When the job is done it looks very accurate. *It is an easy and fatal step to think that the accuracy of our arithmetic is equivalent to the accuracy of our knowledge about the problem in hand* [my italics]. We suffer from "delusions of accuracy". Once an enthusiast gets this disease, he and all who depend on his conclusions for their welfare are damned.'[14]

Examples of how easy it can be to become bemused by the apparent magic power of numbers are legion and are perhaps symbolised for the innumerate by the sight of an equation in a page of text. The sense of inadequacy produced by the failure to comprehend its meaning instantly is matched by an equal sense of awe at the mysterious and often proved power of this language of the wise to reveal the secrets of nature. No doubt the ancient Egyptian peasant had the same feeling when watching a scribe writing down his hieroglyphs. Two examples drawn from the material of this book illustrate the 'delusion of accuracy' which essentially consists of a subconscious process of substituting the qualitatively uniform and complete figures derived from an arbitrary set of facts for the incomplete and non-uniform facts themselves.

In the first example we may consider the use of maps in the study of prehistoric astronomy. It is relatively simple, and a useful technique for the student, to calculate the grid bearing (easily convertible into a bearing from true north) for an alignment from the grid references of the two points concerned on the Ordnance Survey maps. For example, if we have a standing stone (the backsight) at 456789 and a mountain notch (the foresight) at 241998 we know that these two points define the hypotenuse of a right-angled triangle whose sides are discovered by simple subtraction to be 13.36 and 12.99 miles (21.5 and 20.9 km). By dividing the upright by the base we obtain 0.9721, the tangent of the angle between the alignment (the hypotenuse of the triangle) and the E-W grid line. From the tables this

$$\begin{array}{cc} 456 & 998 \\ \underline{241} & \underline{789} \\ 21.5 & 20.9 \end{array}$$

proves to be 44° 11′ and adding 270° gives the grid bearing of 314° 11′. We have to add say 1° 39′ to get true N (the figure is obtained from the margin of the 1 inch OS map) and the resulting bearing of 315° 50′ seems an impressively accurate result and quite capable of being turned into an astronomical declination suitable for a summer solstice observatory once we have the latitude of the stone and the altitude of the mountain notch (chapter 4).

However, it must be obvious that such precision is obtainable only if the original two grid references are *exactly* correct, to within a very few metres. If there is a 50 m error in the position of the backsight for example — which can easily happen if the stone is not marked on the map or if the reference has been wrongly read (in a direction at about right angles to the supposed alignment) the calculated bearing will be off by about 6′. Such an error will be even greater if the alignment is much shorter, and could easily be compounded if the location of the natural mark chosen as the possible foresight is also not exactly pinpointed. Such three-figure references, accurate to the nearest 100 metres, are not intended to give the exactitude of location required for the calculation of bearings to minutes of arc. Two eight-figure references, taken from the 2½ inch OS map after the position of the two points has been exactly defined, would be needed for this. If we start with falsely precise locations the apparent precision of the resulting bearing is obviously an illusion, though it looks very impressive, and so superior to one obtained with a protractor!

The second example involves the assumption — which might be a delusion — that mathematics can be used to infer what happened in the past (and what will happen in the future) on the basis of measurements of present conditions. The whole geological and astronomical theory of uniformity is based on this assumption. For example, the theories on megalithic astronomy discussed in this book depend on retrospective calculations to discover what the earth and the solar system were doing about 4,000 years ago. On the basis of extremely precise measurements of the present rate of change in the obliquity of the ecliptic (defined as the angle between the earth's equatorial plane and the plane of its orbit) it has been calculated by Newcomb and others that at about 1800 BC the sun at the solstices would have set about half a degree further away from its equinoctial position than at present, and such obsolete midsummer and midwinter positions are in fact found at many standing stone sites (chapter 4). The theories about the sites claimed as lunar and stellar observatories depend on even more complex calculations. Yet obviously we do not and cannot *know* from this type of work exactly where the sun, moon and stars were in the sky 4,000 years ago; only a contemporary description or marker of some kind could do that. We assume these prehistoric positions on the basis of our astronomers' exact observations of modern celestial motions and their retrojections of these into the past by skilled mathematical techniques.[15]

A more sophisticated danger than that of 'delusion of accuracy' which can develop from too great a reliance on mathematics was analysed recently by Dingle in relation to physics, but it could apply equally well to archaeology. It might be stated as the error of assuming that mathematics *must* correspond with our knowledge of reality as derived from practical experience, and the relevant part of Dingle's work (which is mainly concerned with the nature of science and the theory of relativity) should be read by all mathematically inclined archaeologists.[15] In essence, his view is that mathematics is a language invented by man and which belongs to the realm of pure thought, and its validity is determined and defined by its success in describing reality. Its enormous success in dealing with practical problems with verifiable solutions, such as the counting and sorting of large numbers of objects efficiently, in all branches of engineering, in navigation and in the sending of men to the moon and retrieving them, is naturally taken for granted. It may be assumed that the pressure of natural selection would quickly eliminate any false mathematics in such fields. But can false mathematics really exist, and is not the phrase itself a contradiction in terms? In fact there are so many simple examples of statements which are mathematically true but which are yet demonstrably false when checked against reality that it must be clear that a mathematical demonstration in a new field cannot be taken on trust without being checked by experience. Much the same points are made by Doran and Hodson.[16]

Dingle gives several examples of which one concerns a cubical vessel with a volume of 8 cu ft. Our mathematical task is to find the length of a side without the aid of a measuring rod. The answer is to find the cube root of 8 and the obvious solution is 2: so the vessel has sides of 2 ft. Yet there are in fact two other solutions to $\sqrt[3]{8}$ which are equally true, mathematically, namely $-1 + \sqrt{-3}$ and $-1 - \sqrt{-3}$, but as neither of these makes any sense at all when applied to the physical problem under consideration they are generally ignored. Yet the extremely important conclusion is that there are no means *inherent in mathematics itself* of telling which of the three solutions is the correct one. The correct one has to be found by relating the mathematical process to a concrete problem, and in this case the valid solution is so obvious that the fact that mathematics can say nonsensical things in terms of the real world is conveniently ignored. But what of fields of knowledge, like theoretical cosmology and prehistoric archaeology, in which the real world is beyond our reach — in the first case for the foreseeable future and in the second forever — so that no experimental checks can be made on the mathematical deductions? It is in such intangible fields that the mathematician's greatest fallacy constitutes the greatest danger and this fallacy is to believe that 'everything that is mathematically true must have a physical counterpart; and not only so, but must have the particular physical counterpart that happens to accord with the theory that the mathematician wishes to advocate.[17] More than a hundred years ago Professor T. H. Huxley, one of the most remarkable scientific minds of the nineteenth century,[18] made essentially the same point in his 1869 Presidential Address to the Geological Society. His concern there was to combat the view of William Thomson (later Lord Kelvin) that he could show by calculation that the age of the earth and the solar system must be much less than had been supposed, thus making severe difficulties for the new theory of evolution of Darwin. 'I do not presume to throw the slightest doubt on the accuracy of any of the calculations made by such distinguished mathematicians . . . But I desire to point out that this seems to be one of the many cases in which the admitted accuracy of mathematical processes is allowed to throw a wholly inadmissible appearance of authority over the results obtained by them. Mathematics may be compared to a mill of exquisite workmanship, which grinds you stuff of any degree of fineness; but, nevertheless, what you get out depends on what you put in; and as the grandest mill in the world will not extract wheat-flour from peascods, so pages of formulae will not get a definite result out of loose data.'[19] Huxley's main point — a correct one as we now know — was that Thomson's assumptions about the chemical source of the sun's heat and the rate of cooling of the earth's crust on which he based his calculations could easily be wrong, thus making the impeccable arithmetic worthless.

In recent years archaeology has provided numerous examples of social theories founded on a mathematical analysis of data, so the problem is particularly relevant to the topics to be discussed later on in this book. Indeed there are two such topics which come exactly into this category and which will be discussed in their proper places: the concept that a uniform 'megalithic yard' was used in laying out the stone circles, and the idea that the short astronomical alignments claimed by Hawkins at Stonehenge were deliberately pointed a little away from the phenomenon they were designed to observe so that the date of this could be determined through two successive sightings. Both these theories involve the assumption that what is true mathematically must have been true in Early Bronze Age times, but in the light of what has just been said, it must be clear that this cannot be assumed on the basis of mathematics alone. Some form of corroborative *physical or historical* evidence is essential if a theory about the Bronze Age, or about any other field of archaeology, which is based entirely on mathematics is ever to be regarded as more than an ingenious speculation. This is a crucially important point which it is essential not to overlook. The first example mentioned above is discussed in a later chapter, but a brief outline at this point of the problem of the 'megalithic yard' will help to clarify the general point.

From exact plans of some 150 stone circles, made in the field over many years, Thom has concluded that a standard unit of length was used by the designers of these sites in setting them out.[20] This unit was inferred to have been equivalent to 2.72 ft (2 ft 8.64 in or 0.829 m) and was deduced entirely by a mathematical technique, devised by Broadbent to detect quanta in apparently random sets of numbers. As is explained in more detail in chapter 2, the lengths used in this analysis consist of the radii of the true circles which best fit the actual stone rings; these radii are then analysed mathematically to determine whether they are composed of multiples of a fixed unit of length.

It is important to distinguish between the two processes in this type of study. The determination of the size of a circle which best fits a prehistoric round structure, and of the accuracy of its fit, is a relatively simple matter, but the detection of a unit in a set of the radii of such circles is much more complex: it also carries more important social implications. An exactly circular figure can have an arbitrary or paced radius and can easily be set out on the ground with a peg and string compass: accurately circular buildings need imply no more about the skills of the society concerned than that such a device was used. However, the discovery that a standardised measuring rod might have been used to measure these radii should imply an altogether higher order of social organisation in which a standardised metrology was devised and taught to a specialist class of surveyors. Because of this, and because of the limitations on the credibility of purely mathematical theories about the past referred to earlier, corroborative evidence for the existence of a measuring system based on the megalithic yard is clearly required. In chapter 3 this problem is approached in three ways, first by examining documented ancient metrological systems to see whether a length of 2.72 ft fits in anywhere, second by looking for physical examples of megalithic yardsticks, and third by surveying another class of prehistoric round structures in the same way to see if a systematic measuring system was used to design these.

RADIOCARBON DATING

The method and the tree-ring calibration

It is fair to say that the development of radiocarbon (C-14) dating by about 1950, and its subsequent widespread application to archaeological problems, has initiated what is probably the single greatest revolution in the study of European prehistory, and indeed in archaeology everywhere, since the invention of the Three Age system in the nineteenth century. The reason is of course that the method has provided a reliable and independent system for the absolute dating of organic remains in archaeological contexts anywhere in the world, on sites of all kinds. Previously, European prehistoric sites depended for their dating on tenuous connections with the urban cultures of the Mediterranean world — civilised societies which had devised their own systems of historical dating and used them in their records. In the European Bronze Age the links were ultimately with Egypt, by way of the Aegean and Crete; in the Iron Age there were connections with Classical Greece and later with Rome. Since objects which could be closely linked with these historical societies are rare except for the last, the majority of European sites had to be dated secondarily, through the occurrence on them of objects which had elsewhere been found with the objects dated by their Mediterranean and Egyptian connections. Moreover, large numbers of sites in the northern regions like Britain lacked even such second-hand aids to chronology and remained in a limbo as far as accurate dating was concerned.

Radiocarbon dating has changed all this and made the historical connections almost redundant as dating aids for the pre-Roman period (with the exception perhaps of the Greek and Etruscan imports to the Hallstatt and La Tène Iron Age cultures of France and Western Germany and of Roman material on native sites everywhere). It has also opened up immense opportunities for the better understanding of the development of prehistoric societies. However it is first necessary to give a brief account of the method itself and how the radiocarbon dating system has been modified in recent years, in a way that at first seemed to cast doubt on its credibility but which has in fact made it much more precise and reliable as a dating tool.

The mechanics of the method have been explained more than once, most recently and lucidly by Renfrew.[21] In essence, the dating laboratory measures the quantity of the radioactive isotope of carbon (C-14) in an organic sample and thus discovers the proportion of this to inactive carbon (C-12) present. During its lifetime an organism continuously absorbs carbon from the atmosphere and returns it by breathing and eating, so that it contains in itself the same proportion of C-14 as is at that time present in the atmosphere generally (the radioactive isotope is produced in the upper atmosphere by the bombardment of cosmic rays from space). The two varieties of carbon are of course chemically indistinguishable. When the organism dies this exchange of carbon with the air ceases and since C-14 decays to nitrogen at a known rate, it is possible to determine the time of death by establishing with scintillation counters what proportion of the carbon in the sample is still radioactive. Carbon-14 has a half life of about 5,730 years, which means that, of a given quantity, half will have decayed after that span of time, half *of the remainder* after another such span, and so on. However, in spite of the most careful counting the date can never be known exactly. This is partly because some background radiation always gets into the counter in spite of massive shielding, but mainly because the disintegration of C-14 is a random and irregular process, and the amount in the carbon sample very small. Thus a long period of counting is needed to get a reasonably reliable estimate of the rate of decay. The longer the count the greater the accuracy, but because of expense, samples are normally counted for not more than four days. The radiocarbon ages are therefore expressed as a statistical probability that the true age falls within a given span of time; the age given is the mean and standard deviation of the error is also quoted (see below).

Clearly one of the most important assumptions of the radiocarbon dating method is that the quantity of C-14 present in the atmosphere has always been the same in the past as it is now. In the late 1960s a method of checking this assumption was devised using the extremely long-lived Bristlecone pine tree (*pinus aristata*) which grows only in the White Mountains of California.[22] By counting the yearly rings in cores taken from living trees which are 4,000 or more years old, and by linking the ring patterns of these trees with those of older, dead trunks found standing and lying nearby, samples of wood were obtained which could be dated exactly to within a year or two, back to before 5000 BC. By performing radiocarbon analyses of this wood it was possible to see how inherently accurate C-14 dates were (or, in other words, how constant has been the atmospheric reservoir of radioactive carbon in the past) back to that time.

The result has been to show that the C-14 dates fluctuate a little in accuracy on either side of the calendar (tree-ring) age back to about 500 BC, but before that time the C-14 dates become consistently and increasingly younger than the tree-ring dated wood with which they are compared. This discrepancy amounts to some eight centuries in the fourth and fifth millennia BC. It is now customary, when referring to dates in radiocarbon years, to use the suffix 'bc' and the prefix 'ad', and to use 'BC' and 'AD' when quoting calendar dates in real (terrestrial) years; this distinction is made throughout this book.

The implications of these discoveries are many, and though there are some unsolved problems about the details of the tree-ring calibration curve for radiocarbon dates, the basic correction does seem to be valid. Tables are available with which C-14 dates can be corrected into calendar year dates[23] though of course the ages remain as time spans and do not become single year dates in the normal historical sense of the word.

Implications for Europe

The most important implications for Old World archaeology of the discovery that C-14 dates before about 500 bc are older than they appear to be have been defined by Colin Renfrew.[24] Many impressive Neolithic structures in Europe, particularly the passage graves, are now seen to be far older than the oldest stone buildings erected by the Mediterranean, Near Eastern and Egyptian urban peoples of the Early Bronze Age, civilised sources from which the inspiration for these monuments (and for many other aspects of European prehistoric culture) were once unquestioningly thought to have come.[25] Renfrew believes that, if the first great technological achievements in Europe occurred before 4000 BC and thus before the first flowering of the oldest known urban civilisations in Mesopotamia and the Nile valley, then they were due entirely to native European developments, and must have been produced without the aid of talented immigrants from the Near East. This explanation has an important implication for the slightly later phenomena which form the subject of this book — the great flowering of astronomical and other intellectual activity in Britain in the latter part of the third millennium BC — but detailed discussions of this must be reserved for another work.

Meanwhile we may note that by 2500 BC advanced urban civilisations had been established for centuries in Egypt and Mesopotamia, and that the effects of these were being felt to the west, in the Aegean and on the Mediterranean islands. These early cities provided environments in which professional wise men of all kinds — astronomers, mathematicians, engineers and so on — emerged and flourished as permanent classes.[26] The existence of these remarkable cultures southeast of Europe cannot be ignored, and Britain, unlike Polynesia and Easter Island, could have been within the range of their influence, unfashionable though it may be at the moment to say so. The question of whether the flowering of the learned orders in Britain occurred independently, or was prompted by these urban societies in some way, is of first importance and has to be faced.

C-14 dating and cultural development

One further aspect of radiocarbon dating has a very great potential for integrating diverse fragments of archaeological evidence and thus for making it possible to construct a coherent picture of cultural development in prehistoric times. This is its capacity not as a system of *absolute* dating but for providing a reliable *relative* chronology which can link in time sites and objects, as well as human and natural phenomena and events, between which there would otherwise be no detectable connection whatever. This is particularly true when a series of dates on well stratified material is available for each relevant site: with only one or two dates there is always the risk present that one of them will be substantially in error for some reason, but this erroneous date should clearly stand out if a series is available.

In the case of the phase of British prehistory which is to be discussed in detail, the overlapping Late Neolithic period and the Early Bronze Age, we are dealing with a relatively short span of time in which a great many things were going on in different parts of the country. Because several of the most important sites belonging to this period now have whole sets of radiocarbon dates available for them, it becomes possible to assert with a high degree of confidence that they were built and used contemporaneously. This in turn allows the suggestion that sites as far apart as Skara Brae in Orkney, the giant henges of southern England like Durrington Walls, and the Grimes Graves flint mines in Norfolk were not only truly contemporary but also all part of a particular phase of development in British prehistoric society and reflect the activities of a particular group of people. When we find that all these sites are also linked archaeologically by the presence of the same specialised kind of pottery, it becomes essential to view them together as a single phenomenon and to explain them with a single hypothesis, otherwise a complete picture of the period is not obtained. In its way this use of radiocarbon dates, hardly exploited yet, is as fundamental a revolution in prehistoric studies as the advent of C-14 dating itself because it may well allow us to begin to write the detailed history — and not a counterfeit one[27] — of the whole country phase by phase, and to link events in Britain with those abroad, at least in time and perhaps even more closely in the same historical context.

PREHISTORIC ASTRONOMY AND SOCIETY

In my view there is enough independent supporting evidence now available to make Thom's general theories (described in chapters 2-4) about the metrological and astronomical skill current in Late Neolithic and Early Bronze Age Britain quite acceptable. While it is possible to argue about the interpretation of individual sites, or the degree of sophistication of some of the work done, it can no longer be denied that a great deal of time and effort, both physical and intellectual, was expended at that time on observational astronomy and on field surveying and geometry and that considerable progress was made in these fields. This at once raises the question of what kind of pre-urban society it was in which such work was done.

There are perhaps two main kinds of rural farming and herding Neolithic societies in which the development of some degree of skill in such esoteric fields could be regarded as plausible. For example a popular current view of prehistoric Britain at that period is that the population had organised itself into what can be termed *chiefdoms*.[28] For these a relatively simple social structure is envisaged, rather like that seen until recently on many Pacific islands such as Tonga, and in which distinct groups of culturally homogeneous agricultural families are loosely linked to a chief, the latter being sometimes elected or chosen in a ceremonial manner. The bonds connecting such groups and extended families to this superior authority are loose and often depend on economically and ceremonially necessary trade and exchanges of goods; there might be some common centre, a combination of market and sanctuary, where the chief performed his functions and held court. Permanently differentiated specialised groups or classes are rarely found except in the sense that individuals emerge or are chosen as chiefs, priests and specially skilled craftsmen. The bonds which hold together such essentially rural and agricultural or fishing societies are those of custom rather than codified law. The skills which may be developed in ceremonial or superficially 'scientific' (intellectual) fields are not usually formalised into a coherent body of knowledge, nor systematically added to by deliberate research nor taught to selected novices to create a learned order. Sometimes specialist knowledge is accumulated to an advanced level for a specific purpose, as with the hereditary classes of navigators in some Polynesian island societies,[29] but such knowledge cannot be thought of as 'scientific' in the sense that it is systematically and deliberately accumulated by people interested, at least partly, in the phenomena themselves. In the case of the long canoe voyages of the early Polynesians, detailed knowledge of how to use the stars for navigation was essential for success, but it was passed on by rote learning, and no further advances in understanding the sky seem to have been made.

Into a somewhat different category falls another group of Neolithic proto-urban cultures such as that of the Olmec and Maya people of Central America in the first millennia BC and AD respectively, the early cultures of Peru down to the Mochica of the early first millennium, and the Uruk culture of the Mesopotamian delta probably of the fifth or fourth millennium BC. Here again we are dealing with primarily agricultural, rural populations, but ones which for a variety of reasons have evidently acquired a semi-civilised organisation whose power centres seem to have been in temple precincts served and staffed by a professional priesthood. In all the examples mentioned, true urban civilisations developed from these temple-building societies: in the post-Classic Maya, the Toltec and Aztec cultures of Central America, the Chimu and Inca cultures of Peru, and the Sumerian civilisation of Mesopotamia a much larger proportion of the population lived in cities and followed full-time non-agricultural pursuits. The point about the preceding proto-urban societies, as they may be called, is that as in the Classic period Maya, a dominating class of priests and chiefs emerged of whom at least the former lived in special ceremonial centres supported by food surpluses grown by the rural population. Its members thus had plenty of time to engage in intellectual activities and to develop systematically a variety of skills — astronomy, mathematics, an accurate calendar, writing, a legal system, elaborate religions and so on — which never seem to appear in the same way in Neolithic societies without this non-agricultural superstructure of 'wise men'. Moreover the resources acquired by the priesthood through its prestige evidently supported other full-time specialist craftsmen — architects, stonemasons, builders, professional potters and artists of various kinds — since a whole range of such new activities is apparent in the archaeological evidence found in the ceremonial centres. Decorated 'luxury' pottery often appears as well as massive masonry buildings, carved stone stelae, hieroglyphs, painted frescoes and so on. One might say that these proto-urban societies had for the first time provided opportunities for individuals gifted in various ways to pursue their specialised activities up to a professional level. They were organised in such a way that they could support permanent classes of such people, and were laying the foundations for the specialised, stratified societies which came to full flowering in the first urban civilisations.

The question that this book attempts to answer is this. Is all the varied archaeological evidence which is now available about the Britain of some 4,000 years ago explained best by assuming that the population of that time was essentially rural, homogeneous and organised into something like chiefdoms? Or can we on the other hand construct a more plausible picture by supposing that it was a much more organised, stratified and technically competent society evolving towards the proto-urban stage? I shall hope to show that the latter hypothesis is at least as plausible as the former, and that it in fact integrates the available evidence better without the need to doubt large sections of it.

PART ONE
The Achievement

2

Prehistoric Metrology and Geometry

One of the most important conclusions arrived at by Professor Alexander Thom about the intellectual and technical capability of certain groups of people within Early Bronze Age Britain was derived from the statistical study of the dimensions of scores of stone circles which he had himself accurately surveyed over many years.[1] Using the analytical methods developed by the mathematician Broadbent[2] to detect the existence of quanta (units of length in this case) among sets of apparently random numbers, he inferred that measuring rods of a standard length of 2.72 ft (0.829 m) had been used to lay out the design of the circles and stone rows. It also appeared that a multiple of 2½ of these 'megalithic yards', equivalent to 6.80 ft (2.073 m) and named the 'megalithic rod', was also used; it was noted to be particularly frequent in the stone rows of Brittany and also in the lengths of the perimeters of the British circles. The same work demonstrated that, though most of the stone rings were laid out accurately as true circles, a large proportion could be interpreted as having been built round other more complex geometrical constructions such as ellipses, egg-shapes, flattened circles and so on; all of these were likewise set out in units of megalithic yards. Other mathematicians such as Kendall[3] have subsequently examined the stone circle data independently and come to similar conclusions.

Moreover an independent study of rubbings made of the Early Bronze Age rock carvings of southwest Scotland, known as cup-and-ring carvings and found in many other parts of highland Britain as well as in Iberia, showed that the pecked grooves of which they are composed also followed precisely drawn circles and other more complex geometrical figures (below). These markings too were found to have been drawn out using a unit of length which proved to be 0.816 in; this is exactly 1/40th of a megalithic yard of 32.64 in and 1/100th of the megalithic rod.[4]

It is possible to make at least two important deductions from these discoveries. In the first place one must conclude that the designers of the British stone circles and cup-and-ring rock carvings possessed a standardised system of linear measurement, one which was moreover perhaps based on a decimal system involving the megalithic rod divided into 100 parts, or perhaps on a vigesimal system involving multiples of 20 megalithic inches (with five of these 'feet' to the rod). The second inference is that they also had an advanced knowledge of geometry, including Pythagorean right-angled triangles, and were capable of skilled practical field surveying in order to set out these large and sometimes complex designs on the ground with a high degree of accuracy.

Several aspects of these theories need to be examined in detail in assessing whether their implications are compatible with the rest of the archaeological evidence available for the period. There is first the question of the mathematical processes by which these discoveries have been made; in effect, of deciding whether arithmetical techniques can be used to reconstruct a vanished measuring system and geometry in this way. A discussion of their mathematical validity is beyond my capacity and within that of only the most skilled mathematicians, so only a few brief remarks on the subject will be made here; the main weight of the argument will therefore fall on the more tangible archaeological and historical implications of the theories.

The second aspect of this part of Thom's work concerns the megalithic geometry itself and its plausibility. It should be clear that, if shapes more complex than circles can be shown to be reasonable interpretations of the ground plans of megalithic rings or other buildings, and if the dimensions of these more complex constructions are also in megalithic yards, then the existence of this prehistoric unit is much more probable. (Slightly more complex geometrical constructions, composed of three or four arcs of different radii, are surely less likely to fit by chance any drawn out in units of megalithic yards.) A third aspect concerns the question of whether any other prehistoric structures can be shown to incorporate the same or a similar unit of linear measurement; if they can, the existence of the megalithic yard in the stone circles is clearly strongly supported, particularly if the other buildings concerned consist of continuous stone walls instead of isolated boulders. Examples of such standardised buildings which come to mind, and which might repay the sort of analysis Thom gave to the stone circles, are the Early Neolithic chambered cairns known as passage graves with their central, often circular, corbelled chambers; the round wooden buildings found in the large henge monuments of southern England (chapter 7); and the Iron Age drystone brochs and duns of the Scottish highland and island zone. Only the brochs have been systematically examined in this way and the results are described in chapter 3.

The fourth, and in some ways the most important, aspect of the problem concerns the independent, non-mathematical historical or archaeological evidence of the existence of the megalithic yard. Are there any traces in the modern or ancient European systems of linear or area measurement of a short yard of about 32½ or 33 in, or of a rod of 6.8 ft (6 ft 9.6 in), or of multiples of these? Have any actual measuring rods of wood, bone, metal or stone been found which might be interpreted as physical examples of megalithic yardsticks? And lastly, are there any traces in the literate civilisations of the ancient world of the megalithic yard or rod? The answer to this last question has implications far beyond that of checking the feasibility of applying Broadbent's theorems to British stone circles, since the discovery that a 'short yard' of 2.72 ft was in use in the ancient world would greatly increase the probability that it was known in Late Neolithic Britain. Also it seems likely to be one of the few ways of tracing any influence from these early urban cultures that may have penetrated into northwest Europe in the Neolithic and Early Bronze periods, or at least into one segment of the European society of the time.

The circularity of prehistoric sites

There are in essence two stages in analysing ancient circular structures for traces of deliberate geometrical construction and systematic measurement. It has first to be decided whether there is a reasonable likelihood that the separate standing stones (or the continuous drystone wall) of such a structure was built along an exactly drawn circle or arc of a circle, and the statistical techniques for finding this out are remarkably simple. The result is a series of circles or arcs worked out as 'best fits' to the buildings, with an indication of the degree of precision with which the stones follow the true circle — that is, the average distance by which the wall or the centres of the standing stones diverge from the supposed exact line. The many radii (or diameters) and circumferences which have been computed during this first part of the work will have provided a set of lengths which can then be searched for quanta, or recurring units of length, with the much more sophisticated mathematical techniques devised by Broadbent. The simplest way to illustrate the first part of the process is by describing an example.

From the 36 brochs whose central courts were accurately planned in 1971 (chapter 3) I have selected one at random, that at Backies in Sutherland (fig. 2). The survey done in the field consists of a series of measurements made with a metric steel tape from a theodolite (set up near the centre of the broch) to the lowest visible parts of the internal wallface. Thus in this case we have 19 angle-and-distance measurements which can be exactly plotted on permatrace at a scale of 1:20. The same exercise could have been done with a stone circle of course, except that there the positions of the centres of the stones would have to be estimated; one would also have to assume that they lay close to the line of the original geometrical shape pegged out on the ground by the designers before the stone sockets were dug. No such estimates are needed for the wall of a broch.

Thom gives a simple method for establishing the exact size of, and the position of the centre of, the true circle which best fits such a circular wall or ring of stones, where these constructions are fairly complete.[5] A circle of arbitrary diameter (13.98 ft (4.26 m) in fig. 2) is drawn on the plan so that its perimeter passes close to the measured marks; to make the operation

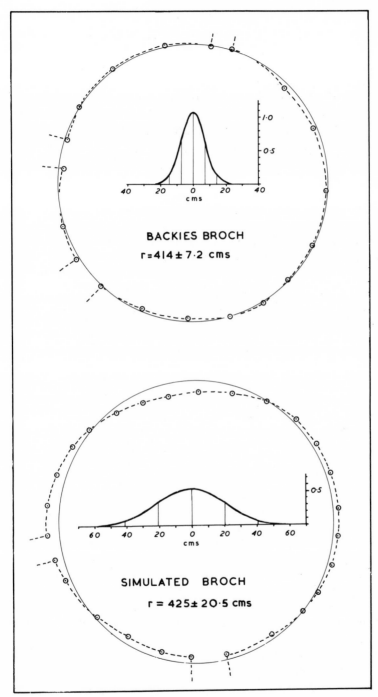

Fig. 2. Accurate survey, and suggested geometry, of the interior of the Backies broch, Sutherland and of an imaginary broch

easier it is best to arrange it so that the circle passes either just outside or just inside all these marks. This arbitrary circle is then divided into four equal quadrants labelled NW, NE, SE and SW and the distance of each surveyed mark from its perimeter is carefully measured, being counted as plus if it is inside and minus if it is outside this circle. The average or mean (m) of these distances is then worked out separately for each quadrant and the difference of the radius of the 'best fit' circle from that of the arbitrary superimposed circle results from the following formula.

$$\tfrac{1}{4} \, (mNW + mNE + mSE + mSW)$$

The four separate means are thus added together, averaged and added to (or subtracted from, as the case may be) the radius of the arbitrary circle. In the case of the Backies broch the result was a radius of 4.14 m which compares excellently with the figure of 13.56 ft (4.132 m) obtained from a computer. (Anticipating slightly, it may be observed that this figure is only 0.59 in (15 mm) less than 5 megalithic yards.)

TABLE 1

Figures derived from calculating the best fit circle for Backies broch. Radius of arbitrary circle 4.26 m (fig. 2)

quadrants	NW	NE	SE	SW		
	−0.32	−0.08	−0.06	−0.25		
	−0.27	−0.01	−0.03	−0.26		
differences	−0.15	−0.15	−0.08	−0.16	Radius of mean	
	−0.08	−0.08	−0.04	−0.09	circle =	4.26
	−0.03		−0.10	−0.15		−0.12
totals	−0.85	−0.32	−0.31	−0.91		4.14m
means	−0.17	−0.08	−0.06	−0.18		

The resulting best fit circle can then be drawn on a separate piece of paper to the same scale and fitted by eye to the broch survey, but the point of dividing the plan into quadrants was to make it possible to work out the correct position of the centre from the data obtained in the following simple manner. The centre of the arbitrary circle drawn originally should be moved to the northeast by $\tfrac{1}{2}(mNE - mSW)$ and to the northwest by $\tfrac{1}{2}(mNW - mSE)$.

The accuracy of fit of the actual drystone wall or ring of monoliths with the calculated mean circle is clearly of first importance when assessing the intentions and skill of the builders since the crudest ring of masonry or stones, even an almost square one, will yield a mean circle by the method described. What are the limits of tolerance inside which we may permit ourselves to assume that the men putting up the monoliths of a stone circle, or the masons constructing a broch, were following as best they could a precisely drawn circle marked out on the ground by an architect or designer? To some extent the criteria have to be arbitrary, and they will depend partly on what one thinks prehistoric builders (as opposed to designers) were capable of. A consistent error of more than 5 parts in 100 (5%) should certainly cause the supposed exact circularity of the design of the structure to be looked on with grave suspicion, and probably the error should be 2% or less before the hypothesis of a precisely circular plan could be accepted. The relevant data for this operation are obtained by measuring the distance of each of the surveyed points from the mean circle.

There are six ways of describing the difference in size and shape of the stone structure from the 'best fit' true circle, two involving averages or means, two involving the concept of standard deviation known as σ (sigma), and two involving that known as the standard error. In the case of the first, one finds the *mean deviation* of the actual measured radii of the structure simply by measuring with a scaling ruler on one's large plan of the site (1:20 at least) the differences in centimetres between each measured point on the wall and the nearest point on the calculated mean true circle. These differences are totalled up and averaged to get a quick and expressive idea of the average discrepancy. With the Backies broch (table 2) we can see that the mean deviation of the wall from the radius r of the 'ideal' circle is here 2.42 in. However, it must be obvious that with a slightly greater mean deviation of say 12 in, it will make a great deal of difference whether the site is large or small: an average discrepancy of 12 in is not much on a stone circle 80 yards in diameter but is a great deal in a broch 8 yards across. For this reason it could be better to express the mean error as a percentage of the radius of the best fit circle:

$$\% = \frac{m \times 100}{r}$$

in the case of our broch the mean deviation of the radii is 1.48%. This seems to be a very satisfactory demonstration of the circularity of the broch wall and one which shows rather clearly that the latter can at no point diverge very far from the mean circle. In fact we can see from the actual figures (table 2) that the maximum divergence is 14.0 cm.

Nevertheless the mean deviation figure is only an arithmetic average and cannot give any idea of the spread or dispersion of the actual individual measurements of the radius. How these are distributed on either side of the mean circle is shown by working out their *standard deviation* as follows. Each of the 19 figures of differences already obtained (for the Backies broch) is squared and the total of these squares added up. This total is then divided by n (19, the number of measurements in this case) and the square root of that figure worked out from the tables. The formula is thus:

$$\text{SD } (\sigma) = \frac{\sqrt{\Sigma(\bar{x} - x)^2}}{n}$$

where Σ means 'the sum of all the values of ', $\bar{x}$ is the arithmetic mean radius, and x is each actual measured radius to the structure; n of course is the number of measurements taken. In the case of our example the standard deviation proves to be 7.21 so we say that the mean radius of the Backies broch is 13.58 ± 0.24 ft (414 ± 7.21 cm; table 2). Alternatively we might express the standard deviation as a percentage of the mean radius: in this case our estimate of the original radius becomes 414 cm ± 1.74%.

It is important to understand exactly what the concept of standard deviation is telling us, though it should be fairly familiar through its long use in expressing radiocarbon (C-14) dates. When a series of measurements of varying accuracy is taken of a fixed quantity such as in recounts of the votes cast for candidates in an election, or of an ongoing but irregular process like the erratic atomic breakdowns of a fixed quantity of radioactive carbon, these measurements will be scattered across a certain range with the majority near the mean at its centre. A similar case is seen in measurements of a variable characteristic, such as men's height. The majority will cluster near the mean but a certain number will be substantially shorter and taller than this. In the case of our broch we may suppose that if a true circle was first pegged out on the ground, the masons subsequently laid each foundation stone of the inside wallface at a distance from the mark which varied slightly according to various factors — their tiredness, carelessness, waywardness and so on.

TABLE 2

Backies broch data   r (mean radius) = 414 cm

point	difference from r (cm)	d^2	d as % of r	%²	
3	11	121	2.66	7.08	
4	07	49	1.69	2.86	
5	02	04	0.48	0.23	
6	07	49	1.69	2.86	
7	07	49	1.69	2.86	
8	00	00	0.00	0.00	
9	05	25	1.21	1.46	Standard deviation of radius
10	12	144	2.90	8.41	414 ± 7.21 cm
11	08	64	1.93	3.72	standard deviation of r as %
12	05	25	1.21	1.46	414 cm ± 1.74%
13	00	00	0.00	0.00	mean error = 6.11 cm
14	03	09	0.72	0.52	mean error as % = 1.47%
15	04	16	0.97	0.94	standard error of radius
16	01	01	0.24	0.06	± 1.65 cm
17	10	100	2.42	5.86	standard error of r as %
18	08	64	1.93	3.72	± 0.40%
19	06	36	1.45	2.10	
1	14	196	3.38	11.42	
2	06	36	1.45	2.10	
n = 19	116	988	28.02	57.66	
means	6.15	52.00	1.47	3.03	
$\sqrt{n}$ = 4.359		$\sqrt{} = 7.21$		$\sqrt{} = 1.74$	

Simulated broch data (drawn freehand at 1:20, mean radius 4.25 m)

1	37	1369	8.71	75.86	
2	30	900	7.06	49.84	
3	18	324	4.24	17.98	
4	05	25	1.18	1.39	
5	15	225	3.53	12.46	
6	31	961	7.29	53.14	
7	40	1600	9.41	88.55	
8	32	1024	7.53	56.70	
9	18	324	4.24	17.98	
10	00	000	0.00	00.00	
11	13	169	3.06	9.36	standard deviation of radius
12	16	256	3.76	14.14	425 ± 20.55 cm
13	16	256	3.76	14.14	standard deviation of r as %
14	15	225	3.53	12.46	425 cm ± 4.84%
15	16	256	3.76	14.14	mean error = 17.57 cm
16	12	144	2.82	7.95	mean error as % = 4.14%
17	05	25	1.18	1.39	standard error of radius
18	02	4	0.47	0.22	± 3.88 cm
19	11	121	2.59	6.71	standard error of r as %
20	19	361	4.47	19.98	± 0.91%
21	22	484	5.18	26.83	
22	20	400	4.71	22.18	
23	15	225	3.53	12.46	
24	07	49	1.65	2.72	
25	02	4	0.47	0.22	
26	14	196	3.29	10.82	
27	26	676	6.12	37.45	
28	35	1225	8.24	67.90	
$n = 28$	492	11828	115.78	654.97	
means	17.57	422.43	4.14	23.39	
$\sqrt{n} = 5.292$		$\sqrt{} = 20.55$		$\sqrt{} = 4.84$	

What we need is a way of describing the distribution of these measurements about their average or mean and this is what the standard deviation gives us. If we imagine that we have taken 1,000 measurements of this wall instead of 19 or measured the heights of 1,000 men taken at random, one standard deviation in effect refers to the number of measurements which should have fallen in about the central third of the total range of distribution of the figures, that is a sixth on either side of the arithmetic mean. According to statistical theory (verified by actual observation on numerous occasions), in a normal distribution 683 of these measurements should have fallen in the central third, 270 more in the two sixths on either side of the central section and the last 47 in the two sixths beyond these. Two in a thousand are likely to lie beyond the range of three standard deviations. Normally one simply says that 68.3% of the measurements should fall within the 1 sigma range, 95.3% within the 2 sigma range and almost 100% (actually 99.8%) within 3 sigma. The standard deviation thus expresses the length of this range or dispersal of the measurements around the mean together with a uniform indication of how they are, or should be, scattered along it.

The way of expressing the probable *reliability* of the measurements, also included in table 2, is known as giving the *standard error of the mean*. The standard deviation simply describes the spread or scatter of the individual measurements on either side of their mean; by itself it does not tell us how many measurements were made or how representative those that were made are likely to be of all possible such measurements. The standard error (of the mean) describes how close this discovered mean value is likely to be to the true value which would be revealed if an infinite number of measurements had been made. It is obtained simply by the formula $\sigma/\sqrt{n}$ or, in words, by dividing the standard deviation of the mean by the square root of the total number of measurements. When n is small, less than about 10, the divisor becomes $(n - 1)$. Thus the smaller the number of measurements taken the larger becomes the mean error, and the less reliable the discovered mean is likely to be. In the case of the two sets of broch measurements the mean error of the radius of the simulated broch (below) is, at ± 1.53 in (3.88 cm), still larger than that of the Backies broch (± 0.65 in or 1.65 cm) in spite of the larger number of measurements made, because of the inherently less circular shape of the former and the consequent larger standard deviation of the radius. The standard error is the appropriate measurement to use, however, as it gives a more satisfactory method of assessing the likely accuracy of the mean values discovered.

Reverting to our broch we now see that we have calculated that almost all the measured radii should fall within 8.52 in (21.63 cm) on either side of the mean circle, the vast majority within 5.68 in (14.42 cm) and two-thirds within 2.84 in (7.21 cm) of it. Of the 19 measured figures we actually find that none are beyond two standard deviations, 4 are within two standard deviations, and 15 within one. This is a slightly better performance than one would expect statistically, but then measurements of a circular or near-circular wall are not entirely random: the figures for the various radii represent physical entities — the positions of massive stone blocks — none of which is very likely in a circular structure to project too far from the mean since each is attached to its neighbour. The statistics, however, treat the positions of the stones as pure numbers and assume that a tiny percentage will be absurdly far out even though this is physically not possible in a continuous wallface. In the case of isolated standing or fallen monoliths in a stone circle, circumstances might well conspire to ensure that the occasional stone was out in the three standard deviation range from the mean. Expressing the sigma value as a percentage perhaps gives us a more evocative indication of the accuracy with which this broch was designed and built, namely 13.58 ft $\pm 1.74\%$ (414 cm $\pm 1.74\%$).

We must recall again the subtle distinction between the standard deviation and the standard error as arithmetical descriptions first of the dispersal in the amount of a given quantity present in individuals of a population (and of the reliability of the mean value found), and second, of the scatter of measurements of a specific quantity. No one claims that the mean figure of men's height in a population is anything but a statistical concept. We do not believe that a Creator intended all men to be, say 2 megalithic yards in height and that individuals have deviated from that ideal for some reason; therefore we do not expect to find the 'correct' height by analysing the figures. We do believe, however, that there is a specific age of a piece of organic carbon, or an exact number of votes cast, which measurement will gradually pin down more precisely; that is, it will give a smaller standard error to it, though in the case of the radiocarbon dates, this will never be exact for reasons already described. We also believe that there are good reasons for supposing that the designer of a broch or a stone circle marked out an exact circle on the ground (probably with a measured diameter, though this is a separate question) and that a study of the scatter of measurements of the actual radii will reveal its dimensions. However, the calculation of the standard error of this radius cannot *prove* that it was measured out on the ground with a central peg round which pivoted a non-stretching cord; it can only say that it is extremely improbable that such a construction could have been set up in its discovered position without such a line for the builders to follow.

A final illustration may help to show why this is so, and will also provide some guidelines as to the acceptable degree of error in a circular building claimed to be exactly planned. I have drawn a broch freehand at a scale of 1:20 and performed the same calculations on it as with the Backies broch (fig. 2). The assumption is that a quick freehand attempt to draw a circle should produce results similar to those gained by laying out the plan of a circular building on the ground by pacing and estimation. The simulated broch is quite markedly irregular to the eye — almost egg-shaped in fact — but, as we shall see, the standard deviation of the measurements of its radius is not vastly greater than that of the Backies broch. The mean circle proved to have a radius of 13.95 ft (425.3 cm) and the maximum distance of the 'wall' away from this was 40 cm: the mean error of the 28 measured radii was 6.93 in (17.6 cm) or 4.14% of the radius. The standard deviation of the radius is ± 8.12 in (20.6 cm), or ± 4.84%, and its standard error ± 1.53 in (3.88 cm) or ± 0.91%. We can at least conclude from this small experiment that we require considerably better results, for a broch at any rate, than a standard deviation of the radius of ± 5%. Certainly no sigma value of over ± 2% for the radius should be considered as evidence that circularity was carefully planned, and one would be happier with one of ± 1% or less.

The two standard deviations of the measured radii of the Backies broch and the imaginary one are shown pictorially inside each plan (fig. 2). The curve is symmetrical about the mean value of these radii, the total length of the curve represents three standard deviations on either side of these means, and the vertical scale indicates the number of measured radii. It can easily be seen how the bell-shaped curve of the real, and more exactly circular, broch data is much taller and narrower than the low broad mound representing the imaginary broch which was not designed accurately. The higher and narrower the curves, the more closely the radii are grouped around the mean and the more precisely the structure has been built around a true circle.

Megalithic yards and mathematics

There are no really controversial aspects of the first part of the exercise, just described, unless it be in the degree of tolerance which should be allowed in the variation of the radii before one concludes that the structure concerned was not systematically set out as a circle. However, in searching for units of length in the mean radii established for many sites certain problems must arise. It is an established fact that spurious units of some size, and having a high level of probability, will appear in almost any random set of numbers quite by chance, so some other means is clearly needed to distinguish likely from unlikely prehistoric yards. It is also clear that the smaller a suggested unit is, the more easily it will divide almost exactly into a radius of several metres. There ought therefore to be a minimum size for acceptable quanta when dealing with structures of the size of stone circles or brochs.

The first problem should be solved by analysing separately structures from different geographical zones since the chances against the same false unit appearing more than once in separate sets of measurements must be very high. In fact, the stone circles of England and Scotland have been analysed separately by Thom, and the stone rows of Brittany form a third distinct group. All three groups have produced the same unit of length independently, with the Breton sites showing a more frequent use of the megalithic rod (2½ MY), so the actual existence of this yard in the past seems that much more probable. Again, a mathematically deduced unit is less likely to have appeared among the data by chance if it can be related to some historically known system of linear measurement: this question is discussed in the next chapter. It is concluded there that a 'short yard' of from 32.6 to 33 in was almost certainly used in the ancient world from Spain to north India, so that its detection by mathematical analysis in the stone circles of Britain and Brittany is, to say the very least, not an isolated phenomenon unrelated to any other system of linear measures.

Although it is beyond the scope of this work, and the competence of the author, to assess the validity of the mathematical process of deducing quanta in sets of measurements, one aspect of the detailed conclusions made by Thom about the megalithic yard, fathom and rod in the stone circles cannot pass without comment. This is his deduction that the evidence plainly shows that the megalithic yard was carried in the form of actual rods of standard length made of wood or bone from one end of

England to the opposite end of Scotland (Ireland has not yet been investigated), and without varying in length more than 3/100ths of an inch.[6] In other words, the metrology and geometry that the circle builders used in their projects was highly organised to the extent that the lengths of the measuring rods were standardised at a single centre: if the rods had been copied from one region to the next errors should have accumulated and the actual variation between the rods of different areas should have been much greater. If it is correct, this deduction must have very important implications for the social organisation of Late Neolithic and Early Bronze Age Britain since it is scarcely conceivable that such a situation could have come about unless there was one major training centre for the wise men of that period where the appropriate knowledge and skills were taught by the wisest of the order and from which the 'graduate' astronomer priests and magicians were sent out all over the country.

Leaving aside for the moment the question of the astronomical skills possessed (chapter 4), one may conclude that if it were not for this particular inference about the absolute uniformity of the rods, it would be possible to assume a lower level of organisation among the 'priesthood' and perhaps to draw an analogy with the Early Christian missionaries and monks in Scotland in the middle of the first millennium AD, who were in general united by their faith but who owed allegiance primarily to local religious leaders, who lacked (with a few exceptions) great intellect and had no rigidly uniform body of doctrine and ritual.[8] A centralised but widespread prehistoric order would be more analogous to the highly organised medieval Roman church with its training colleges and monasteries, uniform doctrine and ritual, and rigid hierarchical organisation.

Pursuing the Early Christian analogy, one might imagine that at 2000 BC there was a body of practical knowledge of, and a religious tradition about, geometry and measurement, perhaps originating among some earlier inspired group, which was carried gradually throughout the country by 'missionaries' of some kind and handed down in local versions or sects through several generations. It would not be necessary to suppose that the specialist class of each generation was trained at a single centre nor that its members were thus closely integrated over the whole country, nor even that the practitioners were a full-time priestly class: part-time shamans and medicine men might suffice. However the concept of an exactly standardised yardstick implies that there was such an integrated class, and it presupposes an altogether more advanced and better organised class of wise men and priests. The evidence for it therefore needs to be carefully examined.

This particular inference about the standardisation of the megalithic yard is based on the fact that the analysis of the mean radii of the English and Scottish stone circles, when treated as separate groups, reveals almost exactly the same values for it.[9] A later analysis of the Ring of Brodgar stone

TABLE 3

The standard deviation of circle radii remains constant with the increasing size of the site
(from Thom (1967), table 5.3)

Group	Diameter	n	$\Sigma \varepsilon_i^2$	$s^2 = (\Sigma \varepsilon_i^2)/n$	$\sigma = \sqrt{s^2}$
1	0-31 ft	35	15.27	0.436	0.66
2	31-54 ft	35	14.53	0.416	0.65
3	54-76 ft	37	19.31	0.522	0.72
4	76-189 ft	38	21.91	0.577	0.76

circle in Orkney (chapter 9), in which the dimensions were exceptionally clearly preserved, again revealed the same almost identical unit.[10] Furthermore, the standard deviations of the radii of individual sites, as indicated by the measurements to separate stones, vary hardly at all in small and large circles (table 3) and this shows two things rather clearly. The first is that the accuracy with which the sites were laid out does not decrease with their size, which it certainly would do if the measurements were paced out. The inference to be drawn from this is that, whether the diameter was 30 ft or 180 ft, the positions of the monoliths in each circle were painstakingly surveyed and marked out in some way on the ground with little error, presumably with stakes, and that the subsequent deviations from circularity were due to mistakes of fairly constant magnitude made by the builders in placing individual stones at the surveyed marks. Only if the mistakes were made fairly uniformly in this way, one by one at separate stones and for separate reasons, would the standard deviations of the radii be so uniform. Second, the question of the uniformity of the yard is also clearly affected by this uniformity of errors in large and small circles since it might be assumed that, unless the measuring rods used in surveying all the sites were identical, the variations from exact multiples of 2.72 ft should surely increase with the size of the circle, though obviously they could not increase by more than half a megalithic yard (1.36 ft).

However, there is one aspect of the mean diameters found in the stone circles which is hard to explain if one is assuming an absolutely uniform measuring rod and this is the undoubted fact that the computed diameters are individually very often well away from whole numbers of megalithic yards. This is something which at first sight is difficult to understand, since people with the degree of skill in mensuration and practical field surveying which is postulated by Thom would easily have been able to overcome the problem of exactly measuring diameters, even on large sites. Indeed we have seen from the uniformity of the standard deviations that they were able to do so perfectly well. Two main explanations can be offered for this state of affairs, revealed pictorially in the histogram of circle diameters.[11] Thom himself explains it as the result of a desire on the part of the circle designers to make the *perimeters* of their sites as near as possible to integral numbers of megalithic rods (2½ MY), and the most spectacular and convincing example of this process was probably Woodhenge (chapter 8).[12] A statistical examination of the diameters was carried out to see whether there was evidence of a preference for their being away from whole numbers of megalithic yards in the appropriate direction to ensure that the circumferences were nearer to multiples of 6.8 ft and this suggested that there was such a tendency. The level of probability (that this result was due to chance) was 6% — too high to be certain about this — but Thom thought the results were a significant pointer in favour of the theory of deliberate diameter adjustment.

An alternative explanation could be obtained by assuming that the megalithic yardsticks were not absolutely uniform all over the country but varied by an inch or two on either side of a mean, which in this case would be 2.72 ft. This would have occurred if there had been no continuing maintenance of standardisation from a single centre, and a consequent gradual 'drift' of the lengths from that of the primeval measuring rod would be expected, as there was in later times. One could assume that the lengths of the rods would have been handed down through generations separately in different parts of the country and small regional differences would accumulate as well as differences over time. If one assumes that the mean diameters of the circles were laid out as whole numbers of these local megalithic yards, and that the length of the perimeter was not important (although the area of the enclosed space might have been), a small variation in the yardsticks would be an automatic conclusion. For example, if we select ten sites at random from Thom's list[13] we can see just how often the mean diameters are not exact multiples of 2.72 ft (table 4). The first four columns are as in the original table: first the site code, second the mean diameter in feet (d), third the nearest multiple of megalithic yards which fits this (MY), and fourth the actual discrepancy between that multiple and the mean diameter (e). A fifth column has been added in which an equation is given to show the length of the yardstick nearest to 2.72 ft which divides exactly into the mean diameter (MY2).

TABLE 4

The variations of diameters from whole numbers of megalithic yards from ten sites

	$d(ft)$	MY	e	MY2
B7/4	10.8	4	−0.08	4 × 2.700
G4/9	20.9	8	−0.86	8 × 2.613
G8/2	23.2	9	−1.28	9 × 2.578
B7/17	32.0	12	−0.64	12 × 2.667
A2/8	44.2	16	+0.68	16 × 2.763
B1/23	57.0	21	−0.12	21 × 2.714
B1/26	67.2	25	−0.80	25 × 2.728
G4/14	82.1	30	+0.50	30 × 2.737
B7/11	103.7	38	+0.34	38 × 2.729
N1/13	188.3	69	+0.62	69 × 2.729

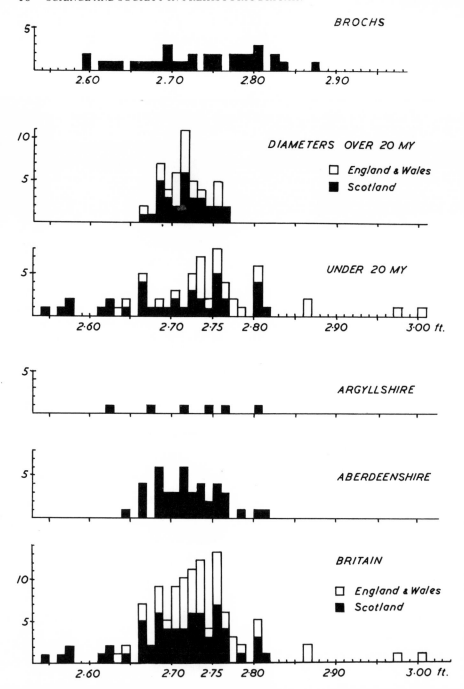

Fig. 3. Histograms of possible variations of the megalithic yard used in brochs and in various groups of stone circles

It can easily be seen that it is possible to assume that there existed a set of yardsticks of slightly varying lengths which fit these diameters more or less exactly. Indeed a histogram of these derived lengths for all the English and Scottish circles on Thom's list (fig. 3) shows something rather like a normal distribution pattern with a high, thick cluster close to and on either side of 2.72 ft and smaller numbers tailing away to the sides with only a few more than 0.1 ft away from the mean.[14] In this case Thom's figure of 2.72 ± 0.03 ft would presumably represent the arithmetic mean of these figures (its actual figure for these measurements is 2.724) and their standard deviation would describe quite well the observed frequencies of different values on either side of that mean.

Another test immediately suggests itself for this hypothesis. If the megalithic yardsticks did vary in this way from area to area one might reasonably expect circles in a restricted geographical zone, whatever their geometrical construction, to have been laid out with the same or very similar local yardsticks. If this was the case the spread of the lengths near to 2.72 ft which divide exactly into the various mean radii concerned should be much smaller for a small zone than for the whole country, unless it was assumed that the sites were constructed over a long period of time during which the length of the local yardstick might have 'drifted' steadily away from the primary figure. However, it still seems unlikely that regional standard yards — the rods for which could be copied directly one from another — would vary as much as those of widely separate regions between which there would, in this view, have been little or no contact after the initial dispersal of the idea.

The two other histograms in fig. 3 show the 'yardsticks' from circles of two restricted, distinct and homogeneous regions, Aberdeenshire and the small counties immediately to the north (Moray, Nairn and Banff), and Argyllshire including the islands. The former region, later to become the heart of Pictland, is a lowland area fringed on the north, west and southwest by the rugged highland terrain of Invernesshire and Perthshire and the circle builders here were certainly a group apart. A characteristic regional type, the recumbent stone circle, is particularly common there, but there are also simpler forms and other geometrical shapes. There are many fewer circles in Argyllshire, but though quite different from Aberdeenshire in terms of terrain and natural resources it is also a relatively homogeneous maritime zone consisting of coastal fringes and islands west of a highland massif.

Only six measured circles are available for Argyllshire, but even so it is noticeable that the rod lengths which might have been used to lay out their diameters are scattered widely and more or less evenly along the scale, from 2.62 to 2.80 ft. On the other hand no less than 42 exactly surveyed circles are listed from the northeast mainland, and yet here again this much larger regional sample shows a marked and very similar scatter of rod lengths, from 2.64 to 2.81 ft with the main mass falling in a solid block between 2.68

and 2.76 ft. This regional histogram looks like a smaller version of the one for the whole country, and one is forced to conclude that, if the rods did vary slightly in length, this variation was much the same within a limited region as it was over the entire country. This would seem to count against the hypothesis of the variable rod and in favour of that of an exactly uniform one maintained at a single centre; the 'inaccuracy' of the circle diameters would then have to be explained in terms of a desire on the part of the designers to make the circumferences integral in megalithic rods. The only other explanation for this fairly uniform variability in the megalithic yardsticks might be to suppose that length altered fairly uniformly over time across the whole country so that the products of the early, middle and late phases of the circle-building period were laid out with rods of different lengths. Such a phenomenon might produce a similar scatter of lengths in all regions, but the hypothesis cannot be checked because of the lack of enough circles which have been sufficiently well dated by archaeological means.

There is one striking fact about the histogram of rod lengths which may give a clue to follow: the circles laid out with yardsticks which vary widely from 2.72 ft are all small ones. If one divides Thom's list of circles into two groups, those with diameters above and below 20 megalithic yards (about 54 ft), the histogram of the rods used in the smaller ones is markedly the more scattered (fig. 3). In fact the 'yardsticks' used in every circle with a diameter greater than 20 MY are tightly clustered between 2.66 and 2.77 ft, a difference of 1.3 in, whereas those of the smaller group extend from 2.54 to 3.00 ft, 5½ in or more than four times the variability of the larger group. This is discussed again below.

It is important to realise that the histograms and calculations just described have no bearing on the validity of the concept of a megalithic yard, which depends on much more sophisticated mathematics. The hypothesis that the 'inaccurate' diameters may mean that the rods themselves varied slightly can only be examined after the existence of the yard has been demonstrated by other means. In fact any arbitrary yard-like length could be divided into the mean diameter in the way described and a meaningless histogram constructed out of the slight fluctuations in its length which would have to be assumed from its failure to fit these lengths exactly. For example, a length of 2.51 ft fitted to the diameters in this way will produce a variety of lengths whose mean is 2.52 ± 0.07 ft, an excellent fit on the whole, but of course it means nothing at all. However, it is noticeable that here again the mean length fits the diameters of the smallest circles worst; in the larger ones the exact subdivisions of the diameters are all very close to 2.51 ft. This is obviously because minute alterations in the basic unit become large differences when multiplied many times (as they have to be with the large diameters), but the same errors in small diameters have to be compensated for by correspondingly large adjustments of the basic unit. For example, a fluctuating unit centred on a mean of 3 ft could only fit exactly into a diameter of 10 ft by assuming it at that site to be 3 times 3.33 ft, but it would fit exactly into a diameter of 100 ft by supposing that there it was 33 times 3.003 ft, a far better figure! If the concept of a megalithic yard of 2.72 ft was not valid, this could of course be the explanation for the greater dispersal of the units from that mean described earlier: that they were being forced to fit the computed circle radii. This worse fit of the megalithic yard in small circles could not, moreover, be explained in terms of the adjustment of the perimeters to integral numbers of megalithic rods since diameters of 4, 7, 8, 11, 12, 15, 16, 19 and 20 MY provide circumferences which are within one-quarter of a whole number of MR (0.625 MY), the criterion adopted by Thom[15] for a satisfactorily adjusted circumference. The lesson of all this is that other independent evidence needs to be taken into account when assessing the validity of the concept of the megalithic yard.

THE GEOMETRY OF THE CIRCLES

Many of the stone rings of Britain are obviously not truly circular in shape and an important part of Thom's work has been to show that most of these can be plausibly interpreted as the results of deliberate attempts to produce more complex geometrical patterns, many of which are based on Pythagorean triangles. These more complicated shapes show two things. In the first place their sophisticated geometry should demonstrate much more plainly than the simple circles that a complex body of knowledge and tradition, well beyond that credible in the context of a society with only local and perhaps part-time religious leaders, was accumulated and systematically taught. Second, the fact that the dimensions of the complex shapes are defined in terms of megalithic yards must, if the shapes are genuine, make it very much more likely that the yard of 2.72 ft was used by the circle builders. There is less room for manoeuvre in fitting an ellipse or an egg-shape drawn in megalithic yards to a ring of stones than there is with a simple circle.

Ellipses

The shape closest to a circle — and the next simplest to construct with primitive equipment — is the ellipse. In prehistoric field geometry an elliptical shape would have been drawn out with the aid of a loop of rope of chosen length rotating round two stakes a measured distance apart. The important part of an ellipse for anyone setting one out in this way is the isosceles triangle (with two angles the same) formed by the rope and stakes; this is in effect two opposed right-angled triangles. The upright common side b is half the short axis of the ellipse, the two hypotenuses c are each half the long axis and the bases $2a$ form the distance between the foci (stakes).

Thus if the ellipse was to be based on a Pythagorean triangle with a, b and c equal to 3, 4 and 5 respectively, the distance $2a$ between the foci would be 6 MY or a multiple thereof, and the length of the loop would be that plus twice the hypotenuse c of 5 MY (or a multiple thereof). The half short axis b would then automatically be 4 MY.

About twenty stone circles surveyed by Thom have definitely proved to be ellipses and some fifteen more are less certainly so because of their ruinous state. There seems to be clear evidence from the dimensions of these ellipses that the builders were concerned either to draw them round perfect Pythagorean triangles or to arrange their dimensions so that the perimeters were at or near whole numbers of megalithic rods. The perimeter of an ellipse is found by the approximate formula

$$2 \pi \sqrt{\frac{b^2 + c^2}{2}}$$

Using as raw data the perimeters derived from the best-fit ellipses of the twenty good sites, together with the perimeters of the egg-shaped rings described below, it appears that even if one assumes no prior knowledge of the megalithic yard, the probability that a length of 6.80 ft was incorporated in these perimeters is extremely high, less than 1% in fact. It may also be significant that in the one known elliptical circle, at Daviot in Aberdeenshire, which seems to be drawn (in half yards) round the sixth of the perfect Pythagorean triangles (namely $12^2 + 25^2 = 37^2$, also seen at Woodhenge), the discrepancy away from an exact multiple of $2\frac{1}{2}$ MY in the length of the perimeter is, at 0.94 MY, by far the greatest observed among the twenty good sites. The next largest discrepancy is 0.39 MY. Thom suggests that at Daviot the perfection of the triangle outweighed in the designers' minds the need for a perimeter integral in megalithic rods and it does seem a reasonable supposition. Another well designed ellipse is that at Penmaen Mawr in Wales which is drawn around a triangle which must have been thought a perfect one by the designers. In terms of half yards it is $19^2 + 59^2 = 62^2$ although this is not quite a valid equation. The squares on the shorter sides add up to 3,842 whereas 62^2 is 3,844: the hypotenuse must therefore be a fraction short, but the error, of 2 parts in 3,800, would never have been detectable on the ground by the circle builders. Here, by contrast, the perimeter is a remarkably good fit in megalithic rods, being within 0.06 MY of 38.

At the Cultoon stone circle on Islay, Argyllshire, it was possible recently to carry out a check on the hypothesis that some of these sites were accurately designed as ellipses. In 1973 Thom surveyed the site for the Islay Historic Works Group and found only two stones still standing upright, nine prostrate and partly or wholly visible, and three more completely buried which were detected by probing. Cultoon was clearly not circular: the monoliths lay along the perimeter of an oval of which the long axis, aligned NE-SW, was about 135 ft and the short axis about 110 ft. An ellipse based on a 3:4:5 Pythagorean triangle fitted the stones quite well, although it was obvious that the many prostrate ones meant that the shape could not be regarded as definite: some of the stones lay 6 ft away from the presumed perimeter.

Excavations at this site in 1974 and 1975 showed clearly that the circle had never been completed. Monoliths had been dragged up close to their intended positions and left. Some stone sockets had been dug yet no monoliths lay beside these, while other prone stones appeared to have no socket beside them. That some kind of destruction may have been visited on the site was suggested by the fact that one of the uprights had been snapped off short and that no fallen fragments were found next to it. However the discovery of twelve sockets around the perimeter of the ring together with the position of the three standing stones allowed its precise shape to be ascertained. It was found that an ellipse measuring almost exactly 44 × 43 megalithic yards — actually 119.69 × 115.23 ft — passed exactly through all these positions, and also that the long axis of this shape was aligned NE-SW towards an astronomically significant mountain peak 50 miles away in Ireland (chapter 4).

The Cultoon excavations showed two things rather clearly.[16] The first point is that it is now possible to turn on its head the argument sometimes heard that the suggested geometrical constructions are improbable because the stones could have moved or been disturbed during the last four thousand years. On the contrary it can now be seen that a wrecked site can, after excavation, prove to be a much better fit to a geometrical construction than could ever be determined from surface indications alone. The second point is that at Cultoon the geometry is linked in a very decisive and satisfactory way to a sophisticated astronomical function, in that the long axis of the ellipse could have been set out to point exactly at a distant foresight. Thus at this site the two aspects of Thom's deductions about the intellectual capacity of Early Bronze Age Britons complement and reinforce each other, and both the design and the situation of the site become comprehensible.

Egg-shaped rings and flattened circles

It has been suggested that two other important geometrical constructions were incorporated in the stone rings[17] and it is difficult to dispute the genuineness of these shapes without making arbitrary assumptions that some stones are not in their original positions, or that the components of the site were built at different times.[18] Two kinds of flattened circles are suggested, in both of which half or more of the perimeter is a circle while the flattened part consists of an arc drawn from a point on the opposite side of the perimeter of the main circle (fig. 4). Several of the sites claimed to have been based on such geometrical constructions are very large: Dinnever Hill and Rough Tor, both in Cornwall, are 45 and 50 yards across respectively

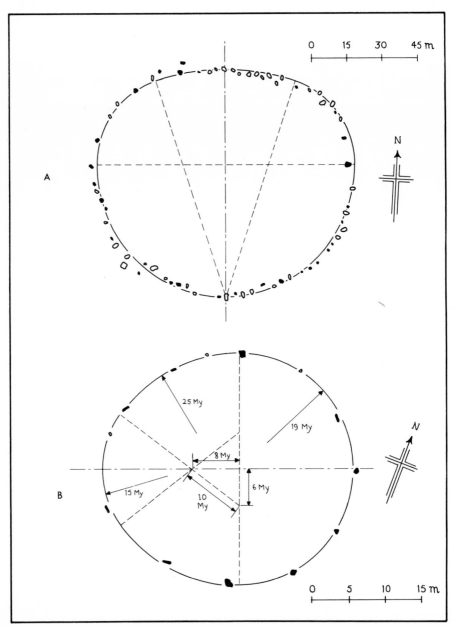

Fig. 4. The geometry of two stone rings after A. Thom: A is a flattened circle (Long Meg) and B an egg-shape (Clava)

while Long Meg in Cumberland measures no less than 117 yards. There is a suggestion that some of the radials incorporated in the flattened circles were aimed in astronomically significant directions, as at Castle Rigg in Cumberland.[19] Also the flattening of one part of the circle could have been due to an attempt on the part of the builders to find a ring whose circumference was exactly three times the length of the diameter. If this was the case, the perimeter of the Type A flattened circle (with two-thirds of the perimeter a true circle) is too large by 2% and the Type B form (with one half circular) is too small by 1.3%.[20]

The two egg-shaped constructions suggested consist of a semicircle, forming the base of the egg, with arcs of larger circles forming the longer, upper part (fig. 4). The suggestion is that this upper part was based on two opposed right-angled triangles. The most spectacular of the claimed geometrical egg-shapes is the construction devised for the post-holes of Woodhenge, described in a later chapter. The egg-shaped rings are particularly noteworthy in that their construction involves the setting out of two opposed right-angled triangles, either with a common base line or with a common hypotenuse (fig. 4). If the egg-shapes are a valid geometrical interpretation of the shape of some stone rings — and that they are is suggested by the occurrence of the same geometry in a few brochs — then a knowledge of the properties of Pythagorean triangles must be assumed for the builders and designers. The triangles, moreover, seem to have been chosen so that the formula of $a^2 + b^2 = c^2$ (c being the hypotenuse) is in whole numbers of megalithic yards (there are of course only a limited number of right-angled triangles which fulfil this condition). Hutchinson[21] gives the figures:

TABLE 5

Dimensions of egg-shaped rings of Type 1 to show the Pythagorean relationship of the sides of the constructional triangle, expressed in megalithic yards

Site	a (base)	b (upright)	c (hypotenuse)	equation			
Esslie major	4	3	5	16	+ 9	=	25
Clava	8	6	10	64	+ 36	=	100
Druid Temple	3	4	5	9	+ 16	=	25
Allan Water	6½	5½	8½	30¼	+ 42¼	=	72½
(in half MY units)	13	11	17	169	+ 121	=	290*
Cairnpapple Hill	16	12	20	256	+ 144	=	400

(* $\sqrt{290}$ is 17.03, but measuring alone would scarcely have revealed the flaw in this triangle.)

Objections to the theory that complex geometrical shapes, set out with a standard unit of length, are incorporated in the stone rings usually rely on the assumptions such as those mentioned earlier, that the stones have somehow moved (by frost heave perhaps) or that elements of the buildings may have been set up at different times. The discoveries at the Cultoon ring in Islay partly answer the first objection, which in any case can only be substantiated by excavating the suspicious sites concerned. No other stone circle to my knowledge has been found to have been disrupted in this way, except Stonehenge (chapter 6). A double stone circle on Machrie Moor, Isle of Arran, appears effectively to dispose of the moving stone argument and to demonstrate clearly that non-circular rings were arranged deliberately.[22] The inner ring is a true circle 14 MY in diameter while the outer one is clearly not circular and yet possesses an axis of symmetry exactly 22 MY long; it can be interpreted as a flattened circle. It is clear that neither soil movement nor any other agency is likely to have selectively disturbed the shape of the outer ring while leaving the inner one intact. A final point is that the existence of complex geometrical constructions in stone circles is supported by their appearance in the much later Iron Age brochs in circumstances which make it very unlikely that this could have happened by chance.[23]

The second objection — that the rings can belong to features of more than one period — hardly stands up. The vast majority of the surveyed sites are simple rings of standing stones, and it seems highly unlikely that they were not planned and built as a single operation. In a few cases like Callanish other features which may be later are included in the suggested geometry, but in the case of the site mentioned the two features are almost independent geometrically.[24] It is also surely wrong to assume that the circle builders were unable to recollect, or somehow to mark out at the site, the important features of their geometrical constructions apart from the perimeter and so carry the knowledge of them over several generations. There really seems to be no reason not to accept as highly plausible the geometrical and metrological theories of Thom about the stone rings, although the more complex or 'compound' rings may be open to re-interpretation.[25] It is a fact, discovered afresh by the writer while analysing broch geometry, that different constructions, and different sizes of the same construction (ellipses for example), can sometimes be made to fit a site equally well, a circumstance which suggests that the maxim to be observed in this field is 'the simpler the better'.

THE ARCHAEOLOGY OF THE RINGS

What light does the variety of other information on the stone circles, obtained by archaeological excavation and research, throw on the geometrical and astronomical hypotheses about them? The answer is 'not much', and this is mainly due to the fact that much of this evidence is irrelevant to the ideas being considered here. One has only to pose the question 'how can one tell what a prehistoric man was thinking about from the debris he left at a site?' to see the point. The evidence of the pottery, graves and other artefacts found at stone circles is telling us about the activities of potters, about the preferred pottery of people at the site, about the burial customs of the times, about flint working techniques and ditch digging and so on, but it does not, and cannot, tell us about the degree of interest in astronomy and geometry.[26] Evidence that such esoteric skills were present in the contemporary population can only be extracted from the sites in the ways pioneered by Thom, by exact surveying and fairly skilful mathematics. However this does not mean that the archaeological evidence *sensu stricto* should be ignored. As will be demonstrated in later chapters, this mass of other data from Late Neolithic and Early Bronze Age sites provides the crucial test for the existence of the kind of society that could have supported the specialised classes required to do the intellectual work.

One obvious check that archaeological evidence can provide is that of dating the stone rings and allied sites: if the dates derived by radiocarbon and associated artefacts agree with the few obtained independently from the astronomical theory by retrospective calculation, then one possible flaw in the new theories is disposed of. Archaeological excavation can also partly confirm or completely disprove specific theoretical geometrical constructions as described earlier, and can sometimes demonstrate whether or not various features of a site are contemporary or of different periods. Burl has recently summarised the archaeological dating evidence for stone circles and will shortly examine the subject in depth.[27] He offers an analysis of the associations between pottery, and a few other well dated artefacts, and 54 stone circles classified by size and geometrical construction. From this study it seems that the great majority of the stone rings belong to the overlapping Late Neolithic and Early Bronze periods — in terms of radiocarbon years between about 2000 and 1500 bc (2500-1700 BC). This is also the time during which, according to retrospective calculations, the stone circle observatories were in use. A few circles are earlier, and the oldest may well be that surrounding, and presumably contemporary with, the New Grange passage grave in Ireland. The construction of this great chambered cairn has been dated by C-14 to 2456 ± 40, 2475 ± 45 and 2585 ± 105 bc, an average date of about 2503 bc (about 3230-3330 BC).[28]

The suggestion is made from this evidence that the earliest stone rings are, as might be expected, the true circles although some flattened circles are also found in the first period. Ellipses only seem to become common after about 1600 bc, judging from the artefacts, and egg-shaped rings also tend to be late (though New Grange, the earliest known ring, may be one of these). The general picture is of primary, large circles with simple geometry and later, smaller ones whose construction is more complex. The fact that C-14 dates have shown that the geometrically highly complex wooden roundhouse at Woodhenge in Wiltshire is later than the adjacent giant henge at Durrington Walls, with its purely circular timbered buildings, also supports this sequence (chapter 8).

The distribution of the stone rings is mainly within the highland zone of Britain, including Ireland,[29] and the geographical distribution of the various geometrical shapes reveals some features of interest. Truly circular rings seem to occur almost everywhere in the stone circle province — from Cornwall to Orkney and in Ireland — though they appear to be absent from the heavy concentrations of ellipses in northeast Scotland. True circles have a distinctively Atlantic and Irish Sea distribution, and the flattened circle also occurs commonly in these regions with marked concentrations in Cumbria and Cornwall. In striking contrast are the elliptical rings, of which nearly two-thirds are in northeast Scotland, one group in Aberdeenshire and the second in Perthshire west of the Firth of Tay; there is another similar concentration in southwest Ireland with a thin scatter in Wales and Cumbria (the determination of the shape of the Irish circles depends on evidence other than that of Thom's surveys). Within these regions nearly all the identified circles are ellipses: other shapes are represented by a few examples only. Moreover the elliptical rings of northeast Scotland and the Cork-Kerry area of Ireland are also linked by the concentration in these same areas of a special type of ring — the recumbent circle — having a massive prone monolith on one part of the perimeter.[30] It may well be that stone circles have more than one origin, or at least more than one line of development. The recumbent circles, for example, could be a peculiarly northeast Scottish derivative from the Clava passage graves and ring cairns in the same area, which have stone circles surrounding them.[31] Why they are also in southwest Ireland is not as clear, but their distribution hints at close connections of some kind between the two areas in the Early Bronze Age.

The origin of all the other stone rings is not clear either, but their occasional presence inside henge monuments[32] could well imply a closer connection with these 'ritual' sites than with the funerary traditions of the Early and Middle Neolithic periods, though the emergence of the basic tradition of the stone ring among the Irish passage graves before 3000 BC still seems clear from the New Grange evidence mentioned earlier. In Wessex an interesting phenomenon can be seen in two Late Neolithic sites, the Sanctuary and the giant henge at Mount Pleasant (further discussed in chapters 6 and 8). Here circles of standing stones were set up apparently to mark the positions of the posts of a decayed wooden roundhouse though the significance of the phenomenon, which has been called, rather unpronounceably, *lithicisation*,[33] is again not at all plain. It may well suggest that the traditions of the stone circle builders of Ireland and the highland zone of Britain arrived in the Wessex area at a specific time, not before about 1800 bc, judging from the dating of the giant henges. The adding of the stone rings to Stonehenge in phases II and III is clear evidence of the same process, which may well be hinting at the origins of the whole metrological and astronomical phenomena of Late Neolithic Britain (chapter 10).

CUP-AND-RING ROCK CARVINGS

Scattered throughout the highland zone of Britain, in Ireland and in Iberia are characteristic rock carvings made by pecking, or pounding the surface with pebbles, which seem to form another element in the intellectual and ritual aspect of Late Neolithic and Early Bronze Age society. The great majority of these carvings are found on glaciated rock surfaces and are therefore not datable by archaeological associations. However the Irish and Breton passage graves have produced more complex carvings, and a few cup-and-ring marks also occur in the Irish tombs, which show that the sculpting skills required to make these widespread and standardised designs were already present in Ireland at the end of the fourth millennium BC; carvings were especially numerous at New Grange.[34] Enough cup-marks and cups-with-rings have been found on standing stones and stone circles in Britain and Ireland to make it clear that the carvings belong broadly to the same period as those; several of the many standing stones in the Kilmartin valley in Argyllshire are decorated in this way, and a fine spiral rock carving was found in 1973 at the Temple Wood stone circle in the same area. Another, finer spiral was found on the same stone in 1975. Cup-marks are found on stone circles frequently only in northeast Scotland where they were carved on some recumbent stone circles and, more often, on the rings surrounding the Clava cairns of Inverness.[35]

A collection of about 60 rubbings of cup-and-ring carvings from southwest Scotland have been subjected by Thom to the same kind of metrological and geometrical analysis that he applied earlier to the stone circles.[36] The rubbings and most of the measurements were made by R. W. B. Morris who has extensively studied the rock carvings of the area.[37] Two important and hitherto unknown properties of the carvings were discovered in this way. The first was that a unit of length had been used to set out the designs which the carvers followed, a length equivalent to 20.73 mm or exactly 1/40th of the megalithic yard. This figure was arrived at by applying the Broadbent theorem to measurements taken from the circular carvings, or rather taken from a line along the estimated middle of the broad pecked grooves, and the exact numerical relationship with the megalithic yard provides important independent evidence that the latter was actually used. The megalithic rod of 6.8 ft (2½ MY) detected in the perimeters of the stone rings and also in the alignments of southern Brittany would of course have contained 100 of these 'megalithic inches'.

The second discovery was that, if the carved rings were not circular, they followed similar methodical geometrical shapes to those found in the stone rings, notably ellipses and egg-shapes. Spirals are frequently found, made from series of half ellipses. Direct evidence — the only so far available — for the knowledge of the 3-4-5 right-angled triangle was even found in a set of five cup-marks on Gourock golf course in Renfrewshire which define two such triangles quite clearly and precisely.[38]

Although the close relationship between these rock carvings and the stone circles is thus clearly established through two independent lines of evidence — archaeological associations and ancient metrology — the function and purpose of the engravings is not at all clear. The distribution of the carved rocks and stones shows marked concentrations in several areas and a complete blank south of central Wales (where there is one cup-marked boulder and another cup-mark not far away in the Four Stones circle at Walton).[39] The carvings are numerous in southwest Ireland, on the south coast of Galloway (southwest Scotland), in Argyllshire and central and northeast Scotland. There are many stone circles in all these areas, though they also occur in regions devoid of the carvings such as Wales and the southern half of England. In the case of much of the latter area the reason for this must be that suitable rock surfaces are rare. The frequent association between cup-marks and stone circles in northeast Scotland has already been noted. At present there seems a definite probability that the carving tradition originated in Ireland among the passage grave builders in the latter part of the fourth millennium BC and, if so, the special knowledge and skills involved in laying out the designs (with measuring rods and trammels) and carving them doubtless spread from there into both Britain and Iberia.[40] This possibility of an Irish origin takes on an extra interest in the light of the discussion later in this book of the emergence of the ceremonial centres of southern England (chapters 7, 8 and 10).

3

The Origins and Affinities
of the Megalithic Yard

Although the use by the British, Irish and Breton stone circle builders of a standard unit of length of 2.72 ft, and a multiple of 2½ times this length, seems highly probable from the mathematical evidence, reviewed in the preceding chapter, the concept of a prehistoric standardised 'short yard' would clearly benefit greatly from some independent confirming historical evidence in order to make it fully acceptable. There is in fact evidence for the existence in the civilisations of the ancient world of such a 'short yard' of 32½-33 in and this must go far to substantiate Thom's metrological claims. Another way of testing the theory of the megalithic yard is to examine another homogeneous group of ancient stone structures in the same way; if these too prove to incorporate a standard unit of length the hypothesis of the megalithic yard is likewise supported. The second part of this chapter reviews such a study of the Iron Age brochs of Scotland, and shows that not only has a unit of length been discovered in them through mathematical analysis, but that this length is also a 'short yard' very close to that found in the stone circles of 2,000 years earlier. Even the more complex geometrical constructions of the Early Bronze Age seem to be reproduced in a few of these brochs.

HISTORICAL PARALLELS

The megalithic yard is not an isolated phenomenon of the Neolithic period in northwest Europe but appears to be closely linked with, and could ultimately be derived from, the ancient systems of linear measurement used in Mesopotamia and perhaps in Egypt as well — sources from which evidently sprang the metrologies of many other parts of the ancient world.[1] These links provide us with an essential and hitherto ignored clue to the origins of the metrological and surveying skills possessed by the circle builders and must inevitably cast doubt on the assumption that the northwest European Neolithic metrology and astronomy was an entirely indigenous phenomenon.[2]

The Iberian vara

The megalithic yard is almost identical to the traditional Spanish unit known as the *vara*, a word meaning 'rod', as Thom himself noted. At

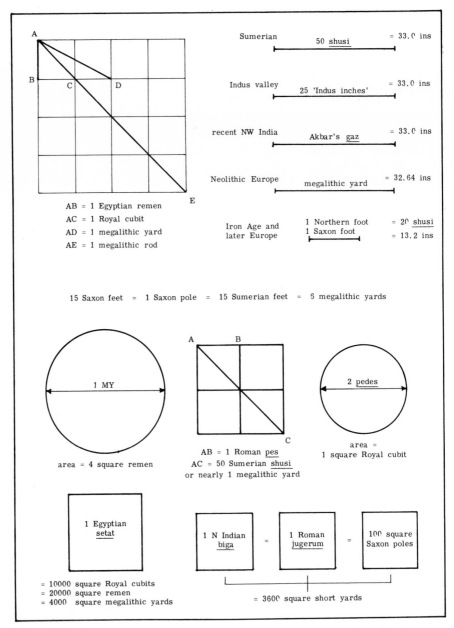

Fig. 5. Units of length of ancient and recent times and their possible links with the megalithic yard

Burgos and Madrid this pre-metric, native yard was found to be equivalent to 2.77 and 2.74 ft respectively.[3] It was also reported to Thom that the *vara* is known in the New World, having presumably been taken there by the Spanish *conquistadores* from the early sixteenth century onwards. In Texas and California (both former Spanish colonies) it was 2.78 ft, in Mexico 2.75 ft and in Peru 2.75 ft.[3] The question then arises, is there any archaeological link between Iberia and Britain in the Neolithic period, before the circle-building epoch? The Early Neolithic chambered cairns known as passage graves are abundant in Iberia, Brittany and the British Isles but have not yet been examined for evidence that a systematic geometry was incorporated in their design nor for the presence of any linear measure in their dimensions. The existence of the *vara* suggests that such a search might prove rewarding, and that the megalithic yard could have been brought to Britain from Spain — or taken in the reverse direction — in Early Neolithic times. However, the apparent links with the Egyptian and Mesopotamian measuring systems, discussed below, seem to make a northwest European origin for the megalithic yard much less probable.

Egyptian and Mesopotamian measuring systems

In ancient Egypt the unit of area used in measuring land was the *setat*, equivalent to a square with sides of 100 *royal cubits* of 20.63 in.[4] This cubit was mentioned by Herodotus in relation to Babylonia and by the Rhind mathematical papyrus of the XVIth (Hyksos) dynasty which was apparently copied from an older XIIth dynasty document dating to early in the second millennium BC. There are carefully graduated stone measuring rods extant from the New Kingdom showing the royal cubit.[5] There was another Egyptian unit known as the *double remen* equivalent to 29.16 in, and it was Sir W. Flinders Petrie[6] who first realised that the two units were geometrically related. The royal cubit is the length of the diagonal of a square with sides of one remen (14.58 in) and, similarly, the double remen is the length of the diagonal of a square with sides of one royal cubit (fig. 5). These geometrical relationships are simple and undoubted, but it is true that the contemplation of ancient measuring systems can sometimes produce extremely fanciful ideas. One such is surely Petrie's notion that the double remen is the length of the string of a pendulum which swings 100,000 times in one day![7]

The purpose of this dual Egyptian system is plain in the light of the relationship between the remen and royal cubit, since the area of a square remen is half that of a square royal cubit which in turn is half that of a square double remen. Similarly the area of a circle with a diameter of 1 royal cubit would be twice that of one with a diameter of 1 remen, and so on. By having the two systems the Egyptians would have been able rapidly to double or halve *areas* of land (measured in squares) without doing awkward calculations each time. Both the remen and the royal cubit were subdivided, the latter into 7 palms each of 4 digits of 18.7 mm, and the former into 40 almost exactly similar digits of 18.5 mm.

A link between the Egyptian and Sumerian measuring systems is not obvious at first sight but becomes apparent when the megalithic yard is considered below. Knowledge of the exact size of the Sumerian units comes from basalt statues of the governor Gudea of Lagash, now in the Louvre, which date to near the end of the third millennium BC. One headless figure has a tablet on its knees on which is the ground plan of a temple and also part of a cubit scale; another tablet is blank but the scale is better preserved. Berriman established that the average distance between the main 'inch' divisions was 0.66 in and he supposed these to be the *shusi* mentioned in the cuneiform texts.[8] Also from the cuneiform tablets the Sumerian cubit is known to have contained 30 *shusi* so its length would be 19.8 in according to Gudea's scale. The Sumerian foot, also mentioned in the texts, contained 20 *shusi* and would be 13.2 in long. The length of the Egyptian royal cubit is thus 25/24ths of the Sumerian cubit, but this need mean nothing by itself of course.

The metrology of the Indus civilisation

The other major Early Bronze Age urban civilisation of the Old World west of China was in northwest India, centred on the valley of the river Indus, and it was flourishing in the third millennium BC.[9] The 1931 excavations at the city of Mohenjo-daro produced a fragment of a shell 2.60 in long which was marked with nine fine, carefully sawn, parallel lines 0.264 in apart; one line is marked with a circle and another, five spaces away, with a large dot, and the space between them — termed the 'indus inch' by Berriman — is thus 1.32 in which is exactly 2 Sumerian *shusi*.[10] This can hardly be a coincidence and would appear to support the derivation of some elements of the Indus urban civilisation from further west, a thesis argued on other archaeological evidence as well as on the general principles of human social and genetic development.[11]

It is a remarkable fact that the megalithic yard of the British stone circles appears to provide a link between the systems of linear measurement of these three oldest centres of urban civilisation—in the valleys of the Indus, the Tigris-Euphrates and the Nile. In northwestern India, but not in other parts, a traditional yard known as the *gaz* was in use from early times as a land measure. The *biga* was a unit of land area consisting of a square *jarib*, the *jarib* being 60 *gaz* in length: the *biga* thus contained 3,600 square *gaz*. In the sixteenth century the Pathan emperor Akbar attempted to standardise the length of the *gaz* and have it universally adopted in his realm, but he was not entirely successful because of internal troubles. In 1823 the British government of India, also wishing to standardise the *gaz* and the measurement of land in general, set up the Silberrad committee to consider the evidence as to what the traditional length was in Akbar's time.[12] The conclusion drawn by the committee was that the *gaz* should be 33 in long (2.75 ft): the megalithic yard is of course 32.64 in in length. The discovery of the scale at Mohenjo-daro more than a hundred years later showed that this 33 in *gaz* was exactly 25 'Indus inches' in length ($25 \times 1.32 = 33$) so it seems highly probable that the traditional yard of northern India is directly descended from the system of linear measurement used by the Indus valley urban civilisation of 4,000 years earlier. The *gaz* is of course exactly 50 of the Sumerian *shusi* found on Gudea's statues. The British megalithic yard as defined by Thom too is only a fraction (0.36 in) under 50 *shusi* in length.

The megalithic yard and Egypt

Geometrically, the megalithic yard can be closely related to the Egyptian and Sumerian systems and hence to the Greek, Roman and later European units of length derived from these. We have noted the relationship between the Egyptian remen, royal cubit and double remen; the second and third units are each equivalent to $\sqrt{2}$ of the one immediately preceding them.

The Egyptian unit of land measure was the *setat*, equivalent to the square on a line 100 royal cubits long: thus the *setat* was 10,000 square royal cubits and 20,000 square remen. Ivimy seems to have been the first to point out that, in a rectangle measuring 1 remen by a double remen, the diagonal measures 32.602 in or almost exactly 1 megalithic yard (fig. 5) ($14.58^2 + 29.16^2 = 1,062.89$: $\sqrt{1,062.89} = 32.602$).[13] Thus one megalithic yard is scarcely distinguishable from $\sqrt{5}$ remen, and the *setat* would be equal to 4,000 square megalithic yards. Moreover, fig. 5 shows that four diagonals along square remens, i.e. four royal cubits, equal 82.52 in, only 0.92 in more than the length of a megalithic rod at 81.60 in.[14] Fletcher has pointed out another potentially important geometrical link between the megalithic yard and the Egyptian units.[15] A circle with a diameter of 32.64 in (1 MY) encloses an area of 836.74 sq in and a square with the same area has sides of 28.927 in or very close to a double remen (29.16 in). Thus the megalithic yard might be related to Egyptian measurement of areas in two ways: it could have been used to make squares five times larger than units of square remens without complex calculations and it could also have served to translate quickly areas in square double remen into circles. That it was used as a 'short yard' in the ancient centres of Bronze Age urban civilisation is strongly suggested by the geometrical relationships just described and by its clear links with the Sumerian and Indus metrologies (being equivalent to 50 *shusi* and 25 'Indus inches'), and plainly shown by its survival to modern times in north India as the *gaz* and in Iberia as the *vara*.

Roman metrology

Several historical metrologists have deduced that the Greek, Roman and later European units of length were derived from the Egyptian and

Sumerian systems and the megalithic yard should therefore relate to these also. Roman linear measurement was based on a foot or *pes* of 11.66 in, a length found carved on several stone monuments including the late first century AD memorial to the young architect Statilius Aper, now in the Capitoline museum in Rome.[16] A white marble slab in the capitol has several scales of measurement engraved on it, including a *pes* of 11.604 in which is surely the same as the Statilian foot; it seems questionable whether the difference of 0.056 in was deliberately intended by the stone carvers. Two later bronze *pes* measures in the British Museum are slightly shorter at 11.50 and 11.60 in.[17] The Roman *pes* was divided into 16 digits of 0.73 in as well as into 12 uncial units or inches. The digit is evidently the same as the Egyptian one in the remen and royal cubit so that 5 Statilian *pedes* are more or less exactly equal to 2 double remen (58.30 in as opposed to 58.32).

The major unit of land area used by the Romans was the *jugerum* (*iugerum*), 800 of which made one *saltus* of about 500 acres (below). The *jugerum* consisted of the curiously unsymmetrical number of 28,800 square *pedes*, equivalent to the square on a line 169.7 *pedes* in length. Fletcher points out that this area is almost exactly equal to the square on a line of 96 Egyptian royal cubits; 1/96th of the side of a *jugerum* would be 20.612 in as opposed to the royal cubit of 20.63 in.[18] Similarly the area of the *jugerum* is extremely close to that of the traditional north Indian *biga*, of 3,600 square *gaz*; the *biga* is about 35 square *pedes* larger. Thus the peculiarly odd number of *pedes* in the side of a square *jugerum* would be nearly exactly equivalent to a *jarib* of 60 *gaz* (1.3 in less in fact) and almost equal to 60 British megalithic yards (in fact 20 in more than the latter). Berriman also realised that the *jugerum* and the *biga* — and therefore the square on 96 royal cubits also — are almost exactly equal to a square with sides of 10 Saxon poles of 16.5 ft (the European linear measures are described in the next section).

Fletcher pointed to another link between the Roman measuring system and the megalithic yard.[19] The diagonal of a square with sides of 2 Statilian *pedes* measures 32.98 in, almost identical with the north Indian *gaz* and 50 Sumerian *shusi* and only 0.34 in longer than the megalithic yard. Similarly a circle with a radius of 1 *pes* encloses an area of 427.19 sq in, almost identical to that enclosed by a square Egyptian royal cubit which has an area of 425.6 sq in: in other words, a square equal in area to such a circle has sides of 20.668 in or 0.038 in more than the royal cubit. We have already noted that 1/60th of the sides of a square *jugerum* is 32.98 in, and this is precisely the same as the diagonal on the square on 2 *pedes* referred to.

Thus it would have been possible for the Romans to lay out a square *jugerum*, or at least to establish its area, in a simple manner using an equivalent of the *gaz*, and the Roman system may have used for area measurement two geometrically linked units of length in the same way as the Egyptian, to make it easy to double or halve areas of land. In this case, however, the diagonal would have produced a square equivalent to 8 square *pedes* (1 diagonal 'short yard' = $\sqrt{8}$ or 2.828 *pedes*).

European Iron Age and Saxon measures

A 'northern foot' was deduced by Petrie to have been in use among the Teutonic tribes of Europe 2,000 years ago and to have become the foot used in Saxon England.[20] The foot was used by the Tungri tribe of lower Germany in the first century BC and was so well established there that the Romans under Drusus adopted it locally. The 'Drusian foot' was recorded by them as being 2 digits longer than their own, or about 13.12 in.[21] The Saxon foot was 13.2 in, and Berriman seems to have been the first to point out that the Sumerian foot of 20 *shusi* (13.2 in) is exactly the same as the Saxon foot and almost identical to the Tungrian one of a few centuries earlier.[22] A similar measurement is also recorded as 13.3 in on five known ancient Egyptian cubit rods.[23] Fifteen Saxon feet made 1 pole, the standard unit for land measurement in pre-Norman England, so that the pole is also equal to 15 Sumerian feet of 20 *shusi* and to 10 Sumerian cubits of 30 *shusi*. Six megalithic yards equal 195.84 in (16 ft 3.84 in) as against the length of the pole of 15 saxon feet of 198.0 in, and of course 6 units of 50 Sumerian *shusi* are also precisely equal to it. Thus 2½ Saxon feet equal a north Indian *gaz* of 33 inches and are only very slightly more than a megalithic yard. The possible implications of all these are discussed at the end of the chapter.

The traditional metrology of the Tyrolean mines

Of particular interest to this discussion is the traditional measuring system used in the mines of the Austrian Tyrol.[24] In recent times the mines of Saxony and the Tyrol apparently belonged to aristocratic proprietors who leased them to many small concessionaires whose operations had to be supervised by a class of official geometers called *Schiner* to prevent unauthorised activity. These men were equipped with finely made measuring instruments, in a style worthy of their lordly employers, and the measurement of distance, direction (azimuth) and dip were done in local units peculiar to the mining industry. The unit of length used in the Tyrolean mines was the *Klafter* of 5 ft 5.88 in, equivalent to two miner's perches of 32.94 in, and it was carried around as a wooden measuring rod bound with brass which could be taken apart into shorter sections for convenience.

The Tyrolean miner's perch is of course only 0.30 in longer than the megalithic yard of 32.64 in, and it is of particular interest, first, to find it used only for a special purpose by a specialised class of mine overseers, and second, in a part of Europe where mining activity had been going on continuously for thousands of years. The salt mines of Hallstatt and the copper mines of the Austrian Tyrol have been exploited at least since the Early Iron Age, in the seventh century BC, and the Early Bronze Age, since well before 2000 BC, respectively. The copper mines seem to have been exploited from the outset by professional miners equipped with previously developed techniques[25] and it seems more than likely that the traditional measuring systems mentioned were handed down directly from the first prehistoric miners. It can hardly be a coincidence that a specialised class of mining engineers, probably with its roots in prehistoric times, used the same short yard as did what we infer to have been a specialised prehistoric class of stone circle builders, surveyors and astronomers.

TWO MEASURING RODS FROM DENMARK

Two examples are known of what seem to be wooden measuring rods from prehistoric Europe. In the Early Bronze Age burial mound at Borum Eshøj in East Jutland three oak coffin burials were found, one in 1871 and two in 1875.[26] Their date is usually estimated as late in the second millennium BC.[27] Next to one of the coffins found in 1875, which contained the body of an old man with a bronze sword, lay a slightly curved, notched hazel rod 30.9 (Danish) inches in length which seems to have been thrown down into the grave at the time of the interment. P. V. Glob thought it might have been used in laying out the dimensions of the circular grave mound.[28] The rod was notched in four places — one space being twice as long as the others — so that it was divided as follows: 1/5, 1/5, 2/5, 1/5.[29] Before the adoption of the metric system Denmark had its own system of linear measurement in which there were about 38 inches to the metre, as opposed to 39.37 British inches.[30] So 30.9 Danish inches would be some 32.01 in or 0.813 m long, and the length of the rod at the time of discovery would be only 0.63 in (1.6 cm) shorter than the megalithic yard. However, the nineteenth century description of the Borum finds gives the length of the rod as 30 Danish inches or 79.3 cm (2.59 ft), 0.79 in shorter than the first measurement mentioned and 1.42 in less than the megalithic yard.[31] It seems reasonable to suppose that since Bøye's figure is 30 and not 30.0 in Glob's measurement of 30.9 is more precise. Allowing for the possibility of a little shrinkage in the rod over the last 3,000 or more years, despite the waterlogged conditions of the grave, it seems possible that Borum Eshøj has produced the only known European megalithic yardstick. If it was one, the divisions are of some interest. Since a megalithic yard seems to have been close to 50 Sumerian *shusi*, each 1/5th of the rod could have been intended to be equivalent to 10 *shusi*, and the longer space to the Sumerian foot of 20 *shusi* and to the later northern foot.

The second wooden rod is of Iron Age date and was found during the excavations at Borre Fen, an island stronghold in Himmerland, defended by a great earthwork and two moats.[32] The oak rod was 53.15 in long, with a button at one end and pointed at the other, and was divided into eight equal parts cut along one edge in the form of alternate convex and concave curves. Each division is given as 6.5 in so that two total 13.0 in. If the whole length of the rod is divided into eight parts these become 6.64 in each and two make up 13.28 in. Both figures are very close to the Saxon and Drusian feet mentioned. Five-eighths of course total 32.5 in (or perhaps 33.2 in), very close to the megalithic yard.

THE METROLOGY OF THE BROCHS

One of the obvious tests for the Thom hypothesis that the stone circles were designed and set out using a sophisticated metrology and geometry, is to examine another standardised class of prehistoric structures in the same way to see whether similar methods will produce comparable results. The Early Neolithic passage graves form an obvious group which could be so examined[33] and the results of the careful measurement of the circular central chambers of the two at Clava, Invernesshire, are described below. However, in 1971 the Scottish brochs seemed to be a more easily accessible and promising group of circular buildings and in that year I undertook a field trip to make exact measurements of as many as possible.[34] Since brochs are Iron Age defensive buildings and unlikely to be older than the first century BC, and are thus totally distinct in time, culture and function from the stone circles,[35] they seemed to provide an ideal subject for a parallel metrological study. Previous work on the brochs strongly suggested that these ingenious drystone tower-forts were built for a variety of Iron Age communities in Atlantic Scotland by professional architects and engineers.[36] Reasons for supposing this include the fact that, although the towers are highly standardised in design, they clearly underwent modification and improvement during the period of their construction, thus implying systematic planning and improvement in the light of experience. In spite of this homogeneity in design the artefacts found in them, particularly the pottery, vary considerably from one part of the broch zone to another, implying that the towers were introduced to pre-existing communities by professional builders. In general the brochs seem the ideal structures to examine for evidence of the presence of specialist groups of builders with unusual skills and traditions. The result of this exercise bears directly not only on the problem of the validity of the mathematical method of inferring prehistoric units of length but also on the whole concept of the existence of highly skilled, learned orders in prehistoric Britain.

Circular brochs

A preliminary study by Dr G. I. Crawford of the dimensions of the central courts and of the overall diameters of about 50 brochs (measurements taken by the writer on field trips in 1963) suggested that the former were laid out as multiples of a definite unit of length but that the latter were not. However, only two pairs of measurements at right angles to each other were

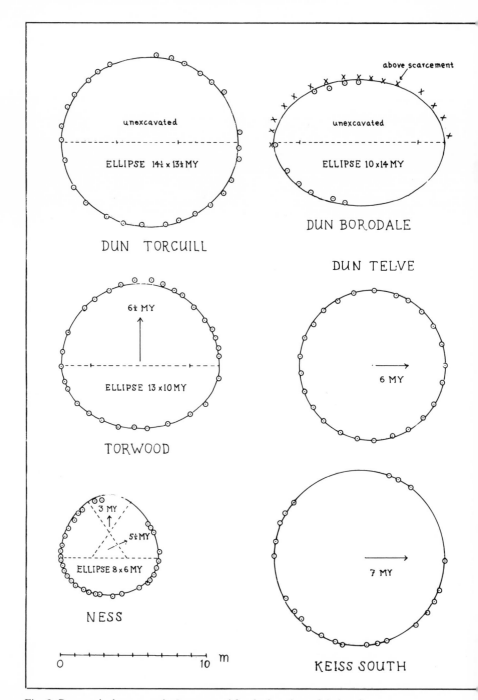

Fig. 6. Geometrical constructions suggested for the interiors of six brochs

available from each site, so it was clear that new, more accurate and complete measurements were required.

In three weeks in September 1971 I travelled throughout the broch province, through Sutherland and Caithness, the Orkney and Shetland Isles, and westward to Skye and the Outer Hebrides. A total of 36 brochs were surveyed, out of a list of about 50 selected in advance as being known from previous visits to be relatively clear of debris. One more, Torwood in Stirlingshire, was added later and two of those in Caithness, Ness and Skirza Head, were further investigated in the autumn of 1972 when another broch (Keiss West) was planned for the first time. The method adopted was to set up a theodolite or plane table in the middle of the broch and to place up to 30 surveying pins against the inner wallface, as low down as possible. The distance from a pin immediately below the instrument or table to each of these wall pins was measured with a steel metric tape and the corresponding angle recorded with the theodolite or the alidade. Dr Crawford prepared a computer programme which could work out the best fitting circle for each of the resulting sets of angles and distances. All but seven of the 37 measured brochs proved to be round, and the precision of their circularity is well illustrated by the figure for the mean error in millimetres. This is the average discrepancy between the actual measured points on the wallface and the calculated best fit true circle and, with circles having diameters varying between 21.65 ft (6.6 m) and 42.65 ft (13.0 m), the mean error in all cases was less than 4 in (10 cm). In most of the brochs (28 out of 30), the mean error was 2.36 in or less, and in five the wallface varied from the circle on average less than 1.18 in. The masons who laid the foundation blocks for the inside wallface placed most of them within 2-3 in of a true circle which must previously have been carefully marked on the ground and which had doubtless been drawn with a peg-and-string compass and checked with a measuring rod. There can be no doubt at all that the brochs were systematically planned as circles.

An analysis of the mean diameters of these 30 circular brochs shows a high likelihood that these had been set out in multiples of a 'broch yard': there was only a 1.4% probability that this result was due to chance. The best fitting length of the 'broch yard' was 2.74 ft or 32.89 in (0.835 m), only 0.25 in longer than the megalithic yard of the stone circles at 2.72 ft. The diameters of some of the brochs, such as Keiss South and Skirza Head in Caithness and Backies in Sutherland, are almost exact multiples of the megalithic yard (fig. 6); others are equally circular, but the units employed in their diameters are a little above or below 2.72 ft. If one treats all the mean diameters (the radii include half yards so are less suitable) as exact multiples of broch yards which varied slightly from one site to the next, a histogram of 30 of these yards could be constructed which would resemble that for the stone circles described earlier (fig. 3).

This histogram is less reliable than that for the circles, in the sense that there are far fewer sites; three or four times as many would doubtless produce the high peak around the mean which is desirable. However, in other ways the broch data is preferable, first because the continuous wallfaces allow the mean circle of each to be computed more confidently (with no doubt at all arising as to where the line on the ground was drawn), and second because of the much narrower range of broch sizes. The diameters vary from 8 to 14 'yards' and the dimensions are thus much more homogeneous. However, it must again be remembered that the deduction that a quantum exists among the broch diameters comes not from this simple process of dividing them into whole numbers but from much more sophisticated statistical techniques.

We find in fact that the mean of the 30 'broch yards' turns out to be 2.745 ± 0.07 ft, a little more than the megalithic yard of 2.72 ft. The smallest 'yard' traced is 2.59 ft and the largest 2.87 ft: the total range is 0.28 ft or 3.4 in. The standard deviation, however, at 0.07 ft is only 0.84 in. The histogram (fig. 3) shows how most of the 'broch yards' might be considered to fall into two major clusters centred on about 2.71 and 2.79 ft. A large cluster at the mean of 2.74 ft is lacking, however, and the yardsticks are scattered fairly evenly along the scale.

It is plain from Dr Crawford's findings on the lengths of the perimeters of the circles which fit the 30 broch interiors best, that it would be difficult to conclude that the lengths of the broch perimeters were deliberately arranged to be in whole numbers of rods, although Clickhimin in Shetland happens to have an internal circumference which is almost exactly 14 megalithic rods. Of the 30 sites nine are within 0.1 rods of an integral number (0.21 m), another nine are within 0.3 rods, while the remaining 12 are (naturally) within 0.5 rods of an integral number. Given the fact that the perimeters cannot by definition be more than 0.5 rods away from a whole number, there seems little evidence for any significant clustering around the integrals.

Elliptical brochs

Of the 37 brochs surveyed, seven appeared not to be set out as true circles but three of these were buried under too much of their own rubble for their exact shape to be ascertained. Of the remaining four, two, Dun Torcuill in North Uist and Dun Borodale on Raasay Island, were oval and two, Ness in Caithness and Torwood in Stirlingshire, appeared to be either egg-shapes or flattened circles of some kind. The surveyed points on the inside wallface of Dun Torcuill were processed by the computer which had been programmed to test such data for the accuracy of their fit to ellipses. As a result the broch was found to have been built very precisely around an ellipse with eccentricity of 0.93. (The eccentricity of an ellipse is defined as the proportion of the long axis of that part of it not between the foci. In the example given the foci are close together and only 0.07 of the long axis is between them.) The fit was particularly impressive because since the broch has never been excavated the survey of the inside wallface had to be done at a height of 5-6 ft above the floor and in places the wall was leaning noticeably inwards. The ellipse exactly fits the wallface where curvature is smooth and diverges from it in those parts where it is obviously leaning in or out. The axes of the best fit ellipse, deduced by the computer through trial and error, were 40.00 ft and 36.85 ft in length and the perimeter 121.33 ft. That the axes are exactly divisible into 15 and 14 by a unit of 2.65 ft can hardly be a coincidence.

The perimeter of this figure is exactly 44½ MY long (121.38 ft); it is 0.2 megalithic rods less than the nearest whole number of these (18). It is worth considering whether the slightly smaller size of the Dun Torcuill 'yards' might be explained as the result of a desire to make the perimeter close to an integral number of megalithic rods. By using axes of 14 and 15 megalithic yards (2.72 ft) the perimeter would have been 123.99 ft or 45.49 MY, that is 0.24 MY more than 18 rods (122.41 ft). Thus there seems no reason to suppose that the question of the number of rods which would be in the perimeter played any part in the calculations of the designer of Dun Torcuill. Neither is the elliptical shape likely to have been dictated by the situation of the broch: Dun Torcuill stands on a small islet in a loch which is little larger than the building itself, but there would have been no difficulty, as far as one can judge, in making it circular if this had been thought necessary.

Dun Borodale on Raasay Island is situated on a high, steep-sided rocky hilltop and is markedly oval in shape; in this case the design may well have been influenced by the restricted area on which it was built. Unfortunately without some clearance of the rubble which fills the interior only a small part of the inside wallface below the level of the scarcement is visible. However, the masonry above the scarcement can be traced for several yards further round and together the two groups of surveyed points span nearly three-quarters of the perimeter. An ellipse of 14 by 10 MY fits these points very well, touching the wall below the scarcement and keeping a distance of about the width of this stone ledge within the other points. The perimeter of this ellipse is 38.23 MY compared with the 37½ MY which equal 15 rods. Such a difference from the hypothetical 'ideal' perimeter, 0.73 MY or 0.29 rods, might be thought small enough to justify a tentative assumption that the shape was designed to aim for a circumference of 37½ MY, but there is no way of knowing, particularly as the quality of the fit between the ellipse and the *base* of the inside wall is as yet unknown. With only two elliptical brochs to consider so far it is impossible to come to a firm conclusion on the subject and the simpler hypothesis is therefore to be preferred. This is that different individual broch designers had slightly different yardsticks with which they laid out their circles and, occasionally, other geometrical figures.

Egg-shaped brochs

When it was first planned the small broch at Ness Head, a sheer-sided cliff promontory on the east coast of Caithness, appeared to fit a type A flattened circle of the kind deduced by Thom to have been incorporated into some stone circles (fig. 6). Only half of the much reduced wallhead remains as continuous masonry, but the curvature of the neatly built inside face proved to be much shallower on one side. It seemed to fit very closely to a circle with a diameter of 8 MY with a flatter segment composed of an arc of a circle with a diameter of 14 MY. Even the 'corner' between these arcs, composed of an arc of a smaller circle of diameter 4 MY, was a good fit.

In order to test the hypothesis that Ness was planned around such a geometrical figure a small-scale excavation was done on the site in September 1972, the assumption being that traces of the inner wallface of the vanished half of the broch might be recoverable and that any such traces should follow the predicted line of the flattened circle. Some paving was found which seemed to support this idea, but a short, new section of wallface was uncovered together with two isolated wall blocks still apparently in position. The line joining these blocks curved inwards and well away from the hypothetical line so that the flattened circle would not fit more than half the perimeter.[37] In spite of the exposed paving there seemed no way to make the new extension of the continuous wallface fit the flattened circle construction, even if the two isolated wall blocks were assumed to belong to the numerous secondary constructions inside the broch. The hypothesis that Ness broch was built round a flattened circle appeared to be disproved.[37]

Eventually the solution applied to the Torwood broch (below) was tried on Ness, and the surveyed points of a selected half of the internal wallface were fitted against half an ellipse having long and short axes of 9 and 8 megalithic yards respectively. Though more than half of the remaining part of the structure has disappeared, the rest of the wallface fits very well to an egg-shape composed of two arcs of a circle with a radius of 5½ MY joined at the top by an arc of 3 MY radius (fig. 6). This egg-shape is based on a Pythagorean triangle with sides of 3, 4 and 5 half megalithic yards. The excellence of the fit of the half ellipse — the standard deviation of the wall foundation blocks measured was ± 1.38 in — leaves little doubt, first, that the megalithic yard was used in laying out the site, and second, that for some reason geometrical constructions inherited from those of Late Neolithic times were occasionally used by the broch designers when laying out the marks for their stone masons.

Torwood broch is the best of the four non-circular sites, being both well preserved and having a complete interior which has been largely free of debris since 1864. The solution to its geometry was not easy: the narrow end was at first easily diagnosed as a symmetrical egg-shape with a 'tip' formed of an arc of a circle 5 MY in radius and the sides, slightly more awkwardly, as arcs of circles 8¾ MY in radius. The base was tentatively assumed to be half of an ellipse with axes of 11.5 and 9.8 MY, but this part did not fit the broch wall base at all well for two-thirds of its length. The bad fit of the lower part, and the need to make several important measurements into fractions of megalithic yards, seemed to make this geometrical solution very unconvincing even though the top half fitted well. Eventually it was realised that if the axis of symmetry was turned through about 110°, then half of an ellipse with axes of 10 and 13 MY would fit the wallbase extremely closely; Dr Crawford's computer programme did an independent analysis of this part of the wall and discovered that half of an ellipse measuring 35.61 ft by 27.63 ft (almost exactly 13 by 10 MY) fitted the stones with a standard deviation of only ± 1.54 in.

The new upper half of the geometrical figure can be reconstructed in two slightly different ways. Half a circle with a radius of 6½ MY (the same as half the long axis of the ellipse) will fit the broch extremely closely except along a length of 20.67 ft around the main entrance, a place where the masonry has been observed to diverge from the expected geometrical figure in several sites. Alternatively, the wall can also be made to fit two almost quarter-circles of radius 7 MY whose centres are on the long axis of the ellipse and 1 MY apart. In this reconstruction the two main axes of the broch should be identical at 13 MY and in fact the distances on the ground are 35.37 ft and 35.30 ft. On the whole the simpler figure, with a semicircular top, seems more convincing and preferable (fig. 6). The perimeter of the second figure is about 15.69 megalithic rods and that of the first described is 15.44 rods: in neither case could one reasonably assume that a circumference of either 15 or 16 rods was intended, and it does not seem likely that the making of the perimeter integral in megalithic rods played an important part in the calculations of the broch designers, as it may have done with the circle builders.

Conclusions

A test was suggested for Thom's theory that a complex Neolithic metrology and geometry, involving the use of a standardised measuring rod of 2.72 ft, was incorporated into the Neolithic stone circles — one which involved the application of the same analytical techniques to another standardised form of prehistoric building. The brochs were chosen, and the results seem to have provided a startling vindication of the theory. Both the geometry and the unit of length evidently reappear in the Iron Age buildings and, because of the nature of these structures, may be said to be more clearly apparent in them than in the circles. The implications of this close link between prehistoric architectural traditions across a gap of two millennia are of great importance and are discussed in the final chapter.

SUMMARY AND CONCLUSIONS

The historical data reviewed in the first part of this chapter shows clearly that a 'short yard' of about 33 in survived in use until recently at opposite

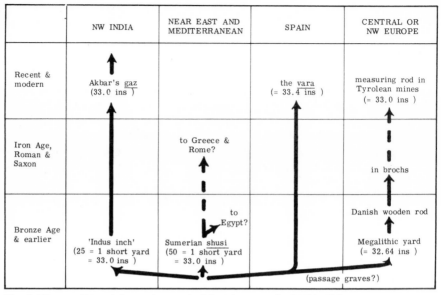

	NW INDIA	NEAR EAST AND MEDITERRANEAN	SPAIN	CENTRAL OR NW EUROPE
Recent & modern	Akbar's gaz (33.0 ins)		the vara (= 33.4 ins)	measuring rod in Tyrolean mines (= 33.0 ins)
Iron Age, Roman & Saxon		to Greece & Rome?		in brochs
Bronze Age & earlier	'Indus inch' (25 = 1 short yard = 33.0 ins)	Sumerian shusi (50 = 1 short yard = 33.0 ins) to Egypt?		Danish wooden rod Megalithic yard (= 32.64 ins)
			(passage graves?)	

Fig. 7. The possible origins and spread of the 'short yard' of 32½-33 in

ends of the Indo-European linguistic province — in northwestern India (but not in other parts of the subcontinent) and in Spain. These two pieces of evidence alone are enough to make the existence in prehistoric Britain of a megalithic yard of 32.64 in much more plausible than if this hypothesis had depended on mathematics alone. However, these historical 'short yards' are also clearly linked to the metrologies of two of the earliest urban civilisations of the Old World, in the valleys of the Tigris-Euphrates and the Indus, and quite possibly to that of the Nile valley as well. In particular the exact correspondence of the 'indus inch' of Mohenjo-daro with two Sumerian *shusi* is of great potential importance, as is the fact that 25 and 50 of these units respectively make up exactly one of the historical 'short yards' mentioned, the *gaz* of northern India. The Sumerian foot of 20 *shusi* also turns out to be identical with the Saxon foot of 13.2 in, presumably brought in from Germany in post-Roman times, and appears to show that a system of linear measurement based on Sumerian units spread into northern Europe at some earlier stage. Thus the prehistoric 'short yard' of northwest Europe could also be related in a straightforward manner to the Sumerian metrology, itself closely linked with that of the Early Bronze Age cities of northwest India. In the third millennium BC, therefore, we have evidence for urban systems of measurement to which the megalithic yard appears to be related and from which it could have been derived.

There seem to be more complex geometrical links between the megalithic 'short yard' and other ancient measures which reinforce this view. The Egyptian remen and royal cubit are distinct from the Sumerian units, but it is nevertheless a curious fact that the diagonal of a rectangle measuring one remen by two is almost exactly a megalithic yard. Moreover, a circle equivalent in area to a square double remen has a diameter again of almost exactly the same 'short yard'. Whether these lengths were actually used by the Egyptians is of course another matter.

Connections are also apparent between the 'short yard' and the Roman systems of linear and area measurement and here it is particularly striking that the Roman unit of land measurement, the *jugerum*, is the same as the north Indian *biga* which measures 60×60 'short yards'. The 'short yard' appears again as the equivalent of $\sqrt{8}$ Roman *pedes*, the diagonal of a square with sides of 2 *pedes*. The survival of the 33 in 'short yard' in the one-time Roman province of Spain, though perhaps from pre-Roman times, has already been mentioned.

The long survival of units of linear measurement over millennia with very little alteration demonstrates that it is difficult arbitrarily to select a particular epoch in the past and to maintain that it was then that there occurred the spread of a particular metrological tradition from its area of origin to some new territory. Only when the circumstances are exceptionally clear, as with the Spanish conquest of the New World, can such an explanation be confidently invoked. The 'short yard' might well be a standardised pace and as such could conceivably have arisen independently in several areas. Yet against this is the precise identity of the subdivisions of the ancient unit of the Indus valley with those of contemporary Mesopotamia, together with the fact that 25 and 50 of these units respectively add up to one of the historically attested 'short yards', the *gaz*. It is difficult not to conclude that this data shows two things clearly, first that skilled specialists took the metrology of Mesopotamia to the cities of the Indus (perhaps with the basic ideas and skills of urban civilisation itself), and second that in places a convenient round number of the small Mesopotamian units was used to produce a 'short yard' of 33 in.

Since a chain of links exists between Mesopotamian metrology and that of ancient Greece and Rome, and of Iron Age Germany and Saxon England, and since the same 'short yard' of 33 in is known in Iberia and is a multiple of 2½ Sumerian and Saxon feet, it seems unreasonable to conclude in spite of all this evidence that the 'short yard' of Neolithic Britain was an isolated standardisation of some local chieftain's pace. It now seems much more probable that the Sumerian measuring system, or at least one based on its smaller units, was brought to northwest Europe at some stage and utilised in the elaborate megalithic standing stone constructions of Britain and Brittany in the third millennium BC. When this happened is not yet clear; presumably it was earlier in the Neolithic period, after the development of settled life and when the appearance of massive stone monuments attests the presence of skilled architects and engineers. Certainly the survival of these ancient feet and short yards over several millennia to medieval times clearly shows with what tenacity a settled people can conserve a measuring system. Yet to suppose that the short yard arrived in Europe with the earliest megaliths in the mid fifth millennium BC brings up the whole question of the age of the Sumerian civilisation itself and whether indeed it is as old as these first European stone monuments.[38] Some of these problems are reviewed again in the final chapter, but discussion of the last is held over for another book.

4

Prehistoric Astronomy

INTRODUCTION

A major part of the new evidence accumulating about the technical and intellectual skills present in Early Bronze Age Britain concerns the practice of relatively sophisticated astronomical observations in those times and on a considerable scale. Thom has claimed that literally scores of standing stones and stone circle sites, from Brittany to the Orkney isles, were set up for this purpose and that not only were the yearly movements of the sun tracked with great precision but also the much more complex motions of the moon were analysed to an extraordinarily high degree. Even if these interpretations are only partly correct, the scale of these country-wide observations — perhaps made over several centuries — together with the elaborate and sophisticated techniques which must have been used to pursue the tasks, must surely imply that the work was done by a learned order possessing considerable skill, authority and prestige. When taken together with the evidence for the advanced geometrical and metrological knowledge and skill possessed by the circle builders (described in the last chapter), this leaves little room for doubt that such an order did exist. It must, moreover, surely have been composed of people who were able to pursue these 'intellectual' studies full time and to an advanced level because they were supported in some way by the agricultural population and in effect did not have to produce any food or support themselves in any way. The existence of advanced astronomical practices in Neolithic Britain on the scale and of the quality suggested by Thom requires that there should be other evidence in the archaeological record of the skilled people responsible. Mrs Hawkes was in effect saying this in her 1967 article;[1] her point — which at that time concerned the astronomical theories about Stonehenge of G. Hawkins[2] — was that the idea of such intellectually sophisticated practices in ancient Britain was incredible because the rest of the evidence we had for that period suggested that the population was incapable of such things and was, in effect, not organised to maintain a class of professional astronomer-priests.

This objection can be construed in two ways. Either it means that no other evidence for such a professional class had at that time been recognised and that it ought to be discoverable if the archaeo-astronomical theories were correct, or it could mean that no such evidence exists so that the theories concerned are untenable. The second alternative is clearly unscientific since it assumes that the 'traditional' kind of archaeological evidence should be given more weight than the archaeo-astronomical data whereas, as we shall see, that data is now quite able to stand on its own merits. It is safer to maintain the simple proposition on which this book is founded: that if the evidence of prehistoric 'intellectual' skills of the various kinds inferred by Thom is valid, then there must be other archaeological evidence in support of the social implications which it carries, even though the relevant sites and finds may have been interpreted in a different way up until now. However, an assessment of the evidence for sophisticated astronomical practices in Britain 4,000 years ago is the first task here.

Before describing some of the standing stone sites claimed as astronomical observatories, it will be useful to outline the principles on which they could have worked. The methods open to a people with a Neolithic technology (one which is incapable of devising accurate small instruments) of making exact observations of celestial bodies are very limited but, perhaps surprisingly, capable of giving excellent results if used in the right way. The whole field of primitive astronomical practices has recently been reviewed.[3]

Elementary astronomy

When considering how these ancient observatories worked it is essential to understand the apparent motion of the celestial bodies which they may have been tracking. The easiest way to visualise these motions is to imagine the sky as an inverted hemispherical bowl on the inside surface of which are the unmoving stars. The constellations of stars provide a fixed frame of reference against which the much nearer sun, moon and planets appear to move slowly. This celestial sphere has an apparent daily or *diurnal* motion caused by the rotation of the earth, so that it seems to revolve from east to west around an axis which is the same as the earth's axis. Just as the terrestrial latitudes are parallel circles, imagined on the earth's surface, which represent angular distances above and below the equator (at latitude 0°) as measured from the centre of the earth, so these latitudes are projected outwards on to the surface of the celestial sphere to give positions of astronomical latitude, or *declination*. These are also measured as angles above and below the plane of the earth's equator so that the celestial equator has a declination (δ) of 0°, the north celestial pole is at $\delta + 90°$ and so on. The information needed to calculate the declination of a point on the horizon (or anywhere in the sky) includes (1) the latitude of the observing point, (2) the azimuth or bearing from this point to the chosen mark on the horizon, and (3) the apparent altitude of this mark as seen from the observing position.

It is very important to remember the difference between the terrestrial and celestial measurements of the positions of an object in the sky as seen from a given point. On the earth, horizontal position (*azimuth* or bearing) is measured on the 360° scale with 0° at true north; *altitude* is the vertical scale above the horizon with 0° being the horizontal. Depending on the latitude of one's position, however, the celestial sphere will appear to spin on an axis which is at a varying angle to the horizon, parallel to it at the equator and vertical at the poles. Thus at the latitude of Argyll (56° N) the parallel circles of declination, along which celestial bodies move with their diurnal motion, meet the horizon at an acute angle (fig. 8). A star of a given δ seen in a mountainous area can thus set at different azimuths according to the height of the horizon. Such a mountainous or irregular horizon also provides observers having only a primitive technology with a convenient fixed frame of reference against which to observe the position of celestial bodies at the time of their rising and setting (fig. 8). Indeed, for people lacking optical instruments and the capacity accurately to build measuring structures, using the horizon in this way is probably the only method for exactly defining the position of astronomical bodies.

How can these observations be made? In the case of the stars, their rising and setting positions do not alter perceptibly over many centuries and all that would be required would be for the observer to note the place of setting, select a convenient nearby natural mark such as the notch between two hills, and adjust his position laterally one evening so that he made the star descend exactly into that notch. This observing position, known as the backsight, could then be marked in some way, with a post or presumably with a permanent standing stone if the site was important. If the stone had a flat face this could be aligned towards the notch concerned to give an indication of where it was; alternatively a second stone a short distance away might point to the foresight. Without some such built-in indication of direction it is difficult to know in what part of the horizon any foresight was intended to be, or indeed if one was intended at all.

THE SUN OBSERVATORIES

The solar motion

The sun, moon and planets, in contrast to the stars, change their declinations over fixed cycles for different reasons, and the techniques for observing these cycles with alignments to the horizon are more complex. The sun, for example, because of the tilt of the earth's axis (fig. 17), appears to alter its position both against the starry background and in relation to the earthly horizon. At midwinter the north pole is tilted directly away from the sun so that the equatorial plane strikes the celestial sphere 23½° (actually 23°27'8.3") above the plane of the earth's orbit (on which the sun of course always is): thus the sun appears to be that distance below the equatorial plane and has a declination of −23½°; it is overhead at midday at the Tropic of Capricorn. At mid-summer the positions are reversed and the sun is above the equatorial plane — overhead at midday at the Tropic of

Cancer — and has a declination of $+23\frac{1}{2}°$. So the sun's real position — not to be confused with its daily motion — each year moves twice across a band in the sky about 47° wide, and this means that its rising and setting positions alter in the same way, back and forth along a specific section of the horizon.

At the equator the sun rises and sets vertically since the celestial sphere appears there to spin with its axis parallel to the horizon: its yearly motion is seen there as a change of nearly 47° in the rising and setting positions, on either side of due east and west respectively. In this case the amount of the change in solar declination is the same as the change in the azimuth (bearing) of position of the disc on the horizon. However the further away from the equator the observer's position, the more the axis of the celestial sphere is tilted upwards in relation to the horizon, until at the poles the axis is vertical with the stars neither rising nor setting. Scotland lies between about latitudes 55° and 60° N (Shetland defining the upper limit) so that the celestial pole is correspondingly between these angular distances above the horizon at any point. The celestial bodies therefore travel on paths which make an acute angle with the horizon so that the 47° change in the sun's position becomes nearly 90° along the horizon in Scotland. In these high northerly (or southerly) latitudes the yearly changes of the sun's position are therefore much more obvious than at the equator, and where the horizon is hilly and uneven the chances that it will occur to a prehistoric people to track these movements by watching the sun rise and set behind a series of prominent natural features should be correspondingly greater.

Techniques for observing the sun

However, though it is easy enough for peasant communities to keep an approximate track of the seasons and the year, by remembering a cycle of risings and settings at a sequence of natural marks, the same basic idea is capable of being used to give very precise observations suitable for professional priest-astronomers armed with the requisite intelligence but only with Neolithic equipment. The problem here is that the *rate* of change of the solar declination is not steady throughout the year; at the equinoxes it appears to move relatively rapidly, more than one solar diameter (32') each day, but as the solstices approach the movement diminishes and finally becomes imperceptible. In the 24 hours before and after the solstice (which is unlikely to occur exactly at the moment of rising or setting) the change in declination is only 12 seconds of arc and this movement increases with the square of the interval (table 6a; fig. 9). How is it possible with the naked eye to detect this tiny movement in the constantly moving sun's real position, a movement equivalent to only 1/160th of its apparent diameter?

A large sundial or gnomon casts a shadow which not only gives the time of day with its angle in relation to the N-S line but also the time of year by the length of its shadow at midday — longest in winter and shortest in summer. However, a very long shadow would be needed to show the

TABLE 6a

The present changes in solar declination around the solstices. The actual changes at the times of sunrise and sunset will vary very slightly because the moment of the solstice varies in terms of terrestrial days. The intervals in 1800 BC would have been a few seconds greater

time from solstice (in units of 24 hrs)	difference from solstitial declination
s	0' 0" (= ± 23°27'8.3")
s ± 1	0' 12"
s ± 2	0' 48"
s ± 3	1' 48"
s ± 4	3' 12"
s ± 5	5' 0"
s ± 6	7' 12"
s ± 7	9' 48"

(diameter of solar disc 32')

TABLE 6b

Base lengths of triangles at various sites formed by the change in azimuth equivalent to a change in declination of 12"

length of triangle (i.e. distance to foresight)	example	change in azimuth	horizontal move at backsight	
260 feet	centre of Stonehenge to Heel stone	23"	0.35	in
1000 yards	(at same latitude)	23"	4.0	in
1 mile	Duntreath to Strathblane hills	23"	7.1	in
10 miles	(at same latitude)	23"	5.9	ft
19.1 miles	Ballochroy to Jura	27"	13.2	ft
27.2 miles	Kintraw to Jura	27"	18.9	ft
30 miles	(at same latitude)	27"	20.8	ft

extremely small solar movement at the solstices — when the shadow ceases to shorten and begins to lengthen again, or vice versa — and because the sun is a disc, the longer the shadow is the more blurred its edge becomes. Thus precision is impossible with really large gnomons unless quite sophisticated devices are added, as at the eighteenth century solar observatory at Delhi in India.[4]

An alternative method is to use a distant foresight on the horizon as described earlier, so that the solstitial sun is seen to rise or set behind a mark when the observer stands at a specified position. The Heel Stone at Stonehenge is probably the most famous example of such a possible *solstitial alignment* (chapter 5); when an observer stands at the centre of the site on June 21st he sees the midsummer sun rise and almost immediately pass directly above the tip of the stone so that only the top of the disc is visible.[5] The dubious aspects of this alignment as a useful observing instrument are described in the next chapter, but here it is sufficient to note the two major drawbacks, the relative nearness of the foresight and the lack of any exact indication of where the observer should stand. The stone is only about 87

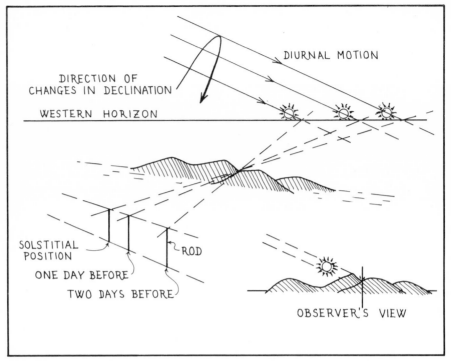

Fig. 8. How a megalithic observatory to watch the midsummer sunset might have been established (the intervals between the setting positions are exaggerated)

yards from the featureless centre of the site — the assumed backsight — and at this distance it is quite impossible to detect the tiny 12″ change in the sun's declination which occurs in the 24 hours before and after the moment of the solstice. Unless this movement can be detected the exact number of days in the year cannot be determined, and so a precise calendar, essential for astronomical work, cannot be constructed. This small solar movement represents a change in the position of the observer's eye at Stonehenge of only about 0.2 in at the times of the two successive sunrises. In other words, a dawn observer at the centre of Stonehenge at midsummer would see exactly the same phenomenon of the sun coming up over the Heel Stone for at least eight days, four on either side of the solstice; even a week before and after this date the sun is less than a third of its diameter away from the solstitial position (fig. 9; table 6a). However, since the changes in declination are seen as movements *along* a fairly level horizon instead of as they really are — at right angles to the direction of daily motion — the problem is not quite so difficult as it sounds. Yet the bright disc over the stone certainly appears to be in the same place on at least six successive midsummer dawns at Stonehenge and perhaps on more.

The problem is really one of a triangle with an angle at the tip of only 0.2′, or nearly 0.5′ if we are dealing with a movement along the horizon at the latitude of the British Isles. The length of the triangle represents the distance between foresight and backsight, and the base the distance on the ground separating the observer's position at two successive sunrises, one of which is the solstitial one. How far away should the foresight be before the tiny change in declination can be detected? Table 6b gives information for alignments of various lengths, and we can see that the foresight should be well over a mile away before there is any hope of separating out the two sunsets concerned. Two standing stone sites in Argyllshire which have been identified by Thom as solar observatories have indicated alignments which are 19 and 27 miles long, and another in Islay may be 50 miles long. These sites also solve the problem of the brightness of the solar disc, which is difficult to look at directly.

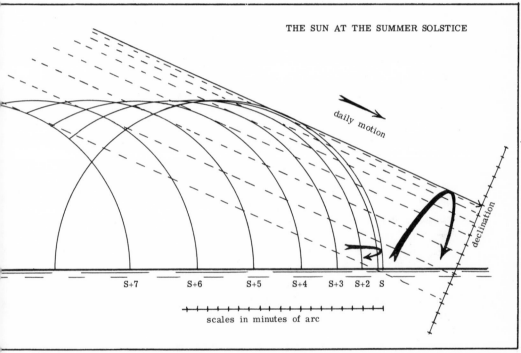

THE SUN AT THE SUMMER SOLSTICE

daily motion

declination

S+7   S+6   S+5   S+4   S+3 S+2 S

scales in minutes of arc

Fig. 9. Diagram to scale showing the changes in the sun's declination, and in its setting position on the horizon, for several days around the solstice

Ballochroy

A description of one of these sites, the three standing stones at Ballochroy on the west coast of Kintyre, will serve to illustrate both the method of solstice detection described above and also how the ideal solstice observatory could have worked in prehistoric times.[6] The three stones stand in a NE-SW line, each about 4 ft from its neighbour, and two of them have very flat northern faces aligned NW-SE. Thus there are four possible directions indicated by the stones, two along the line and two at right angles to it. However, two of these can quickly be eliminated as the horizon in the northeast and southeast is only a few hundred yards away and almost featureless; the stones stand about 100 ft above the sea and the ground rises rapidly inland from them. On the other hand, distant views across the sea are to be had in a wide arc from the southwest round almost to the north.

The western edges of the three stones are approximately in line and seem to be pointing to the southwest, towards a massive megalithic cist (box grave) made of stone slabs 40 yards away and to Cara Island some 7 miles distant in the same direction. If one ignores the possibility that the cist was originally covered by a cairn, in which case the view to Cara Island would have been blocked if the cairn was set up before the stones, the possibility emerges that one peak on the island may have been a distant marker for the setting sun at midwinter. In fact Thom's careful measurements with a theodolite have shown that, if the sun was setting so that its upper edge just grazed the right end of the island, the centre of its disc (the point by which its position is defined) would have a declination of $-23° 54'$, suitable for the calculated midwinter position at about 1800 BC. A recent independent re-measurement of this foresight gave a figure of $-23° 53' 09''$.[7]

The island of Jura lies in the northwest and the three prominent and distinctive mountains known as the Paps of Jura form a conspicuous skyline about 18 miles distant across the sea. When facing these mountains the right-hand stone slab, the shortest of the three, has a flat northern face which is accurately directed towards the right slope of the most southerly of the Paps, Beinn à Chaolais, while the tall central stone is similarly clearly oriented towards Corra Beinn, a smaller peak just to the right of the Paps.[8] Assuming that the sun was setting behind the mountains with its upper edge just showing at the foot of their right slopes, it would have a declination (at the centre of the disc) of $+19° 53'$ at Beinn à Chaolais and $+23° 54'$ at Corra Beinn. The latter foresight has recently been independently re-measured[9] and found to be $+23° 53' 09''$ (although this must be an example of the 'delusions of accuracy' mentioned in chapter 1: the difficulties with terrestrial refraction, discussed by Thom,[10] can hardly allow such precision). Corra Beinn thus marks the position of a prehistoric summer solstice, calculated to have existed at about 1800 BC. It is the equivalent position north of the celestial equator to that possibly marked by the tip of Cara Island (described above), and also by the second long solstice alignment to be described below, at Kintraw some 40 miles further north. The reason for the equally clear alignment towards Beinn à Chaolais from the Ballochroy stones is not understood at present.

The long northwest alignment at Ballochroy is capable of defining the solstice to the exact day, though under modern climatic conditions refraction and temperature changes would have ruined many of the observations. The position of the site could have been established, and the

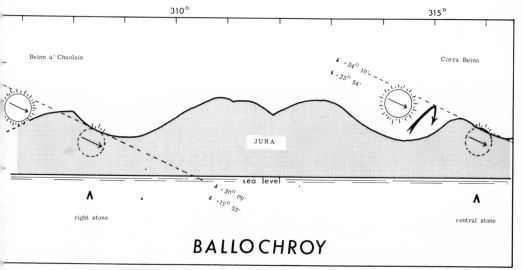

Fig. 10. Profile of the northwest horizon seen from the Ballochroy standing stones, Kintyre

observatory used for accurate work, in the following manner. Initial exploration and observation, perhaps over several years, would have discovered that suitably distant and prominent mountain peaks were to be seen in the midsummer sunset position from that part of the west coast of Kintyre. A couple of weeks or more before one particular midsummer — the time of which would have been approximately known — the sightings would have started: as the sun set on each successive evening the observer would have stationed himself so that it disappeared behind Corra Beinn. As the disc went down he would have quickly adjusted his position so that the very edge of the sun briefly reappeared as a flash at the right slope: this slope is about parallel to the angle of the sun's descent. (Ideally a smooth and slightly concave right slope is required so that there is only one unambiguous point at which the minimum flash of the edge of the sun will reappear: Beinn à Chaolais is such a suitably shaped peak, and it is difficult to understand why it, or Beinn Shiantaidh just to the left of Corra Beinn, was not used as the solstitial foresight. Corra Beinn has a slightly irregular, straight slope which allows for some ambiguity in the sun's position.) It is quite easy for one person to perform this manoeuvre in the half minute or so which is available, but a line of observers would be more convenient, the first (or last) one to see the sun's edge marking the correct position with a peg or stake.

On the following evening the procedure would be repeated, and since the sunset position is gradually moving to the north (the right as seen from the Ballochroy backsight), the second peg defining the line from the mountain to the observer would be put in some distance to the left, or southwest of the first one (fig. 8). As the solstice approaches, the rate of the sun's declination change diminishes so that the interval between the successive stake positions grows steadily less. However, because of the great length of the northwest alignments at Ballochroy, even this final, very small declination change of 0.2 minutes is represented by a lateral distance of about 13½ ft at the stones, quite big enough to distinguish between the two sunsets concerned (Table 6b). When the nightly stake positions had ceased to move to the left and begun to move back to the right, the observer would know that the solstice had passed: presumably a permanent marker such as a standing stone would be set up at the most southerly peg so that the time of the solstice could be checked in future years. If a flat-sided stone was available it could be orientated towards the correct foresight for the guidance of future generations of observers.

This method of establishing a solstitial observing position, or indeed any astronomical observation position, is simple but effective and accurate, though a number of years of such midsummer observations may have been required to establish the correct position with certainty since some of the

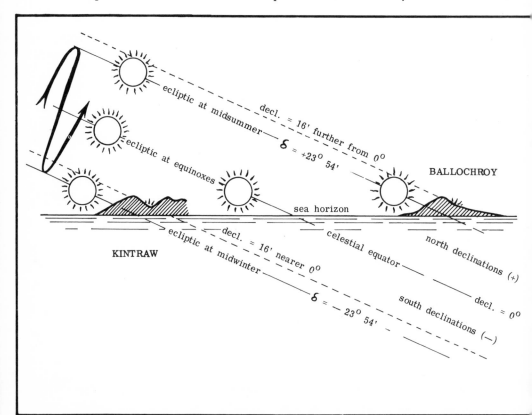

Fig. 11. Diagram showing how the sun's declination (marked by the thick arrow) changes annually and what adjustments have to be made at midsummer and midwinter to obtain the declination of the centre of the disc from that of the horizon marker

crucial sunsets would certainly have been obscured by bad weather or rendered inaccurate by refraction and temperature changes. With an observatory such as Ballochroy the foresight mountain completely conceals the sun in the final moments of setting so that the observer is not dazzled when the crucial observations have to be made. The stone thus marks the most southerly point at which the sun will just flash at the right edge of the mountain; on all the evenings before and after no flash would have been seen from that position, the sun being completely behind the peak.

Kintraw

The conditions are slightly different at midwinter sunset sites where the sun's real position (not its daily motion) is descending from top right to lower left and then back up again (shown by the black arrow in fig. 11). Here, on the evenings before and after the solstice, more of the solar disc will be visible in front of the right slope of the foresight mountain, so perhaps the technique here was to so arrange things that the sun just failed to reappear on the evening of the solstice. A good example of such a potentially highly accurate, long midwinter alignment is the standing stone near Kintraw farm in mid-Argyll, some 40 miles north of Ballochroy.[11] Here a single stone 11 ft high together with a large and a small cairn stands in a flat field on otherwise sloping ground rising up from the end of Loch Craignish. The large cairn was excavated in 1959 and 1960 but no major burial was found.[12] Looking southwest down Loch Craignish one has a long view (in fine weather) towards the Paps of Jura 27 miles away and to a conspicuous V-shaped notch between two of these peaks, Beinn Shiantaidh on the left and Beinn à Chaolais. As seen from the stone, the sun setting with its upper edge just showing at the base of this notch (the left side slightly steeper than the sun's path) would have a declination of −23° 54', numerically identical to that of the Corra Beinn alignment at Ballochroy and suitable for the calculated midwinter sunset at about 1800 BC. One must recall furthermore that the declinations marked by the two foresights concerned are not themselves numerically identical, being more than half a degree apart at +24° 10' and −23° 38' respectively. They only become identical if one assumes that the real measurements are to the centre of the sun's disc when its upper edge is exactly at the two measured points. This is because the sun has an apparent diameter of 32' when seen from the earth and also because the upper edge, which touches the assumed marks when the solar disc is almost completely hidden, must have a declination of one solar radius (16') *closer* to the equinoctial position than the centre of the disc at midwinter and the same amount *further away* from it at midsummer (fig. 11). It is very difficult to believe that the two hill slopes could by chance turn out to have identical solar declinations in this sense, and this piece of evidence, from two of the best sites claimed as solar observatories by Thom, is almost sufficient on its own to demonstrate the existence of accurate solar observation points in prehistoric times. The two sites are moreover exceptionally clear and convincing. At both the Paps of Jura are the only really prominent, distant mountains which are suitable for solstitial foresights; views in other directions are to closer and more featureless horizons. At Ballochroy the mountains are actually indicated by the orientation of two of the stones, and the foresight at Kintraw may also be an indicated one as is described below. Yet at first sight Kintraw exhibits a major difficulty for the astronomical interpretation, but one which in fact provided a unique opportunity for a test by excavation of Thom's controversial general theory.

THE ASTRONOMICAL ALIGNMENTS

The histogram of alignments

In his first book Thom presents the results of the measurements made at about 150 standing stone and stone circle sites at which there was some built-in indication of a preferred direction towards the horizon.[13] Each item on the histogram (fig. 12) is the equivalent astronomical declination of a point on the horizon — usually a notch or a hill slope — which seems to be indicated, and the resulting picture shows immediately that astronomical considerations must have played an important part in the plans of the builders when the positions of the stones were being chosen. The declinations are not random but fall in very clear peaks of which, moreover, many are at astronomically significant points. If only the azimuths of these suspected alignments had been plotted the histogram would have shown a much more random distribution: for reasons already explained the declination of a given celestial body as seen from Scotland, rising or setting along a slightly curved path which makes a relatively low angle with the horizon, can be equivalent to several different azimuths in a hilly terrain. Thus the histogram by itself is a highly significant body of evidence. Strong peaks of declinations are visible at the solstices and equinoxes, and also at the four limiting positions of the moon (below). Other smaller peaks can be reasonably explained as intermediate points in a solar calendar having 16 'months' of 22 or 23 days, while yet others fit well with the positions of some of the bright stars calculated back to about 4,000 years ago. To assume that this histogram is meaningless — the only way the basis of the astronomical interpretation of the standing stones could be fundamentally challenged — it would have to be maintained that most of the horizon markers clustered by chance into peaks when converted to astronomical declinations. Since the data is compiled only from sites with some fairly clear, built-in indication of a preferred direction, it cannot be supposed that these horizon positions were themselves chosen from preconceived ideas about where they ought to be to fit an astronomical theory. While the interpretation of

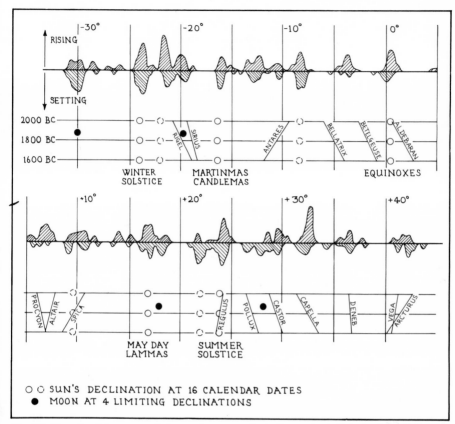

Fig. 12. Gaussian histogram of observed astronomical alignments in Britain up to 1966, after A. Thom. It should be noted that all the alignments included here incorporate some built-in indication of the direction of the horizon marker, or foresight (individual sites not shown)

individual sites can obviously be challenged, it is impossible, without deliberately ignoring hard evidence, not to conclude from this data at the very least that it was important to Early Bronze Age man to orient his ceremonial sites towards the rising and setting positions of a variety of celestial bodies. To deny the evidence of this histogram would simply show that it is extremely easy to cast doubt on any theory provided that one does not feel obliged to specify the exact reasons for the doubts. Nevertheless the astronomical interpretation would clearly benefit from confirmation from some entirely independent piece of evidence.

Questions to be answered

Postponing for the moment any discussion of the more complex problems associated with the standing stone sites claimed as lunar observatories, we may isolate the various general questions which arise when the implications of the histogram of declinations are considered. First, and most obvious, is there any independent evidence which can support or refute the astronomical hypothesis? Second, have all the chosen alignments been identified objectively, or are there other possible lines at some of the sites? Have any of these alignments been selected because they were expected from the theory to be in a particular place? Third, does the fairly precise dating given to some of these sites on astronomical grounds fit the archaeological dating evidence? Fourth, do the assumptions about astronomical observation and expertise implied by these interpretations require either a technology or methods of recording or storing information which are not plausible in a Neolithic, non-urban social context? Fifth, were all stone circles and standing stones erected primarily to mark astronomical observation points or only a proportion of them, and is it reasonable to suppose that proto-scientific 'research' on such a large scale was carried out in Late Neolithic and Early Bronze Age Britain? Attempts to answer some of these questions are better deferred to later stages of this work, but there is some independent evidence from two sites which is of crucial importance for the astronomical theory and which it is appropriate to discuss at this point.

TESTS FOR THE ASTRONOMICAL THEORY

The excavations at Kintraw

At the Kintraw standing stone, claimed by Thom to be an extremely accurate observatory for the winter solstice as already described, the topography of the site presented a formidable difficulty for his interpretation (fig. 13). About a mile in front of the stone a tree-covered promontory juts out from the east side of Loch Craignish and obstructs the view to Jura from the field in which the stone stands (fig. 14b). It is just possible to see the col between Beinn Shiantaidh and Beinn à Chaolais from beside the stone, but as soon as one moves to the left or southeast of it, i.e. in the direction on which the preliminary sightings leading up to the solstice would have to have been taken, the col is obscured. Thom thought that the nearby cairn might once have been high enough to serve as a platform from which an observer could have seen over the obstructing ridge (an extra elevation of only a few feet is needed) and surmised that much of the cairn material was probably robbed to build the nearby sheep enclosures.[14] However, he recognised that this supposition would not solve the problem of how the position of the backsight was established in the first place since the necessary preliminary sightings cannot be made from the field.

A few yards northeast of the stone is a steep-sided gorge with a stream in it and beyond that the hillside rises sharply up to well above the level of the

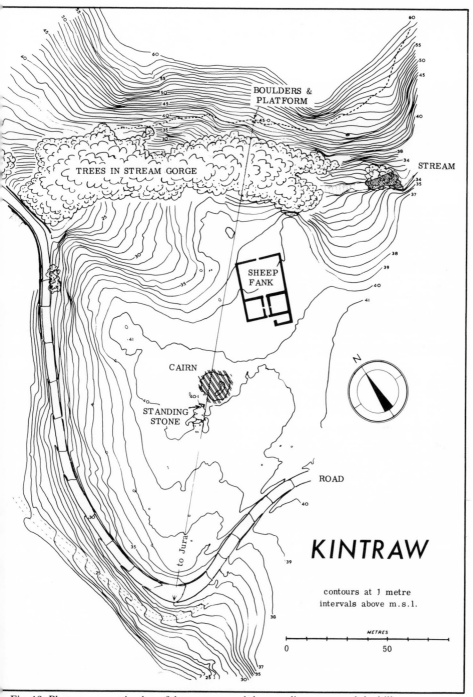

Fig. 13. Photogrammetric plan of the area around the standing stone and the hill platform at Kintraw, Argyll

field. A narrow, more level grassy ledge with a sheep path runs parallel with the stream and several yards higher than the field and the stone, and Thom suggested that the preliminary observations could have been done from this ledge, on which there is plenty of room for the rapid sideways movement which would have been necessary to pinpoint the sunset in the col on Jura.[15] He found a large boulder lying on this ledge, more or less on the line from Jura through the standing stone, and surmised that this was once an upright marker. I discussed Kintraw with Professor Thom and Dr A. E. Roy in the autumn of 1969, and the former was kind enough to let me read

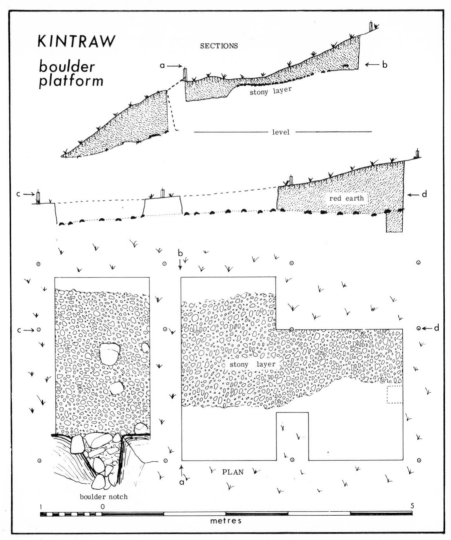

Fig. 14a. Views in section and plan of excavations on the hill platform at Kintraw showing the extent of the rubble floor

the manuscript of his new book in which the discussion of the hill platform and boulder at Kintraw occurs.[16] It quickly became clear that the site was presenting what might be a unique opportunity for an archaeologist to test the astronomical theory. If Thom's interpretation of the stone as a very accurate solstitial observation point was correct, evidence of a construction of some kind — a standing stone or post-holes or perhaps an artificial platform — might well be found at the specific spot on the hillside ledge dictated by the assumed alignment to Jura. If an artificial observation point was found there this would be as near to direct proof of a hypothesis about an archaeological site as one could hope to obtain since there is no other obvious reason for expecting traces of Early Bronze Age activity at that particular spot on the sloping ledge — at the foot of a steep hillside and immediately above a precipitous gorge.

Excavations were carried out at the appropriate spot on the hillside ledge in 1970 and 1971, next to the 'solstice boulder'.[17] Two other similar boulders were found on the edge of the hill ledge, one about 22 yards downstream where the path was very narrow and the other 50 yards upstream at a point where the ledge broadened out into a sloping platform about 14 yards wide (fig. 13). There was no reason to select the central

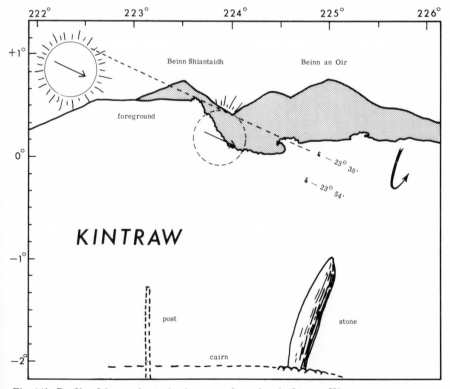

Fig. 14b. Profile of the southwest horizon seen from the platform at Kintraw

boulder for investigation rather than one of the others except that it was on the hypothetical solstice alignment. The trenches around the central boulder quickly showed that it actually consisted of two large rocks lying together, the pointed ends of which were touching and forming a prominent notch. No sockets were found and there was no evidence that the stones had ever stood upright: they were solidly embedded in deep red earth. Between this boulder notch and the rapidly rising hillside to the northeast was an approximately level layer of small stones, about 6 in thick and at a varying depth below the turf. It appeared to come to an end just beyond the downstream end of the boulders, but excavations traced the layer as a stony path for at least 7 yards upstream (fig. 14a). In this direction the layer remained more or less level even though the turf was steadily rising; immediately behind the notch its surface was only a very few inches deep but at the upstream limit of the trenches some 80 cm of red earth covered it. Similarly along the line of the alignment the stone layer rose gently and uniformly at an angle of about 10° but the turf rose more steeply. The layer abutted against the two boulders, which formed a revetment for it, and ran into the notch itself. The two rocks forming the notch lay in red earth and it was not possible to tell for certain whether they had been placed in position deliberately or whether they had rolled down the slope and by chance had come to rest in contact. The chance explanation seemed somewhat improbable, and investigations at the other two boulders failed to reveal a comparable stone layer, although a considerable thickness of red earth containing many randomly scattered stones lay behind and around the upstream boulder as it did around the central one.

No trace of human activity in the form of flints, potsherds, post-holes or charcoal was found, so the question of whether a human or natural origin for the stone layer was the more probable depended for an answer on the nature of the layer itself, leaving aside the effects of the astronomical interpretation of the site as *sub judice*. Comparable layers of stone of natural origin, a few inches thick and not far below the surface, are known from various parts of Scotland; they appear to have been formed by frost shattering and soil creep under the extremely cold climatic conditions found on the edge of an ice sheet and should therefore be 10,000 years old or more in Scotland. A method of studying the stones of these layers statistically — and thus distinguishing for example between such soliflucted layers and deposits from raised beaches — has been developed by geomorphologists and termed petrofabric analysis.[18] Essentially it consists of measuring with a magnetic compass the orientation or azimuth, and the angle of dip with a clinometer, of the long axes of a hundred adjacent stones and plotting the results as contour diagrams in a circular frame known as a Lambert polar equal-area net (fig. 15). On this the scale of dip runs from 90° (vertical) at the centre of the circle to horizontal at the circumference, the shallower angles being compressed like the equatorial circles of latitude on a globe seen from above the north pole. The azimuths

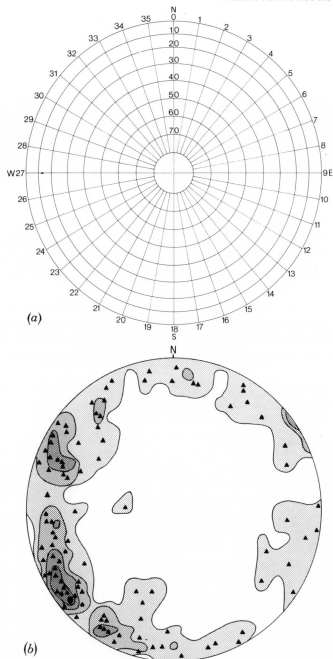

(a)

(b)

Fig. 15. Petrofabric analyses of the rubble floor of the hill platform at Kintraw (b and c, *overleaf*) compared with those of a man-made cobbled floor inside a hillfort (d), a deposit of scree on Broad Law, Peebles-shire (e, *overleaf*) and a natural soliflucted platform, also on Broad Law (f, *overleaf*). The diagram at (a) shows the Lambert polar equal-area net on which the stones are plotted

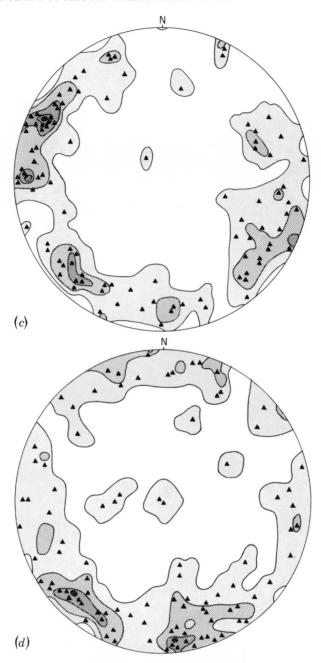

(c)

(d)

are plotted on the 360° scale represented by the circumference, top being 0° (N), right being 90° (E) and so on. The technique was applied to the Kintraw stony layer, and two sets of measurements were made and compared with the diagrams of two other natural deposits of stones on

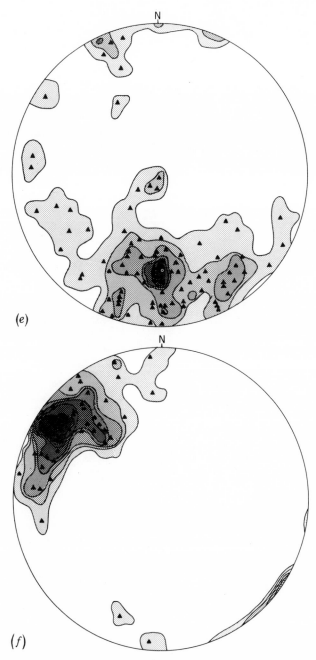

(e)

(f)

Broad Law, Peebles-shire; the first of these was a deposit of scree and the second a solifluction layer.[19] It can be seen from these diagrams that there are marked differences between the Kintraw diagrams and the other two: the natural accumulations show strong orientations in the direction of the slopes together with a fairly low angle of dip, whereas the Kintraw rubble, though it shows a slight concentration of azimuths in the direction of the shallow slope, was much more randomly scattered. These stones also had fairly gentle inclinations. There was never any question of the Kintraw stony layer being an accumulation of scree, deposits of which always come to rest at an angle of about 30° to the horizontal: the stones on the ledge lay at an angle of about 10°. Thus the most useful comparison is with the solifluction layer on Broad Law which shows an even more marked contrast with the Kintraw diagram than does the scree analysis.

The final check was to compile a petrofabric diagram for a stony layer known to be man-made, and fortunately one was readily available, inside the Sheep Hill hill-fort in Dunbartonshire. This had pottery and other artefacts lying both on and under it and was composed of rubble from the ruins of an earlier vitrified wall:[20] the diagram obtained from it is shown with the others (fig. 15d).The resemblance with the two Kintraw patterns is remarkably close, especially when one considers that the materials from which the two layers are made are quite different, the former being mainly slab-shaped pieces of schist and the latter wedge-shaped fragments of basalt. This evidence leaves little room for doubt that the stone layer behind the 'boulder-notch' at Kintraw was made by man, and the implications of this discovery are profound. An artificial observation point, consisting of a level rubble path running southeast from a massive and conspicuous megalithic notch, was found in exactly the position required by the astronomical interpretation of the nearby standing stone, and this theory seems to be thereby decisively vindicated. By implication, therefore, Thom's general theory about standing stones and stone circles being the markers for astronomical observatories should also be vindicated. We can see now that Kintraw and Ballochroy form a complementary pair of the clearest and most convincing of the solstitial group of these sites, which were set up at a time when the earth's axis was tilted a little further away from the vertical than it is now, at 23° 54' instead of 23° 27'. Kintraw itself also becomes a more plausible and comprehensible such site now that the massive observing platform is known. If this platform was in fact the primary observation point (and it is quite easily reached from the road bridge) at a height of 16.08 ft above the surface of the nearby field and stone, then all the difficulties previously associated with the site disappear and the stone itself would be pointing the way to the col on Jura (fig. 14b), making the alignment into an indicated one like those at Ballochroy.

The Cultoon stone circle

This is the second site which may be said to have provided some independent evidence concerning the Thom interpretations, not in the same decisive way as Kintraw — by producing a feature predicted by an astronomical interpretation — but because it was surveyed and excavated

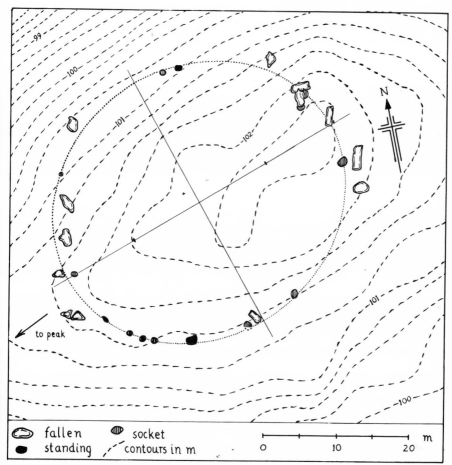

Fig. 16a. Plan of the Cultoon stone ring, Islay, showing the contours of the ground and the ellipse that best fits the stones and sockets

with no preconceived ideas about what kind of observatory, if any, it might be. Its exploration can therefore be regarded as a test of the general application of Thom's ideas by other workers. The excavations have already been briefly described in chapter 2: no astronomical function was inferred during the first season of excavation in 1974, but the complete horizon profile was drawn as seen from the centre of the elliptical ring. In fine weather this included a prominent mountain approximately in the southwest, tentatively identified as Slieve Snaght (2,019 ft) some 50 miles away in Co. Donegal. In 1975 the azimuth of this peak was worked out in relation to the Ordnance Survey's national grid and also by means of measurements of the sun with a theodolite: the peak proved to have a bearing from the centre of the site 223° 235′. From this it is possible to calculate that the concave right slope of the peak corresponded to a

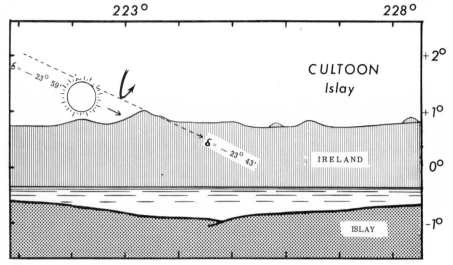

Fig. 16b. Profile of the southwest horizon seen from Cultoon. The final measurements still needed may produce an alteration of a few minutes in the declination of the peak

declination of −23.7° so that the sun, when it set with its upper edge just at this slope, had a declination of −24.0°; this is a good correspondence with the Kintraw alignment. The great distance of the mountain means that the position from which to see the same phenomenon on the evenings before and after the solstice would have been 40 ft or more to the southeast and that Cultoon is likely to have been one of the most accurate solar observatories so far known. Some further measurements at the site are however necessary.

It is difficult to deny that the position of the Cultoon elliptical ring was chosen to obtain this exact relationship with the Irish peak and the design of the site confirms this. Though it is not now possible to establish the exact orientation of the long axis of the ellipse, it must point almost directly at the mountain. It is likely that two stones were to have marked the opposite ends of this axis (fig. 16a). The contours of the shallow elevation on which the site stands show that the ring is not placed symmetrically in relation to the summit, which actually lies in the northeast quadrant of the ring. To deny the primary connection between Cultoon and the winter solstitial sunset would be to assume that all these features — the distant mountain apparently in the right position, the long axis of the site pointing at it and the non-symmetrical placing of the circle on the hillock — were coincidences. The great distance and frequent invisibility of the mountain also reminds us that the function of a stone circle as a solstice observatory may not be immediately obvious in modern climatic conditions; fine weather and careful measurement are usually needed before such a possibility can be adequately investigated.

General conclusions from the solstice sites

There can be little doubt that the high quality of the three solar sites described, in which immensely long and therefore potentially accurate alignments are combined with very conspicuous mountain foresights and with some kind of built-in indication of the direction of these, confirms in a rather striking way that the level of practical astronomical activity carried on in Argyllshire about 38 centuries ago was well beyond that to be expected in, and needed by, a normal unstratified pre-urban peasant society, concerned primarily with the agricultural cycle. Such instruments as these, capable of defining the solstices to the day, imply a considerable outlay of time, energy and intellectual effort as well as a notable organisational achievement. The realisation of the full potential of the simple process of watching the sunset positions slowly change against the background of a hilly horizon surely implies moreover a qualitative jump in thinking, from the level of purely practical, almost casual, observations up to one involving abstract thought aimed at defining and presumably explaining the observed phenomena.

In order for Neolithic man to have progressed to the level of envisaging sites like Ballochroy and Kintraw, certain conclusions about the sun's movements have to be drawn and their potential for providing an exact calendar realised. Presumably there must also be a definite desire for such a precise yearly calendar. In the first place the relatively simple inference must be drawn that the limits of the sun's movements along the horizon — the solstices — mark the turning points of the year, and of the seasons, and that they offer a simple way of telling when midsummer and midwinter have arrived. In the second place an intellectual effort, probably a much greater one, is required to realise that if one deliberately selects an observing position, instead of, for example, watching the horizon from the door of one's hut all the year round, one will get much better results because it is then possible to arrange for the sun to rise or set behind specially conspicuous markers at the chosen times. One may suppose that at this stage a part- or full-time specialist in sky watching was active since deliberate and time-consuming efforts to discover and arrange such observing positions have to be made. Moreover, the failure to pinpoint the time of the solstices better than to within several days would have become apparent. The further realisation would then have been needed that really long sight-lines were necessary and that a great deal of time and trouble to find and establish these would be required; one might suppose that this marks the point at which the work would be given up unless there was some special reason for continuing. Only a class of professional astronomer-priests, wanting to construct an exact calendar and physically and mentally able to consider all these problems at length and in detail, is really likely to go further. They must have first experimented over many solstices with various foresights — artificial and natural — and have worked out the routine of establishing the successions of minimum flash positions and marking these with pegs. Second, they must have concluded that only really long lines of sight to well-shaped mountains would give the necessary accuracy. Third, they must have explored the countryside for months if not years searching for suitable long views to distant mountains in the four appropriate directions. Fourth, they must have spent several solstices at the finally chosen sites to overcome the handicaps of weather and atmosphere, and working to pinpoint the position of the backsight exactly. Finally they must have had enough authority to obtain help to erect one or more massive standing stones, or even a complete ring of them, at the backsights. The long solstice sites by themselves are surely showing quite plainly that a specialist class of wise men was in existence in Britain in the Early Bronze Age, and even if only part of what Thom claims about the more complex lunar observatories is correct (below), this conclusion is abundantly confirmed by the remainder of the sites.

OBJECTIONS TO THE ASTRONOMICAL THEORY

A variety of objections have been raised against the whole idea that many if not most stone circles and standing stones were deliberately positioned in relation to astronomically significant foresights, though these are rarely articulated in print. One misconception which can quickly be disposed of — if indeed it exists in any quarter — is that it is claimed that *all* such sites were built as observatories for something like a prehistoric version of the Royal Astronomical Society. It is of course perfectly possible that many of the circles were not designed as observing instruments at all but were merely oriented, approximately or fairly exactly, towards well known astronomical positions for religious or ceremonial reasons. It is useful to make this distinction between an *orientation*, which need imply no more than a ritual requirement for some part of a building to be aligned in a certain direction (just as Christian churches always face east), and an *alignment*.[21] The latter would consist of a backsight (the site itself) and an indicated foresight which was capable of being used to make useful and accurate astronomical observations: in other words it could have been an observing *instrument*. Moreover, there are standing stone sites with reasonably clear, indicated long alignments the declinations of which yet have no obvious astronomical significance. One such is the stone at Loch Nell in Argyllshire which has recently been re-measured:[22] in spite of a conspicuous horizon notch apparently indicated by two flat slabs no plausible astronomical explanation for this line suggested itself. Others can be spotted on the histogram (fig. 12). It is quite reasonable to suppose, first, that many stone circles were not erected primarily as observing *instruments* as already noted, and second, that there may be some apparently good, indicated long alignments which cannot yet be explained astronomically. The real point is that a sufficiently large number of such sites *have* been plausibly identified as useful observing instruments — and that independent evidence is available in support of this from two sites — to make it quite clear that careful and precise observation of the heavens played a very important part in the activities of certain sections of British society some 4,000 years ago.

Another objection often heard, and occasionally seen in print,[23] is that a stone circle has so many potential alignments to the horizon, i.e. from each stone to all the others in both directions, that some of these are bound by chance to point to 'significant' astronomical positions. It must be admitted first that Thom has never used a method based on this belief and second that the assertion could well be true. If one allows oneself an unrestricted choice of potential alignments in this way and if one ignores any built-in indications of preferred directions and also the nature of the surrounding horizon, one will almost certainly come up with something, especially from a large circle with many stones. However, everything that has been said so far surely shows that it is important to be selective, to work on the assumption that any important lines planned by the circle builders were likely to be marked by some conspicuous aspect of the site's design. If the ring is clearly laid out as an ellipse, an egg-shape or a flattened circle then the axes of the geometrical construction could be oriented towards the important direction and the foresight; otherwise an outlying stone might do this. In any case it is particularly important with a stone circle to recognise that many of even such clearly marked directions may be simple orientations and not functional alignments with a distant foresight. The example of Cultoon suggests that very long alignments may often be present and indicated by the geometry of the site but will not become apparent without a careful search.

Another illustration is provided by the very large flattened circle known as Long Meg and Her Daughters in Cumbria which lies astride a farm road northeast of Penrith.[24] Here the axes of the flattened circle have not been identified as pointing to anything in particular but the ruins of a small circle in the northeast, and what appears to be an arbitrarily chosen pair of stones forming a NNW-SSE diameter, are claimed to indicate astronomical lines. The former can be interpreted as an intermediate calendar date for the sun. The tall outlying stone (Long Meg) is outside the southwest quadrant and is an obvious indicator of an important direction, but Thom's plan of the site does not show a declination for this line though it does for the other two mentioned.[25] I visited the site in November 1973 when the late afternoon mist turned the setting sun into a red ball and prevented a clear view to the southwest, though it was obvious that the land was more open in that direction and the horizon far away. The 'list of observed lines' reveals that a southwest line from the centre of the circle, marked by Long Meg, has been identified and measured and it gives a declination of $-24.2°$ equivalent to $-23.9°$ ($23° 54'$) for the centre of the solar disc and probably right for the winter solstice at the time the ring was built.[26]

A look at the 1 inch map reveals that Helvellyn, the highest mountain in the Lake District (3,118 ft), is about 20 miles from the site and almost exactly in the southwest: the intermediate ground is much lower and open. Judging from the contours, a suitable sloping northwest face is provided by the peak known as Lower Man, slightly northwest of Helvellyn, and the summit of this has a true azimuth of 226.6°, calculated from the two grid references. However, the azimuth of the southwest line given by Thom is 223.4° with an altitude of +1.1°, which in fact points to slightly further southeast. Presumably this peak was seen and measured from the site but I have not yet had an opportunity to check the southwest horizon with a theodolite. We now see that Long Meg could have been positioned primarily to act as an accurate midwinter solstice observation point and that no clear indication of the potential importance of the site in this way is given by Thom. One is unable to distinguish from the data given whether the site has a short, purely 'ritual' southwest orientation, as the symbol CO suggests ('circle to outlier'), or whether a long, potentially accurate alignment is involved. The lesson to be drawn here is that the astronomical potential of stone circles must never be underestimated simply because a small scale plan with some suggested lines on it looks arbitrary to a sceptic. Visits to the sites on clear days are required and the horizon profiles of potentially accurate, distant indicated foresights need to be drawn and measured. The strength of the evidence for the astronomical theory is often understated in Thom's works.

If stone circles like Cultoon, and probably also Long Meg and many others, were positioned primarily in order to make use of distant natural foresights as solstice markers (and because of present climatic conditions this is usually one of the hardest things to verify by direct observation on the sites themselves on a single visit), then most of the other lines detected at these circles are likely to be orientations rather than alignments. It is conceivable that the position of a backsight could sometimes be determined by the crossing of two separate astronomical lines worked out in relation to useful natural foresights, but it seems rather improbable that more than two could be made to cross at the same point more than very occasionally. It should be possible to determine which was the primary alignment at a site, with a little care and good weather conditions.

This brings us to the third of the objections to Thom's astronomical interpretations, mainly voiced by G. S. Hawkins though not specifically as such.[27] He suggests applying the following criteria to establish the validity of suggested astronomical alignments. (a) Construction dates should not be determined from astronomical alignments. (b) Alignments should be restricted to man-made markers. (c) Alignments should be postulated only for a homogeneous group of markers. (d) All related celestial positions should be included in the analysis. (e) All possible alignments at a site must be considered.

In the light of the earlier discussion it must be clear that the approach dictated by these criteria is not well adapted for unravelling the details of practical astronomical functions built into prehistoric sites. Points (b) and (e) in particular almost guarantee that plausible long alignments will be missed, first by ruling out any natural foresights, and second, by an undiscriminating use of numerous arbitrary lines running from each stone or feature to every other. As we have seen, the latter approach is almost certain to produce some 'significant' astronomical declinations in any stone circle. In fact one might wonder whether the two criteria singled out here were devised to provide a justification for Hawkins's theories about Stonehenge — which have been severely criticised on both archaeological and mathematical grounds[28] — and possibly by implication to deny the relevance of the more thorough and wide-ranging work of Thom, which has proved more acceptable to archaeologists.[29]

Hawkins began the modern phase of astronomical theorising about Stonehenge (chapter 5) and his initial approach was to list all the directions which were detectable in the numerous pairs of features at the site (including features of all the different phases), producing the fantastic total of 27,060 lines between 165 positions![30] This host of lines was later narrowed down, by inspection of plans of the site, to 120 'likely' lines between pairs of points (again chosen with no regard to their position in the established site sequence) the azimuths of which were then converted to astronomical declinations by a computer. This selection produced frequent correlations with the positions of the sun and moon — mainly the solstices and equinoxes and the four important lunar declinations — retrojected (by computer again) back to the early second millennium BC. However, all these 'alignments' were of course short and inaccurate, being between stones and other points within a ditched circular site the overall diameter of which is only about 117 yards. No matter how often apparently significant lines turn up these could not be regarded as observing instruments unless they pointed to precisely placed, distant foresights on the horizon, unless the 'crossing the stone' technique (below) was used. It is more probable that, if Stonehenge was indeed deliberately designed to incorporate such sight-lines (which is by no means certain), then these lines should be orientations in the sense defined earlier, a method perhaps of storing basic astronomical information in an important site. Really long alignments may well exist at Stonehenge, and are discussed later in this work, but Hawkins has not so far been concerned with these.

However, the main point is that this method of semi-automatic searching of all possible lines in a stone circle for astronomical targeting is unlikely to reveal any of the really important alignments to distant natural foresights which may exist *unless* the horizon is carefully examined for prominent indicated natural marks at the site itself. As we have seen, the use of the distant, clean-cut natural notch or peak was almost certainly the only really reliable method of exact astronomical observation which was available to prehistoric man in Britain, and now that we know this — and also of sites like Kintraw where such foresights can satisfactorily be shown to have been used — it seems arbitrary and pointless to rule out natural marks in this way. The criteria to be adopted for accepting such natural foresights reasonably confidently are two: that they are unambiguous, clean-cut and distant (10 miles or more away for the sun), and that some prominent artificial part of the sites concerned is pointing clearly towards them.

The systematic examination of standing stones and stone circles for indicated, distant natural foresights is in fact one of the most promising programmes of investigation for those interested in the practice of astronomy in ancient Britain, and indeed it provides us with another objective test of the Thom interpretations which does not so far seem to have been carried out by anyone. One can approach the problem of the credibility of the claimed natural foresights in reverse as it were, by starting with potentially useful features and then looking for standing stones so situated that they could have made use of these as accurate solstice markers. There are many places in Scotland, and doubtless in the highland areas of England and Wales also, from which conspicuous mountains or isolated hills can be seen from afar and it is easy to identify these on the 1 inch Ordnance Survey maps. By drawing lines to the northeast, southeast, southwest and northwest of these hills (in whichever direction long views are to be had) one can search the maps for standing stones or stone circles on or near these lines. The bearing of a peak from a stone can easily be calculated from the pair of grid references, and the apparent altitude of the peak as seen from the site is obtained from the contours and from Thom's formula.[31] The approximate declination of the peak can then be established, either by calculation or from tables already in print,[32] or with a simple mechanical calculator. If stones are consistently found in this way to be in positions from which accurate solstitial observations could have been made using the peaks concerned (when the solstitial declination was about $\pm$ 23.9°) there can be little room for doubt that this was the result of deliberate intention on the part of the builders. Of course visits to the sites are essential in order to check that mountain and stone are intervisible and to make more precise measurements of the supposed foresight.

One brief example of this procedure may be cited. In 1973 I noticed on the Ordnance Survey 1 inch map of Dumfriesshire that the Iron Age hillfort known as Burnswark was situated on top of a prominent, isolated rounded hill with slightly concave sides, standing nearly 800 ft above the surrounding flat terrain (grid ref. NY/1884 7888). A search to the southeast of it revealed the historically important Lochmaben stone (possibly the remnant of a circle) 11.12 miles away (grid ref. NY/3123 6596), and using the contours and the grid reference in the way described, the hill proved to be on a bearing of 312.9° from the stone with an apparent altitude of 49.5′ as seen from it. Preliminary calculation of the resulting declination of the peak from this data gave a figure of +24.2° for the peak (+23.9° for the centre of the sun's disc) which makes the stone seem eminently suitable for an accurate summer solstice marker. In the summer of 1975 I visited the stone, which is at the top of a slope running up from the north shore of the Solway Firth. Though some distant woods partly conceal Burnswark Hill now, the ground is open and flat to the northwest and the view unrestricted. Thus the first attempt to approach the problem of checking Thom's theories in this novel way — by finding a suitable foresight first — has shown well its potential value.

THE MOON OBSERVATORIES

There is space here for only a brief account of the standing stone sites claimed by Thom as lunar observatories,[33] partly because they are both more complicated to understand, and more controversial, than the solstice sites, but mainly because the case for a sophisticated astronomical function for many standing stones must depend primarily on the solar sites, for reasons already set out. It would perhaps be difficult to make out a really plausible case for the lunar observatories by themselves and this is particularly unfortunate, since if only a proportion of what Thom has suggested about them is correct, the moon sites provide us with abundant evidence of the existence of a really skilled and intellectually advanced class in the Early Bronze Age, able to progress to the level of the prediction of eclipses and perhaps even to their understanding.[34] However, the fairly clear evidence just reviewed in favour of accurate and sophisticated solstitial sites must make it more probable that more advanced work on the moon was undertaken, though there will always be room for doubt about the level of this for the following reasons.

Two major difficulties appear to prevent a clear-cut case being made out in favour of the lunar sites. First, the complexities of the moon's orbit are such that there are a large number of 'significant' declinations to choose from at which alignments could be aimed. Second, the moon is a relatively dim body by comparison with the sun, and its declination changes much faster; this has the result that relatively short alignments of a mile or two are sufficient to pinpoint its position and that the conspicuous, distant peaks characteristic of some solstice sites are not required. Hence the genuineness of the lunar foresights is bound to be more a matter of dispute than that of the solar ones because almost any minor notch or small hill slope on the horizon will do if it is in the right position. In these cases one has to rely heavily on the horizon marker being clearly indicated by the standing stone site.

The moon's movements

The present apparent motions of the moon are considerably more complex than those of the sun, which means that a prehistoric people, using the primitive observational techniques described earlier, would have needed to expend a much greater amount of time and energy in unravelling them than on the sun. There is another major difficulty confronting any primitive astronomers interested in the moon in its present orbit, which derives from the fact that the satellite goes through the complete cycle of its changes in declination much faster than the sun, in a month instead of a year. Hence the chances of the moon being at its maximum or minimum declinations at the moment it rises or sets — the only times when it can be tracked in the manner described earlier — are correspondingly much smaller. Furthermore, some of the other present lunar motions, described below, have long periodicities of up to 18.6 years, so that one must assume that decades or even centuries of patient observation (not to mention the massive effort involved in erecting standing stones) would have been required if all that Thom claims was in fact carried out in prehistoric Britain and Brittany.[35]

If the moon's orbit was in the same plane as that of the earth, its cycle of monthly changes in declination would be the same as those of the sun over a year; it would run along the ecliptic 13 times faster than the sun, eclipsing it at each new moon and being eclipsed by the earth's shadow every full moon. Each month it would rise to the same northerly declination as the sun's at the time and then sink to the same southerly one. The greatest declination it could then reach would be that of the sun at the solstices — conventionally represented by the Greek letter epsilon (ε) — and now equal to $\pm 23° 27'$.

However, the moon's orbit is tilted in relation to the earth's, the angle between them, represented by the Greek letter iota (ι), being $5° 9'$. Thus the moon's declination can be as much as $5° 9'$ greater than that of the sun at the solstices and up to the same amount less than ε. These maxima and minima of the lunar declinations are referred to as $\varepsilon \pm \iota$. Such extreme positions will of course be reached only if the moon is at the part of its orbit which is furthest above or below the plane of the earth's orbit at the same time that the sun has attained its greatest declination, i.e. at midsummer and midwinter (fig. 17).

As seen from the earth, the moon swings between its extreme northerly and southerly declinations and back again in a period of 27.32 days, the 'lunar year' (technically the *tropical month* and not to be confused with the *synodic month* — from one new moon to the next — of 29.53 days). However, because of the tilt of the lunar orbit already referred to, these limiting declinations themselves alter from $\varepsilon + \iota$ to $\varepsilon - \iota$ over a period of 18.61 years (fig. 17); the monthly swing reaches a minimum range of twice $18° 18'$ ($\varepsilon - \iota$) and, 9.3 years later, has achieved the maximum range of twice $28° 36'$ ($\varepsilon + \iota$). Thom calls these minima and maxima in the extreme monthly declinations the *minor* and *major standstills*, respectively. When the moon is at the latter point in its complex cycle at midwinter, for example, it is above the horizon for a large part of each 24 hours at every full moon for some

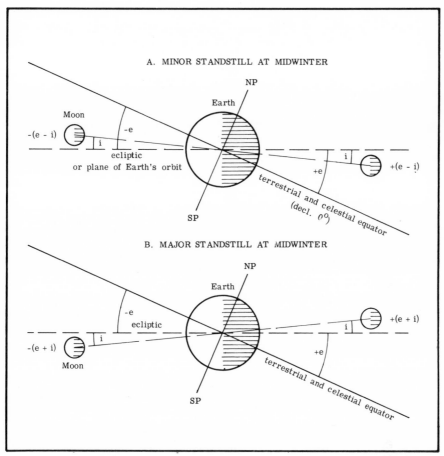

A. MINOR STANDSTILL AT MIDWINTER

B. MAJOR STANDSTILL AT MIDWINTER

Fig. 17. The relationships between the orbital planes of the earth and moon at the time of the major and minor midwinter standstills

months around midwinter and below it for most of the time at new moon. Similarly at the minor standstills (fig. 17) the full moon is much lower and the new moon much higher (the positions are of course reversed at midsummer).

Superimposed on top of these movements is a 'wobble' of ± 9 minutes with a period of about half a year (173.3 days) and represented by the Greek letter delta (Δ). This tiny movement is thought to have been suspected by Arab astronomers in the tenth century[36] but was discovered and measured by Tycho Brahe in the latter part of the sixteenth. It is caused by the extra 'downward' pull of the sun on the moon when the latter is above the ecliptic and nearer the sun than the earth. The maximum effect occurs when the moon is at the nodes — the points where the planes of the terrestrial and lunar orbits intersect and where eclipses occur — so that a knowledge of this wobble can be of great importance in the prediction of eclipses. The moon's limiting declinations can therefore be up to 9' more or less than the amounts given above; for example, the position for the major standstill could either be $\pm(\varepsilon + \imath + \Delta)$, $\pm(\varepsilon + \imath)$ or $\pm(\varepsilon + \imath - \Delta)$ and that for the minor standstill could be either $\pm(\varepsilon - \imath + \Delta)$, $\pm(\varepsilon - \imath)$ or $\pm(\varepsilon - \imath - \Delta)$. This totals 12 positions, but because either the rising or setting points could be used to mark each one, this total becomes 24. It is possible to mark the position of the moon with an alignment by using either the edge of the upper limb, or that of the lower, or even the centre of the lunar disc against a horizon mark, thus expanding the number of possible 'significant' declinations of the moon to 72.

Of course the value of ε seen in the megalithic sites claimed as lunar observatories would have to be similar to that inferred from reliable solstitial sites like Kintraw and Ballochroy, that is about $\pm 23° 54'$. In fact, Thom believes that moon alignments were laid out between about 1800 and 1500 BC, so the value for ε (found through the retrospective calculations of Newcomb) can vary from about 23° 54' 28" to 23° 52' 29". If one lists the 72 'significant' lunar declinations for each of the four dates 1800, 1700, 1600 and 1500 BC, there are thick clusters between about $\pm 28°$ and $29\frac{1}{2}°$ and again between about $\pm 18°$ and $19\frac{1}{2}°$ (because of the relative nearness of the moon to the earth the phenomenon of parallax has to be taken into account, and the actual lunar declinations seen from the latitude of the British Isles are slightly different from those given here).

It could be argued that any notch or mark in the appropriate position, i.e. within the four narrow bands on the horizon where the moon rises and sets at its extreme northerly and southerly declinations, would be very likely to fit one of the four sets of 72 declinations quite closely. It might also be argued that there is a good chance of a notch being visible in a 'significant' position from a point chosen at random in a hilly terrain — a contention which it would be easy and useful to check in a fieldwork experiment. However, if the horizon marks are actually indicated at the site by a flat-sided slab or by a pair of stones the chances are obviously much greater that they were intended as astronomical alignments, and if several such lines at the same site point to such 'significant' declinations, then it clearly becomes more difficult to dismiss the arrangement as one resulting from chance.

Two lunar sites

We may now examine briefly two standing stone sites which Thom has claimed as complex lunar observatories, noting in advance that none of these sites has yet presented an opportunity for a practical test of the theory such as was carried out at Kintraw.

The standing stones at Nether Largie and Temple Wood are one mile south of Kilmartin in mid-Argyllshire and five miles south of the Kintraw solstice site described earlier.[37] The site consists of a stone circle in Temple

Wood and, 327 yards to the southeast, an alignment of five standing stones running from northeast to southwest; the latter (Nether Largie) is 80 yards in length and consists of a pair of stones at each end and a single stone in the centre. The members of the pairs are about 10 ft apart and point approximately NW-SE, back towards the stone circle. The site is on flat ground in the centre of the narrow northern end of the Kilmartin valley with hills visible not far away in nearly all directions.

The two pairs of stones pointing to the northwest indicate a hilly horizon about 1¼ miles away on which there are several small natural notches. From five positions along this alignment (of which three are marked by standing stones or, in one case, a group of small boulders) one of these notches marks five declinations suitable for the moon setting at its greatest northern declination $+ (\varepsilon + \imath)$, including the minute fluctuation in the extreme position caused by the 9 minute 'wobble' (Δ). In addition, the long axis of the alignment, pointing to the southwest, indicates the small but conspicuous Bellanoch hill, and several of the notches and clefts next to this have declinations suitable for marking the moon setting at its greatest southerly declination (the 'major standstill' at $-(\varepsilon + \imath)$). This site is claimed to be particularly important because of the number of indicated sightlines there which now point to significant lunar positions retrojected 37 centuries into the past.

The second claimed lunar site to be described briefly is at Ballinaby on the island of Islay, Argyllshire.[38] Here an exceptionally tall and thin stone slab about 18 ft high is oriented exactly towards two conspicuous crags 1¼ miles away in the northwest. The slope of the right crag has a notch with a declination corresponding to the moon's setting position at the major standstill with the 9 minutes wobble added, $+ (\varepsilon + \imath + \Delta)$. The base of the slope has a declination 9' less at $+ (\varepsilon + \imath)$. The orientation of the stone towards the natural marks is exceptionally clear at this site.

5

Stonehenge

INTRODUCTION

Among the numerous, unusual and impressive prehistoric sites on Salisbury Plain, a region which was evidently at the focus of the intellectual and ceremonial activity so clearly manifested in the standing stone sites of Britain, the jewel is undoubtedly Stonehenge. Here the simple architectural and engineering traditions of the henge and circle builders ultimately reached an extraordinary zenith and the latest monuments on the site are unique in prehistoric Europe. Stonehenge has been described and discussed many times and it has seldom been doubted that it was one of the most important temples and sanctuaries of ancient Britain; until recently, however, it had not been fitted satisfactorily into the new framework built up by Thom. Now it has been surveyed afresh and some new insights into its geometrical qualities and astronomical potential gained.[1] The date of the earliest structures on the site has been drastically revised backwards because of the recalibration of its radiocarbon dates and the implications of this also need to be considered.[2]

Stonehenge stands on a slight eminence amid rolling downland and its situation is not visually impressive; there are no obvious horizon markers visible, for example. Large numbers of Neolithic and Bronze Age burial mounds dot the downland in every direction and this great concentration of tumuli — many of which have yielded rich grave goods — is perhaps the most vivid evidence of the paramount religious and ceremonial status that Stonehenge once enjoyed.[3] Other major sites like the Cursus,[4] Durrington Walls and Woodhenge are less than two miles away and this cluster of important sites is matched only by another about nineteen miles to the north which includes Avebury, Silbury Hill and the Kennet barrows (fig. 18).[5]

THE DEVELOPMENT OF THE SITE

The sequence of construction at Stonehenge was worked out in detail by Atkinson using evidence obtained from the excavations of Hawley from 1919 to 1926[5] and those of himself, Piggott and Stone, which were carried on from 1950 to 1958.[6] The earliest Stonehenge was found to be a Class I henge, with a single entrance, a ditch and an unusually internal bank

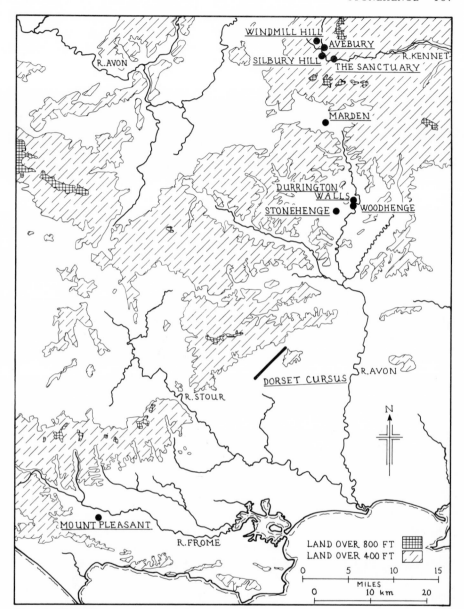

Fig. 18. Map of important sites in the Wessex area

enclosing a circle of 56 pits known as the Aubrey holes. The Heel stone was
set up further out with four timber posts near it and a cluster of posts was
erected on the causeway of the entrance. The four station stones, assumed
by Hawkins[7] to belong to phase I, are assigned archaeologically to a later
phase.

Features of phase I

The outermost earthwork is the irregularly cut ditch, the main purpose of which was presumably to demarcate the enclosed area and to provide material for the bank: it encloses an area about 115 yards in diameter. On the base of the ditch were found several antler picks, one of which gave a C-14 date of 2180 ± 105 bc (I.2328), equivalent to about 2850-2870 BC in real years (p. 19). It probably dates the inception of the site quite accurately and we may conclude that Stonehenge I was built in the 29th century BC and was contemporary with the Old Kingdom in Egypt and with the Early Dynastic period of Sumerian Mesopotamia. Also on the ditch floor and in the primary silts were several sherds of Grooved ware which give a valuable clue, discussed later, to the identity of the builders. The lowest layer of the ditch silt was coarse and had accumulated rapidly; it had never been cleaned out, confirming that the site was not a defensive one.

The bank within the ditch is now much denuded but may once have been about 20 ft wide and at least 6 ft high, tall enough to serve as a good viewing point for any audience watching ceremonies in the interior. The mean diameter of the centre of the bank is about 320 ft. A section through it revealed that the buried old turf line was about a foot higher than the present turf elsewhere, showing that the chalk surface has been lowered by weathering by that amount since early in the third millennium BC.[8] As a result, an observer standing at the centre of the site in 2800 BC would have had a slightly higher viewpoint and, for example, would have seen the tip of the vertical Heel stone just touching the horizon instead of rising slightly above it as at present.

The entrance to the site is in the northeast and consists of a gap in the bank, about 35 ft wide, with an undug causeway across the ditch in front of it. There seem to have been two standing stones in the gap and several rows of posts on the causeway; their function is discussed later.

A large standing sarsen boulder, the Heel stone, stands about 80 ft beyond the entrance and is still 16 ft high although it now leans slightly towards the site. It is inferred that this belongs to phase I because a narrow ditch dug round its base yielded a fragment of one of the bluestones which were brought to the site in phase II; the inference is that the ditch was a symbolic barrier to protect the already standing Heel stone in phase II when the avenue was dug past it. Pieces of Beaker pottery were found in fine earth fill in the socket next to the stone itself and in such a position that they could only have got there after the stakes lining the socket had decayed, that is some time after the erection of the stone. Other evidence shows that Beaker pottery did not appear on the site till phase II, so this piece of evidence also supports the assignation of the Heel stone to phase I. This stone marks the approximate position of midsummer sunrise when seen from the centre of Stonehenge.

The 56 Aubrey holes form a ring just inside the bank and were visible as slight depressions in the seventeenth century, when they were described by John Aubrey. Thirty-four have been excavated and it is clear that these holes never held stones or posts. They vary in width from 30 to 70 ins and in depth from 24 to 45 ins; most of them had been quickly refilled with the clean chalk that had been dug out of them but many had been re-excavated later and then filled again with varied deposits of burnt soil containing fragments of charred wood. Most of the holes contained deposits of cremated human bones — sometimes in the clean, primary refilling but more often in the later deposits — and bone pins and small, rod-like flint implements were found with some of these burials. A C-14 date on charcoal from one of the *secondary* cremations turned out to be 1848 ± 275 bc (C-602), equivalent to about 2190-2290 BC. This date could imply that the holes are earlier than the phase II stone circle (below) and this is supported by the fact that the centre of the circle on which they lie is about 3 ft away from that of the later stone circles.[9] However, the large standard deviation of this early Chicago date means that one cannot be certain about this and that the holes may not be one of the earliest features of the site.

The Aubrey holes are of some interest because of the relative rarity of this kind of feature in henge monuments and also because of the complex astronomical explanations which have been offered for them (below). Though it is clear that they never held uprights of timber or stone they do seem to have been positioned and dug as a single operation and it seems reasonable to assume that this operation was primarily to establish their positions so that they could be used over a long period of time. Their positions could easily have been kept visible by keeping them free of grass and there seems no reason why they should not have served a dual purpose, first as a cremation cemetery for the people who designed and used Stonehenge I and secondly for some more esoteric purpose. Some possibilities for the latter are discussed later.

Stonehenge II

The second major phase of building activity is symbolised by the appearance of two new kinds of artefacts in the secondary levels of the ditch fill and elsewhere, namely Beaker sherds and flakes and chips of the bluestone monoliths which had evidently just been imported on to the site. These chips were found no lower than 'slightly above the rest level which marks the end of the first phase of rapid silting in the ditch'.[10] Observation at the experimental earthwork on Overton Down has shown that, whereas the primary silting in a chalk-cut ditch with steep sides occurs quickly — within a few years of the excavation — the secondary silt above it accumulates much more slowly.[11] An interval of 'as much as fifty years' between the digging of the ditch and the arrival of the bluestones was thought quite likely in 1960. However, as is described in the section on chronology, the recalibration of the C-14 dates for Stonehenge must mean that this interval was in fact far longer. Presumably a milder climate is the explanation; if it is the silting would have occurred more slowly than at present.

The main features of Stonehenge II are the avenue, the double stone circle represented by the Q and R holes and probably the four station stones (though these last are described with the third phase).

The avenue consists of a long road or processional way, about 40 ft wide and bounded by a low bank and a shallow ditch on either side; it approaches the site from the northeast and joins it at the original entrance. From this point it runs straight for about 500 yards, turns sharply to the east to run uphill for some distance and then turns again towards the south to descend more sloping ground to the River Avon: the total length is about 1.9 miles. The latter part, beyond the straight stretch, is now visible only on air photographs. The avenue was shown to be later than the phase I henge by Hawley's excavations, which discovered that it was wider than the original entrance. The last 25 ft of the ditch on the east side of the causeway had been deliberately filled with chalk rubble (probably derived from the adjacent bank), obviously to make the entrance fit the new avenue. In 1954 an unweathered fragment of bluestone was found in the ditch on the west side of the entrance, on top of the 'rest layer' overlying the primary silts and thus on the same layer on which lay the deliberate blocking in the east terminal. This seems to confirm that the bluestones were brought to the site at the same time that the avenue was built.

The question of the axis of the avenue, and of its possible astronomical significance, is discussed in the section on astronomy later (p.126). We have already noted that the ditch around the Heel stone was probably a feature of Stonehenge II, designed to protect the stone when the avenue was being constructed.

The main feature of the second phase of construction was the double stone circle inside the henge. The transportation for this purpose of the 82 monoliths, weighing up to 4 tons each, from southwest Wales to the centre of Wiltshire was surely the most remarkable event in the whole history of the site. Indeed, as far as we know it was an event unique in the prehistory of the whole of Europe. There is no doubt about the geological origin of the stones (which are now arranged in a different pattern from that of phase II).[12] There are five main varieties of bluestones at Stonehenge and four can be matched together in a single restricted location in the Preseli mountains of north Pembrokeshire.[13] Early ideas held that ice sheets transported the stones southeast from Wales to Wiltshire and recently this idea has been revived.[14] Its great drawback is that no other pieces of the rock have been found on Salisbury Plain and it strains credulity to suggest that every fragment, small and large, was collected by circle and barrow builders in ancient times. The theory that the bluestones were brought from Wales by man has everything to recommend it — not least the vague confirmation of legends (below) — and the ice hypothesis very little.

We should, however, note the possibility that the habit of importing Welsh bluestone into Wiltshire may have begun much earlier. Although the fragment found on top of Silbury Hill in 1970 is now known to have come from Cornwall, not Wales,[15] a boulder of spotted dolerite has long been known to have been built into the Neolithic long barrow known as Bowls Barrow, about 11½ miles west of Stonehenge. Radiocarbon dates for such barrows suggest that they were not built after about 3000 BC. However, there is no reason to doubt that the Stonehenge bluestones were transported towards the end of the third millennium BC.

The route by which this unsung Odyssey travelled, and the methods by which the 82 stones were floated and hauled 185 miles from the Preseli mountains to Stonehenge, have been reconstructed by Atkinson[16] and need not be repeated here. It must be emphasised, however, that the motives which impelled this giant project to go forward must have been extraordinarily powerful and, in this context, it is worth mentioning again the remarkable legend about the building of Stonehenge that was set down by Geoffrey of Monmouth in about 1136.[17] Ambrosius Aurelianus was king of the Britons in the fifth century AD and probably of Roman descent, a successor to Vortigern.[18] At about 475 there is supposed to have been a massacre of British chiefs by the Saxons under Hengist and these were buried at Ambresbury (Amesbury). Ambrosius wished to honour their memory and sought the advice of Merlin, the great wise man and prophet, as to a suitable monument to erect. Merlin advised that a stone structure known as the Giants' Dance existed at Killaurus, a mountain in Ireland, and that if this was brought over to England its great stones would stand for ever. The stones were also supposed to have medicinal virtue. The expedition to Ireland was commanded by Uther Pendragon and by Merlin himself, and after defeating the Irish, it set to work to dismantle the stones. Little progress could be made until Merlin had designed special machinery; thereafter the work proceeded rapidly. The stones were then carried back to England by sea and re-erected, again with Merlin's skilled supervision, at Stonehenge.

This story — written down in the twelfth century, presumably from Welsh oral traditions still alive at the time — could preserve a fragment of a genuine folk memory of one of the greatest prehistoric human achievements in Europe of which evidence has survived. One might argue that most legends about great events could contain a core of truth, however distorted, but the chances of finding independent confirmation of such stories is rare. In this case, confirmation of the foreign origin of the stones is provided by geology and we may assume the folk memory to be genuine. Naturally, over the centuries the elements of the tale have become garbled and conflated; the event has been brought forward in time to the early historical period and two separate undertakings at Stonehenge, the bringing of the bluestones and erection of the larger sarsens with ingenious machinery, have been combined. Nor should we forget the part played by the prophet

Merlin. The identity of the Neolithic wise man or men who surely managed the project has been grafted onto that of a famous legendary seer of the post-Roman period[19] and this element in the story surely points to the existence of equally great but anonymous leaders 2,500 years earlier. What the contemporary events were to which such men harnessed their willpower and authority one can only guess.

The first setting of bluestones was a double circle which was later dismantled; the discovery of part of a ring of dumb-bell shaped stone sockets, known as the Q and R holes, revealed their position. Various intersections of these holes with others showed that they were earlier than the sarsen stone structure and earlier than the final bluestone setting. Although the impressions of heavy stones were found in most of the Q and R holes, showing that the double circle was partly built, the discovery of unfinished holes in 1956[20] showed that it was unfinished at the time it was dismantled, and the sockets filled with rammed chalk. An antler pick from an unfinished R hole gave a C-14 date of 1620 ± 110 bc (I-2384), or about 2080 BC in calendar years.[21]

Twelve of the double sockets have been excavated and two more identified and if their spacing and curvature is extended one has a double circle of 38 pairs of stones with mean diameters of 74 and 86 ft. On the northeast, four of the socket trenches are longer, the inner two having room for four stones and the outer two for three. This elongated entrance to the ring faced almost exactly down the avenue and along the axis of the later sarsen circle. The total of stones brought from Wales to be set up would thus have been 82 and this is in fact the number of bluestones in the final setting.

Stonehenge IIIa

The third great phase of building at Stonehenge, the second involving stone circles, was in many ways the most remarkable and the result was a structure that seems to have been unique in the Old World when it was created. The two main new elements are the outer circle of 30 sarsen uprights, joined by a continuous row of 30 lintels, and the inner horseshoe of trilithons of the same stone, forming five free-standing lintelled archways. Also probably belonging to this phase are the other sarsen stones further out (except the Heel stone), namely the four station stones spaced around the ring of Aubrey holes and the pair which once flanked the entrance in holes D and E — the slaughter stone and its vanished companion. The positions of these last two are symmetrical to the phase II enlarged entrance but not to that of phase I. The original total of sarsens would have been 81, 82 if some early reports are correct in describing a fifth station stone on the southwest near Aubrey hole 28.[21] These huge rocks, the larger of which weigh up to 50 tons, were dragged overland at least 18 miles from a region near Marlborough to the north where sarsen blocks are still visible thickly scattered on the ground.[22] That the sarsen circle was later than the Q and R holes is shown by the fact that the socket for stone 3 of the outer circle cuts through the fill of Q hole 4. An antler from one of the sarsen sockets gave a C-14 date of 1720 ± 150 bc (BM-46), which is equivalent to about 2150 BC. Although this date and the one for the first bluestone setting seem to be in the wrong order they are in fact not distinguishable statistically and seem to confirm that phase IIIa followed phase II very quickly.

The unique and sophisticated architecture of Stonehenge III has often been described[23] and until quite recently the cultural context of the site seemed clear.[24] Now, however, its revised earlier dating to the end of the third millennium must mean that Mycenaean architects could not have been responsible for it and that perhaps Early Bronze Age Wessex chiefs did not pay for it. The lintels of the trilithons and the outer circle have sockets in their under sides which fit over bosses on the uprights; in addition the circle lintels each fit into their neighbours with a tongue-and-groove joint and are curved to match the curve of the circle. The whole structure was evidently carefully levelled; the heights of the remaining outer circle lintels do not vary over more than two or three inches. The butts of the uprights are still sunk into the chalk to a depth of up to 5 ft — presumably 6 ft originally — an extent unusual in other standing stone sites. Great care was taken with dressing many of the sarsens and many large hammerstones were found on the site.[25]

Stonehenge IIIb and IIIc

The final two phases of building activity at the site can be quickly described. In the first place, several of the bluestones in their final setting (phase IIIc) bear clear signs of having been carefully dressed: two have a pair of sockets in one side and were evidently lintels, one has the remains of a boss to fit such a socket and two others evidently formed a pair connected by a remarkable tongue-and-groove joint along one side of each. There are marks of frictional wear on some of these dressed stones so they were evidently set up for a period of time.[26] However, there are clear signs that some of these dressed features were later battered off before the monoliths were put in their final IIIc positions, so it seems reasonable to assign the dressed bluestone setting to phase IIIb. Also belonging to this phase is the double circle of the Y and Z holes (fig. 20) which lie well outside the sarsen circle but which can be shown to be later than that structure. This double ring too was unfinished, Y7 being very shallow and Z8 missing, and the sockets were left open and unfilled: the deposits in them were the fine silts characteristic of slow, natural weathering. There were evidently intended to be 60 stones in the Y and Z holes and the remaining 22 seem to have formed part of the dressed setting, the location of which is not known. This is in fact the number of bluestones having signs of dressing.

The final phase of construction apparently followed quickly after phase IIIb since the sockets for the latter were, as we have seen, never completed.

The dressed setting was dismantled and all 82 bluestones were erected into their present arrangement — a circle lying inside the sarsen circle and a horseshoe within the five trilithons. Both constructional phases are presumably dated by the antler pick found on the base of Y hole 30: this gave a C-14 date of 1240 ± 105 bc (I-2445), equivalent to about 1510-1560 BC. This pick must have been thrown into the abandoned Y hole before silting had started and is therefore likely to date the transition between phases IIIb and IIIc quite accurately. The gap of perhaps five centuries which is now revealed between phase IIIa and phase IIIb is not allowed for in the original reconstruction of the site's history and is commented on again in the final section of this chapter.

THE GEOMETRY OF STONEHENGE

The various features of Stonehenge exhibit signs of careful planning and accurate surveying reveals that systematic geometrical constructions often underlie the layout of the stones. The most recent work on this aspect of Stonehenge is that of the Thoms.[27]

Stonehenge I and II

The only feature of the earliest phase of the site which lends itself to geometrical study is the circle of 56 Aubrey holes. These lie accurately along the perimeter of a true circle with a mean radius of 141.8 ± 0.06 ft (or 283.6 ft in diameter): the perimeter is about 891.0 ft or almost exactly 131 megalithic rods of 6.8 ft (890.08 ft).[27] The standard deviation of the centres of the holes from this circle is ± 0.45 ft and the average distance between the holes is 16 ft (just under 6 megalithic yards). In fact the angular distance separating the holes, if they were equally spaced, is 6.43°, but the standard deviation from this figure is ± 0.32° or ± 0.79 ft; thus the Aubrey holes are placed more accurately on the perimeter than they are spaced around it.

One might suppose, rather than assuming that the length of the perimeter was most important to the designers of the Aubrey holes, that they were aiming at something different. If the diameter of the circle was 104 MY the perimeter would be 282.88 ft, only 6 in less than that of the calculated mean circle. In this case a right-angled triangle with a diameter forming the hypotenuse and with sides in the proportion of 5 to 12 to 13, will exactly link Aubrey holes 56, 7 and 28 and every other corresponding set; its sides would be 40, 96 and 104 MY.[28] It is worth noting that the four station stones form two identically opposed such triangles so this theory of the geometry of Stonehenge I may be the more probable.

It has not been possible to deduce anything about the geometry of the double circle of Stonehenge II other than the diameters already mentioned. The main problem of this phase of the site is the direction of the axis of the

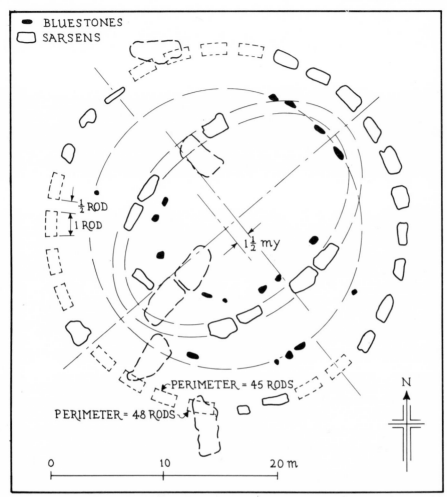

BLUESTONES
SARSENS

½ ROD
1 ROD

1½ my

PERIMETER = 45 RODS
PERIMETER = 48 RODS

N

0   10   20 m

Fig. 19. Plan of the sarsen temple of Stonehenge III showing the suggested geometrical constructions of the outer circle and of the horseshoe of trilithons: after A. Thom, A. S. Thom and A. S. Thom

avenue and its possible astronomical significance; this is dealt with in a later section.

Stonehenge IIIa

The recent studies of the Thoms have added a new dimension to our understanding of how the sarsen structure was planned and laid out; the new geometrical scheme is shown in fig. 19.[29] It has always been clear that, since the inside faces of the 17 remaining uprights of the sarsen circle are carefully dressed, the circle around which they were set up touched these faces. This true circle is 97 ft 4 in in diameter.[30] The uprights themselves have an average weight of about 26 tons, an average width of 7 ft and vary in thickness from 3 to 4 ft. The odd internal diameter of the circle, equivalent to 35.78 MY, makes sense if it is assumed that a *perimeter* of 45 megalithic rods was intended. This divides into 30 segments, each of 1 rod in length and separated by gaps of half a rod, and it is remarkable how well the surviving stones fit this scheme. The diameter of a circle with such a perimeter is 97.41 ft, extremely close to the measured one. The Thoms suggest that the stones were intended to fit into the 'boxes' created by these segments cutting two circles, the outer of which had a perimeter of 48 rods. However, in view of the undressed nature of the outer faces it may simply be that the stones were intended to be about half a rod thick.

Considerable care and planning must have gone into the design of the sarsen circle. Each of the 'stone boxes' so created subtends an angle of 8° from the centre and each gap one of 4°: moreover the true N-S line on the site clips the east edges of two opposing 'boxes' indicating that the geometry was set out in relation to the meridian. The centre of this circle can now be seen to be some 2 ft north of the centre of the Aubrey hole circle.[31] We may assume that 30 stones were wanted in the sarsen ring for some reason and that their standard widths, and the standard interval between them, were also prerequisites of the design. The setting out of the meridional line would have been fairly easy — it might have been done with the sun's shadow — but a fair amount of trial and error measuring must have been done before the exact radius was discovered which would produce a 45 rod circumference to take the 30 stones in the desired way. There would seem to be no alternative to repeated experiments with circles of different radii, the circumferences of each being carefully measured round with the graduated staffs which were surely used. We may note too that the axis of Stonehenge III, dictated by the construction of the circle and the horseshoe (below), passes through the middle of one of the gaps in the outer circle on an azimuth of 50°, running almost down the middle of the avenue of phase II. This not quite perfect match of axes is commented on again later.

The geometrical construction for the sarsen horseshoe suggested by the Thoms is not so simple or relatively obvious as that deduced for the outer circle, mainly because only four of the ten upright stones concerned (nos. 51-4) are known to be standing unaltered in their original positions, and two of these are leaning inwards (nos. 53 and 54). Here again the inside faces of the stones seem to have been dressed, in contrast to the other sides, as if to fit closely along some predetermined outline. As can be seen from the plan (fig. 19), the uprights of four of the trilithons fall neatly between two concentric ellipses the axes of which are 30 × 20 and 27 × 17 MY. The centre of these ellipses lies on the main axis of the site but is 1½ MY northeast of the centre of the sarsen circle, which lies on the same line. From his studies of ellipses in other stone rings Thom concludes that the designers usually tried to arrange for the perimeters to be in whole numbers of megalithic rods and for the two axes as well as the distance between the foci

1. The central stone of the Nether Largie alignment, Argyllshire, showing the cup-markings with one cup-and-ring

2. *Top* View of the five stones of the Nether Largie alignment, looking southwest

3. *Above* The Wayland's Smithy chambered long barrow, Oxfordshire

4. *Top* Aerial view of Stonehenge from the northeast with the Heel stone and part of the Avenue in the foreground

5. *Above* View of part of the sarsen structure of Stonehenge looking approximately northeast: the horseshoe of trilithons is in the foreground and the outer circle beyond it

6. *Top* Aerial view of Silbury Hill, Wiltshire

7. *Above* View of the bank and ditch at Avebury with the outer stone circle beyond

8. *Opposite top* Aerial view of the Dorset Cursus at the Pentridge terminal: the Cursus is the straight line running across the picture from left to right with a long barrow just beyond it

9. *Opposite* Aerial view of Grimes Graves, Norfolk: the shallow depressions are the sites of filled-in flint mine shafts

10, 11. *Top and above left* Aerial views of Durrington Walls, Wiltshire. The excavated strip was in the top left part of the site, beyond the road crossing it (*top*). View of the excavated strip showing the post-holes of the southern round-house after clearance (*above left*)

12. *Above right* Aerial view of Woodhenge, Wiltshire. The concrete posts mark the positions of the post-holes, and the surrounding ditch, with the causeway across it in the foreground, can be clearly seen as a dark crop-mark

13. *Opposite top* Aerial view of Skara Brae, Orkney

14. *Opposite centre* Hut 7 at Skara Brae, Orkney

15. *Opposite bottom* The Ring of Brodgar stone circle, Orkney, with the silted-up ditch in the foreground

16. *Top* View of the Maya ceremonial centre Xunantunich, Belize,
Central America, looking from the palace building A-11 towards the much larger
palace building A-6
17. *Above* Carved stone stela at the Maya site Tikal, Guatemala, depicting
a priest or chief with a feathered head-dress and cloak. In front of the stela is a
carved disc-altar

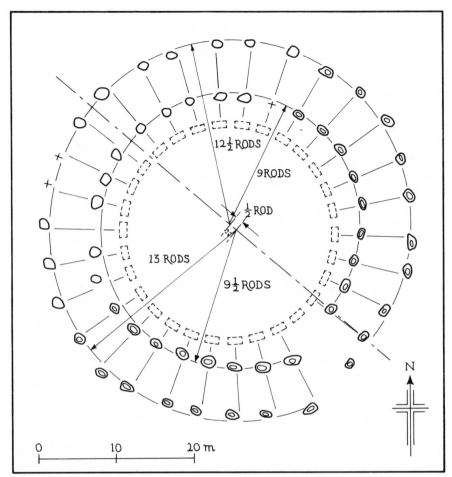

Fig. 20. Plan of the Y and Z holes of phase IIIb at Stonehenge, showing the spiral geometrical construction, linked to the sarsen circle, that fits them: after A. Thom, A. S. Thom and A. S. Thom

to be integral in megalithic yards.[32] In the case of the hypothetical trilithon ellipses, the perimeter of the inner one proves to be within an inch or two of 28 rods. The long axes of these ellipses, when fitted to the actual plan of the stones, coincide extremely closely with the 50° axis independently deduced for the outer sarsen circle.

Phases IIIb and IIIc

Examination by the Thoms of the detailed plan of the Y and Z holes (the second double circle of bluestones) made during the excavations of the 1950s led to some interesting conclusions about the shape of this uncompleted stone setting. The stone holes are seen to lie on two spirals, each formed of two opposed semicircles, a type of geometrical construction first identified in cup-and-ring rock carvings.[33] The radii of the two semicircles on the west are 9½ and 13 MY respectively and, since their centres lie ½ MY apart, the radii of the corresponding two on the east would have to be 9 and 12½ MY. This construction fits the stone-holes best if the axis (the line on which the adjacent diameters lie) is on an azimuth of about 130°.

The size of the circle of bluestones of phase IIIc could not be exactly discovered as too few stones remain in position. The Thoms adopt Atkinson's suggestion that there were 60 stones in this ring and suggest that these were spaced 1½ MY apart. This would give a perimeter of 90 MY (36 rods) and a diameter of 28.65 MY. Such a circle fits the 9 remaining upright bluestones of this ring quite well. The construction suggested for the bluestone horseshoe is a curious figure formed of an intersecting ellipse and circle but neither of the suggestions for the geometry of phase IIIc have the same degree of plausibility as that suggested for the sarsen structures because of the poorer state of preservation of the latest bluestone settings.

THE ASTRONOMY OF STONEHENGE I

The astronomical function of Stonehenge has caused discussion and argument for many years, but most of the early views are out of date because they were framed before it was realised — after the excavations of the 1950s — that the site had a long history and that different features of it are from different ages. The recalibration of the radio-carbon dates has rendered even the most recent astronomical interpretations more controversial than they were, because most of these theories concern Stonehenge I and that site is now known to have been built early in the third millennium BC. This is much earlier than the majority of the other standing stones and stone circles, from which the bulk of the archaeo-astronomical evidence has come, and Stonehenge is indeed now the earliest site so far known in England, Wales or Scotland which might be classed as a professional observatory as well as a temple. Only the New Grange passage grave in Ireland is at the same time definitely older and thought to have some calendrical or astronomical function built into it;[34] the earlier radio-carbon date for the Duntreath standing stones in Stirlingshire does not conclusively date the stones themselves.[35] Much of the evidence for an early origin for any specialist classes of priests, astronomers and wise men in Britain before the Late Neolithic period thus depends on Stonehenge.

The axis of the site

The axes of many prehistoric structures seem to have been orientated towards astronomically significant directions[36] and Stonehenge is no

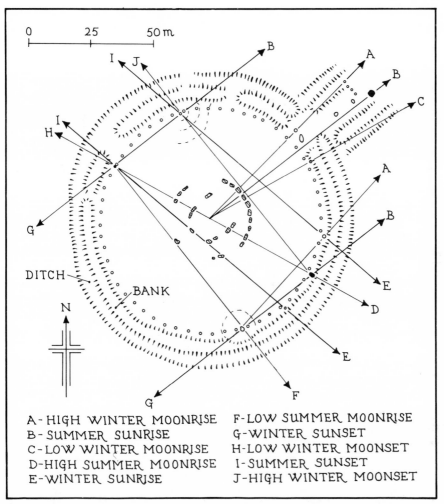

A - HIGH WINTER MOONRISE   F - LOW SUMMER MOONRISE
B - SUMMER SUNRISE   G - WINTER SUNSET
C - LOW WINTER MOONRISE   H - LOW WINTER MOONSET
D - HIGH SUMMER MOONRISE   I - SUMMER SUNSET
E - WINTER SUNRISE   J - HIGH WINTER MOONSET

Fig. 21. Plan of Stonehenge I and the station stones showing the astronomical alignments claimed by G. Hawkins

exception. In the case of the earliest structure on the site the only definable axis not hitherto commented on is that running through the centre of the entrance causeway from the geometric centre of the Aubrey holes. The line from the same point through the Heel stone is slightly different and is discussed below. The entrance axis is a little to the left of the Heel stone and seems to pass between the second and third of the A holes (fig. 21), giving an azimuth of almost exactly 45° or due northeast. If the causeway post-holes were set up for an astronomical purpose (below) this may be the explanation for the northeast orientation of the henge entrance.

The Heel stone

The most widely known of the possible astronomical aspects of Stonehenge is the fact that the midsummer sun now rises slightly to the left of the Heel stone when viewed from the centre of the sarsen circle (which is, as we have seen, only about 2 ft from the centre of the Aubrey circle) and, a few moments later, passes directly behind the stone with the upper rim showing.[36] The tip of the stone is now slightly above the horizon, but in 2800 BC, when it was standing upright and the ground surface on the site was at least a foot higher, its tip would have been about level with the horizon. This can hardly be a coincidence and suggests that the stone was deliberately set up to act as a foresight for watching some celestial phenomenon, possibly the sunrise at the summer solstice.

In chapter 4 it was explained that the exact time of the solstices cannot be detected at megalithic sites except with very long alignments, preferably of more than ten miles, so that the Heel stone could never have pinpointed the time of the solstice with an accuracy of better than one or two weeks. Might it then have been a symbolic marker, designed to present a dramatic spectacle to an audience by priests who already had detailed knowledge of the solar calendar? Neolithic crowds would doubtless have found the spectacle even more awe-inspiring than do modern visitors, especially if it was accompanied by some impressive ceremonial to emphasise the power and skill of the priesthood. Few could have realised then — as most do not now — that the sun can be seen rising in the same awesome way on several mornings before and after the solstice!

The main problem with this interpretation of the Heel stone is that at present the position of the solstitial sunrise is moving very gradually towards the east and that, if this movement is retrojected 5,000 years, the sun would have made its first dramatic appearance some way to the left (north) of the Heel stone.[37] Since the sunrise, to be impressive, needs to occur exactly over the stone, and since this could easily have been arranged, it is hard to understand why the stone is so badly offset if it was intended as a sunrise marker. Hawkins gives the declination of the sun rising over the stone as $\pm 23° 54'$[38] — suitable for a solstice in about 1800 BC — but it is not clear which spot on the horizon is being measured (the solar declination is defined as that of the centre of its disc, 16' from the rim). It is clear from his photograph[39] and Hadingham's drawing[37] that the figure should actually be considerably less than that of the *present* solstice ($+23° 27'$) if by 'sunrise' is meant the first flash of the disc on the horizon. Stone made the same point with characteristic clarity.[40] Thus if the tip of the Heel stone touched the horizon early in the third millennium BC the first flash of the rising sun would have occurred exactly over it when the solar declination was not much above $+23°$, a rising position many days before and after even the present solstice and even more days away from the prehistoric one. The inaccuracy of the declination given by Hawkins serves only to show how unacceptably wide was the degree of tolerance which he gave to his 'significant' alignments.[41]

An alternative explanation for the Heel stone was suggested by Hoyle[42] which accounted for the apparent 'inaccuracy' of this and other alignments at Stonehenge. Short alignments could be used to pinpoint the time of the solstice accurately if they were aimed a degree or two *inside* the midsummer or midwinter positions; then sunrise or sunset would occur over the marker twice, while the position of the disc on the horizon was still changing perceptibly from day to day, and the time of the solstice could be obtained by halving the interval between the two observations. If the stone was set up at about 2800 BC the declination of the sun at the solstices should have been just about 24.0° and we have seen that the tip of the stone marks a rising sun with a declination of about +23.1°. Thus the difference is about 0.9° and, from table 6a, we can see that at present this represents a sunrise about eight days, or a little more, before and after the solstice. Viewed as a movement along the horizon this represents about three solar diameters and at that time, moreover, the daily change in the sun's position along the horizon is a little over one diameter. Thus the Heel stone might well have been used to isolate two sunrises about eight days before and after midsummer and to give in this way the date of midsummer day itself. The only objections to this theory are, first, the possible existence of longer and more accurate solstitial alignments at the site described below and, second, the fact that the stone seems more plausible, judging from its setting, as an impressive ceremonial marker of midsummer morning. However, the latter explanation comes up against the awkward fact of its odd declination.

Hawkins suggested that the Heel stone may have been set up to act as a device to predict lunar eclipses.[43] The winter moon rises over the Heel stone twice in each of its cycles of 18.61 years, that is about every 9¼ years, and Hawkins plotted the positions of the highest winter moonrise for the period 1600-1400 BC — computed retrospectively — as seen from the centre of Stonehenge. In the same way he computed the occurrence of winter eclipses of the sun and moon for the same epoch and claimed that an eclipse always followed high winter moonrise over the stone.[44] But no more than half of them would have been visible from Wiltshire. He concluded that the stone was designed to help the priesthood forecast eclipses and that the Aubrey holes were used as a counting device to help with this, there being a 56 year cycle of eclipses which the 56 holes could have helped to count.

It has been argued that this theory is improbable because the Aubrey holes never held the uprights that would have been needed as moveable markers. However, it is undoubtedly true that large boulders of dark- and light-coloured stone could have been moved round the filled holes for many years provided that these were kept clear of turf. A more serious objection to Hawkins' theory is the fact that the number of eclipses which could be predicted by such a device is a pathetically small proportion of those which actually occur and are visible from Wiltshire. Only once every nine years would the conditions have been right and even then — as Hawkins' diagram itself shows[44] — eclipses could have occurred even when the moon rose up to 3° away from the stone (six lunar diameters) and these would presumably have gone undetected. Indeed the moon could have risen right over the stone without an eclipse occurring[45] and only about half of those detected in every ninth year would have been visible from Wiltshire! It can be argued that any Stonehenge astronomer would have seen only a random array of moonrises in the northeast and subsequent eclipses and would not have been able to make any systematic deductions from such observations. There is also doubt about the existence of a 56 year eclipse cycle.[45] It is a fact, too, that any midsummer sunrise marker will automatically point to the centre of the 18.61 year cycle of maximum winter moonrises and could therefore appear to have a sophisticated moon-observing function which was not intended at all by the designers. The original function of the Heel stone still remains uncertain.

The causeway post-holes

A much more convincing interpretation of Stonehenge I as· a lunar observatory has been offered by Newham[46] who thus gave the first explanation of the rows of post-holes discovered on the causeway by Hawley.[47] There are about 53 such holes arranged in six short rows or ranks which appear to radiate from the centre of the site (fig. 22); they lie within a 10° arc immediately north of the alignment to the Heel stone. This arc defines the left hand of the sector of the horizon at which the moon rises at the northerly limits of its monthly swing as these limits vary over the 18.61 year cycle (chapter 4). In the lunar terminology of Thom the arc extends from $+ \varepsilon$ to $+(\varepsilon + \iota)$ with the Heel stone being at about $+ \varepsilon$: the other half of the arc ($+ \varepsilon$ to $+ (\varepsilon - \iota)$) would be to the right of the stone and does not seem to have been recorded in this way. Moreover the number of holes in any one of the six ranks does not exceed nine, the number of extreme risings which could appear north of ε in any one lunar cycle; in the second nine years of the 18½ year cycle the most northerly monthly moonrise would occur to the right of ε and the Heel stone, as noted.

Newham compared the pattern of the azimuths marked by the post-holes with records of extreme northerly moonrises for nine periods between 1871 and 1954 (fig. 22) and also with the same phenomena computed for the period 1814 to 1712 BC. Though naturally not identical the pattern of the post-holes does bear a marked resemblance to the other two sets of azimuths; even the gaps in the Stonehenge markers are reasonably interpreted as observations missed because of the weather. Also striking is the similarity between the irregular spacing of the post-holes in their ranks — contrasting with the relatively regular intervals between the ranks — and the similarly irregular azimuths in the diagram of actual moonrises. Because of the relatively rapid change in the moon's declination every 24

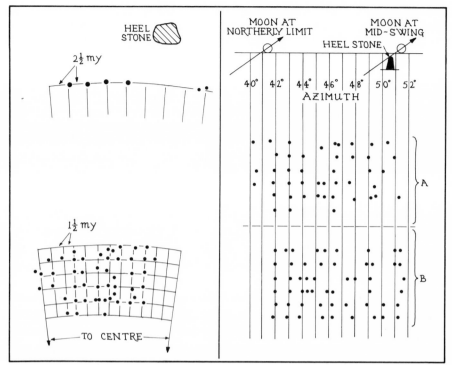

Fig. 22. Plan of the post-holes on the causeway entrance of Stonehenge, probably of phase I, with two suggested interpretations of them — Thom's view of them as a fan-shaped sector of posts (left) and Newham's idea of moonrise markers (right). In Newham's diagram A represents the post-holes as found and B the corresponding positions for observing moonrises at the site between 1871 and 1954

hours, only rarely would it be at its most northerly declination at or near the moment of rising, the only time any Stonehenge observers could have recorded its position. It would thus require observations to be taken over several eighteen year cycles before the extreme northerly position ($+(\varepsilon + i)$) became obvious from the posts at the left end of each rank.

In general, Newham's hypothesis seems highly plausible, particularly in that it has the virtues — not often found among astronomical theories about Stonehenge — of explaining features on the ground in a simple and practical way and of assuming only the minimum of empirical knowledge and technical ability on the part of the prehistoric observers. Two minor drawbacks may be mentioned. First, why was only the left half of the northeast sector of moonrises recorded in this way, and second, why were these posts, which must have stood in position for decades, set up right in the middle of the entrance to the henge when they could have been erected more conveniently further out? Still, these small objections do not seriously detract from what must be the first really plausible detailed theory that has been offered about Stonehenge astronomy.

An alternative explanation for the causeway post-holes has been given; this sees them as part of a fan-shaped arrangement of markers, similar to the stone rows of Caithness, which could have been used in lunar observations, as an aid in detecting the extreme declinations from the rising and setting points[48] (fig. 22). Such a theory would imply that there were longer alignments at Stonehenge with which the actual observations were carried out, a possibility discussed shortly.

The positioning of the site

Perhaps the most ambitious claim about the skill shown by the builders of Stonehenge I — apart from the more fanciful speculations of Hoyle[49] — was one made by Newham.[50] He suggested that the fact that the long and short sides of the rectangle formed by the four station stones pointed at significant solar and lunar declinations was not a matter of chance. The long sides point to the extreme north setting position of the moon in the northwest and to its most southerly rising position in the southeast (fig. 21). The short sides point to the summer solstice sunrise in the northeast and the winter solstice sunset in the southwest. At present these solar and lunar positions are at right angles to one another at the latitude of Stonehenge (54° 11' N), as well as at the corresponding southerly latitude, provided that one has a low and fairly level horizon. Further north or south, this rectangle becomes progressively more diamond-shaped and the assumption is that Stonehenge was sited where it is because the builders wished to take advantage of this feature of that latitude.

There seems to be no adequate way of checking this idea, as it depends mainly on assumptions about the knowledge and beliefs of the builders of a unique site nearly 5,000 years ago. On the whole it seems more probable that this feature of the site did not determine its position in the first place; if a line towards the midsummer sunrise were set out, the reverse direction (on flat terrain) would point automatically to midwinter sunset and lines at right angles to this would give the other directions in the same way. The other assumption involved in this theory — that the builders of Stonehenge I had the option of a site in a variety of latitudes — is not open to proof, and neither is there any positive evidence that the station stone rectangle was an original feature of the site.

Long astronomical alignments

A more promising field for investigation is the existence or otherwise of distant astronomical foresights visible from Stonehenge. The normal procedure for arranging and laying out such long lines — described in chapter 4 — was probably, first, to establish the approximate direction of the rising or setting phenomenon concerned, second, to choose or make a suitable distant foresight on the horizon in about the right direction and, third, to fix the backsight in relation to the foresight by prolonged and systematic observation. If several such long lines crossing at the same backsight were required the task would be much more complex, especially in undulating terrain like the chalk downs where the distance of the visible horizon can vary sharply with changes in elevation of a few feet. Several possible distant artificial foresights have been tentatively located at Stonehenge, but these need to be checked by excavation and, if possible, radiocarbon dating.[51]

About 3,000 yards northeast of the site, on the summit of the high ground which forms the horizon in that direction, is a small, possibly artificial mound 6 to 8 ft across and only a few inches high.[52] Its azimuth from the centre of Stonehenge is 49° 47.6', very close to that of the centre of the avenue (below), and its declination is +23° 59.8'. The sun rising with its upper edge at the little mound would thus have a declination of half a solar diameter (16') less, that is +23° 43.8', equivalent to its midsummer position in about 300 BC. If one supposes that the sun was intended to rise with its centre at the mark — thus having the same declination as the mound — we arrive at the solstice of about 2700 ± 400 BC, surprisingly close to the date for Stonehenge I obtained from radiocarbon. Yet the fact is that the highland solar observatories are interpreted as having foresights which almost completely hid the sun so that its upper edge was at the mark concerned (chapter 4), so it is perhaps a little arbitrary to assume a different technique at Stonehenge. Also, of course, a sun more than fractionally exposed is very bright and it seems doubtful whether it would have been possible to observe it satisfactorily against such a small mark. To set up a backsight using the centre of the sun's disc against the horizon mark, two observers would have been needed, one establishing the 'first flash' position of the sun against the mound and the other the place where the lower edge of the disc grazed the mark; halving the distance between these points would give the required position.[53] However, the glare would be a severe problem for the second observer. The same difficulties arise if the Heel stone is thought to mark the backsight: the centre of the disc at the mound gives the solstice of 3330 ± 400 BC and the 'minimum flash' position that of about 900 ± 400 BC.

Clearly there is a considerable problem here. On the one hand long alignments at Stonehenge are the only really plausible and accurate astronomical instruments but, on the other, to make Peter's Mound fit the prehistoric solstice of Stonehenge I it has to be assumed that the unlikely procedure of using the centre of the sun's disc was followed.

The car-park post-holes

In 1966 the car-park at Stonehenge was enlarged and in the process three massive post-holes were found in the chalk, some 285 yards northwest of the centre of the site.[54] The holes are 30 to 40 feet apart and lie on a line running

E-W: an examination of their contents showed that they had once contained huge wooden posts up to 2½ ft in diameter and traces even of the wedges which had supported them were noted. Such massive timbers could easily have risen to 30 ft, where their tops would have been level with the horizon when viewed from the main site, and they were the first clear indications found that long sight-lines were used at Stonehenge. There may be many more on the surrounding downs but they are unlikely to be discovered without a systematic search.

Newham discovered that when these three posts are viewed from the Heel stone and the four station stones they mark significant astronomical positions on the northwest horizon. The last gleam of the midsummer sunset ($\delta + 23.92°$) and of the two mid-quarter sunsets ($\delta + 16.0°$) — half way between the equinox and the summer solstice — are effectively marked by no. 1 post when seen from the Heel stone and station stone 91 respectively.[55] The maximum and minimum midwinter moonsets, at $-(\varepsilon + \imath)$ and $-(\varepsilon - \imath)$, are similarly marked from the other station stones. It seems quite reasonable therefore to suppose that the car-park posts were set up as accurate astronomical sight-lines although there are no means of deciding at what stage in the site's history they were put up. Such wooden foresights could have been planted in relation to already fixed backsights at any time.

THE ASTRONOMY OF STONEHENGE II AND III

The structural features assigned to phases II and III at the site show, with two exceptions, no features of astronomical interest. The exceptions are the station stones and the avenue. The station stones have already been discussed and it remains to consider the orientation of the final straight stretch of the avenue and its possible significance. Hawkins suggested that there were astronomical alignments running from the centre of the site through several of the archways formed by the lintelled sarsen structures[56] and, while certain features of the building may have been orientated deliberately towards significant rising and setting positions, no sort of precision could have been obtained in observation with such lines.[57]

The axis of the avenue

The line of the centre of the straight stretch of the avenue has an azimuth which is close to, perhaps identical with, that of the axis of the later sarsen circle (p. 117) and distinct from either of the possible phase I axes mentioned. Both Lockyer[58] and Stone[59] measured this azimuth, the former by estimating two widely separated sets of centre points and surveying them and the latter by constructing a row of pegs from a large number of such points. This second attempt gave a result almost identical to Lockyer's first measurement which was 49° 35.85'. However, the line finally chosen by Lockyer to define the axis was a supposed extension of the one measured on the ground eight miles to the northeast to an earthwork on Sidbury Hill. This is now known to be of Iron Age date and is not even visible from Stonehenge![60] Lockyer presumably assumed that this extension was intended by the builders and found its azimuth to be 49° 34.3'; this point on the horizon gave a declination of +23° 54.5', suitable for a midsummer sunrise at about 1800 ± 200 BC.

It must be obvious that the exact edges of the avenue cannot be known until the flanking ditches are extensively excavated and without this information, the azimuth laid out by the builders cannot be exactly determined. It is certainly not legitimate to try to deduce the date of the avenue from such information. We have seen that there is a possible distant artificial foresight, Peter's Mound, in the same direction and this, rather than the avenue, would have served as a sunrise marker if there was one. It is more probable that the avenue was laid out towards the northeast partly because the direction of midsummer sunrise was ritually important but also because this was the best direction for the last part of the road up which the bluestones were being hauled from the river Avon. The importance of the northeast orientation is confirmed by the direction of the axis of the sarsen temple of Stonehenge III, already described. The latter is 50° in our terminology and this direction is strictly determined by the link between the phase III geometry and the meridian. It may be therefore that the axis of the avenue was intended to be the same but that an error of about 24' accumulated as the original line was prolonged over 600 yards.

DISCUSSION OF STONEHENGE

The new information which has accumulated about Stonehenge in recent years — particularly on its dating, geometrical design and possible astronomical function — seems to require a fresh assessment of the significance of the site.

Function and purpose

There is no doubt of the uniqueness of Stonehenge; among the hundreds of stone circle sites in Britain and Ireland it is paramount both architecturally and in the sophistication of its geometrical design. This conclusion is reinforced by the nearness of several other large and obviously important ceremonial sites in the same region of Wessex (fig. 18) and by the multitudes of rich Early Bronze Age barrows which cluster round the site. The parallel with medieval times, when lords and churchmen were buried in and near the great new abbeys and cathedrals, is surely an apt one. Neither do we know of any other such site which was used over such a long

THE STONEHENGE SEQUENCE				
NEW DATING C-14 dates	real years	events at the site	old phases	suggested new interpretation and phases
	3000 B.C.	nothing on site		
2180 b.c.		BANK & DITCH constructed	I	STONEHENGE I Simple bank and ditch henge monument, perhaps sited to serve as an universal astronomical backsight as well as a ceremonial centre.
		Heel stone also?		
	2500 B.C.	STONEHENGE I		Aubrey holes dug slightly later period of stability
1848 b.c.		AUBREY HOLES dug		
1620 b.c.		BLUESTONE DOUBLE CIRCLE started but not finished (Q and R holes)	II	STONEHENGE II FIRST PERIOD OF CRISIS construction of Avenue: transport of Welsh bluestones and partial building of double circle: plans changed and sarsen stones erected: bluestones elsewhere.
1720 b.c.		SARSEN STRUCTURE built	IIIa	
	2000 B.C.			period of stability: most bluestones off the site and unused: some used for dressed bluestone setting.
1240 b.c.	1500 B.C.	SECOND BLUESTONE CIRCLE started but abandoned (Y and Z holes)	IIIb	STONEHENGE III SECOND PERIOD OF CRISIS Start made on double spiral setting of bluestones (Y & Z holes) but abandoned. Destruction of dressed bluestone setting and circle-and-horseshoe built.
		THIRD BLUESTONE SETTING completed (circle & horseshoe)	IIIc	
				No more constructional activity.

Fig. 23. A new scheme for the development of Stonehenge, based on the correction of the radiocarbon dates

period and which was altered and added to so often: again the parallel with the greater medieval churches seems apt.

Obviously we cannot be certain what was the primary purpose of the phase I henge monument when it was set up at about 2800 BC but there seems a distinct possibility that it was intended as much as a relatively advanced astronomical observatory as a temple. It is true that there are difficulties in interpreting the purpose of the Heel stone and of the possible long alignments which have been identified; nevertheless the causeway post-holes and those in the car-park seem fairly clear evidence that precise astronomical observations were made from the site. Moreover, even though one may doubt whether the many alignments identified by Hawkins could ever have served much practical purpose, it is a fact that so many pairs of features at the site do form lines towards significant rising and setting positions of the sun and moon that this can hardly have come about by chance. It seems very likely that such lines were deliberate orientations, either for ritual purposes or as a method of storing information, or both. The Aubrey holes could have served as a counting device of some kind (as well as being receptacles for cremation burials) though it is probably impossible either to confirm this or to determine their exact significance.

The development of the site and its chronology

The detailed history of the site was worked out by Atkinson and Piggott from the results of the excavations of the 1950s, and subsequently given precision with four good radiocarbon dates. At first these dates seemed to confirm the relatively short history of the site deduced earlier, which was thought to last only a century or two.[61] However the tree-ring calibration of C-14 dates has altered this picture drastically by making the site about a millenium older than was originally conceived and an alternative interpretation of its history, based on the new dating, is presented in fig. 23.

As we have seen, the site was probably founded in the 29th century BC and the fact that the enormous mound of Silbury Hill was built at about the same time (chapter 6) can hardly be a coincidence. The implications of this are explored in the next chapter but it does seem that at this time there began the development towards major ritual sites and ceremonial centres which may well reflect a transformation of the rural Neolithic society of southern England into one which was able to produce the hundreds of stone circles and standing stone observatory-temples of the Late Neolithic period.

If the calibrated dates are about accurate there must have followed a period of several centuries during which no more constructional activity took place, although the Aubrey holes may have been added some time after the site was first established. The second major phase of building can be described, with the third, as the response to a series of crises of some kind which occurred in quick succession. It seems to have begun in the 23rd century BC and gone on until about the 21st, though of course the inherent inaccuracy of the radiocarbon method may mean that this 'first period of crisis' lasted a much shorter time. The events of this new period II include the bringing of the bluestones from Wales, the digging of sockets for them and their partial erection into a double circle, the dismantling of this ring before it was complete and the filling of the sockets, and finally the hauling to the site of 81 or 82 enormous sarsen blocks and their erection into the magnificent building of Atkinson's phase IIIa. Now that we know that the final alterations to the site — during the 'second period of crisis' (below) — took place several centuries later it seems logical to put both the original phases II and IIIa into the first main period of stone circle building and to suppose that a long period of stability followed the successful erection of the first sarsen temple.

At present we do not know when and where the setting of the 22 dressed bluestones was erected but it may have been at the same time as the sarsen building: the similarity of the mortice and tenon joints on both might support this view. However the other 60 bluestones seem to have been off the site until a new period of crisis arose and fresh alterations to the site took place. The calibrated C-14 date for the Y and Z hole setting — the abandoned double spiral of bluestones of the original phase IIIb — now falls into the sixteenth century BC, perhaps five centuries after the completion of the sarsen structure. The unused bluestones were evidently to be put into this setting of 60 stones, so it may be that the dressed bluestone setting belongs to this later period also. But plans were quickly changed again and before any stones had been set up in the double spiral, all 82 were erected into the present circle and horseshoe. The dressed setting was dismantled, some of its carved joints battered off and the members used again as simple standing monoliths. Thereafter the site was left undisturbed, though doubtless continuing for centuries as the paramount religious site of the area.

The social significance of Stonehenge

The significance of Stonehenge I in terms of the evolving Neolithic society of Wessex is more fully discussed in the following chapter. Of more general interest perhaps is the social significance of the transport of the bluestones and the erection of the sarsen temple, especially now that the dating of the first period of crisis makes them far too old to have been the responsibility of a Mycenaean architect. At present there seems no alternative to assuming that the sarsen temple, remarkable and unparalleled as its architecture is, was the creation of Late Neolithic or Chalcolithic Wessex society and indeed we now know that its construction, and of course the bringing of the bluestones, follows quite closely on the establishment of major ceremonial centres like Durrington Walls, Marden and Mount Pleasant (chapters 7 and 8) and after the arrival of the Beaker people in Britain. The fact that all these major cultural changes and events seem to have occurred at around the same time can hardly be a coincidence, but it is difficult at present to do more than guess whether any general explanations are appropriate.

In the framework of the old theory about Stonehenge, in which Mycenaean architects played an important part,[62] the motive for building sarsen Stonehenge was supplied by the concept of a territory of rich Early Bronze Age chieftains living on the downs in the middle of the second millennium BC, amassing wealth from trade and having distant contacts along the trade routes as far as the civilised world of the Aegean. The clusters of Bronze Age barrows around the site, the 'Mycenaean' dagger found carved on one of the uprights and the architectural resemblances with the Lion Gate at Mycenae, all seemed to confirm this view.[62] At present there is dispute as to whether the Early Bronze Age Wessex culture — to which the barrows belong — is contemporary with Mycenaean civilisation[63] or earlier;[64] if the latter is correct the sarsen temple could still be a creation of that culture, but if not it would antedate the rich period of the Early Bronze Age altogether and would have been built by the Late Neolithic people or the Chalcolithic Beaker folk.

The alternative view now is to see Stonehenge II and IIIa — or the structures of period II in the new site history offered here (fig. 23) — not as the barbarian temple built by an imported architect for rich chieftains but as the great cathedral and observatory of an outstanding class of astronomer priests and wise men, built for powerful religious and astronomical motives which are the more impressive for being only partly divined. It would thus become the finest achievement of the stone circle builders and would surely indicate where the power and authority of that class was concentrated — on Salisbury Plain. We shall see in the following chapters that the theocratic governing class which might have been responsible for Stonehenge and the many other circles could well have lived not far away and these comments conveniently lead into the second part of this work, a consideration of the kind of society which might have existed in Britain at the time concerned.

PART TWO
The Society

6

The Beginnings of the New Order

The first part of this work has reviewed evidence for great technical and scientific achievements in Neolithic Britain involving both considerable intellectual prowess and practical skill up to what one could call a professional level — particularly towards the end of the period and at the very beginning of the Bronze Age. With the outstanding exception of Stonehenge this evidence is gained primarily from non-domestic sites in the highland zone, remote from the great concentrations of population in the eastern and southern lowlands of England. These sites are well preserved, obvious, long-lasting and megalithic — a kind that can only rarely be expected in the lowland areas — and it seems reasonable to suppose that advances in our understanding of ancient astronomy and metrology were bound to be more rapid among them than among the diffuse, grass-grown earthworks of the lowland areas, the precise designs of which can only be revealed by skilled excavation. It seems unreasonable to suppose on the other hand that the 'advanced' activities detected among the standing stones and stone circles were characteristic only of the Neolithic cultures of the highland zone and not of those lowland areas, and indeed Stonehenge and the sites around it do suggest strongly that it was in Wessex that the 'intellectual', as well as the technical and organisational, aspects of Late Neolithic culture reached their peak.

Yet if this was so should there not be abundant evidence from the many well excavated and impressive Neolithic and Early Bronze Age sites on the southern English chalklands that a rather special type of skilled society or class did exist then? No suggestion that southern Britain between 4,500 and 3,500 years ago was inhabited by anything more complex than rural tribal communities, ruled no doubt by chiefs and witchdoctors and sometimes perhaps by a High King, has ever been made from a study of the evidence.[1] Yet when considering questions of this kind one must be clear about what kind of evidence archaeology might discover which could support or deny the conclusions drawn for example by Thom from data collected in the field by a wholly different set of skills based on theodolite surveying, exact measurement and advanced arithmetic. We can leave aside any cases of other workers discovering similar astronomical properties on Wessex sites using similar techniques,[2] and any archaeological checks on predictions made at standing stone 'observatories' by the astronomical theory.[3] Archaeological techniques of the standard kind are unable to detect evidence for advanced intellectual activities of the sort being discussed, but they ought perhaps to be able to detect the kind of site from which one could infer that a special class of wise men was in existence at the time concerned, as well as evidence for the appropriate economy and social organisation.

It has often been concluded from the mere existence in Wessex of many huge Neolithic and Early Bronze Age sites which required tremendous labour to build that the peoples of the Wessex area at those times were highly organised in some way, but this need imply nothing specific about the mental skills of their leaders except that they were effective leaders and practical organisers. The only way we could hope to find direct archaeological evidence for a full-time class of wise men, priest-magicians, bards and their families and retainers would be to detect any specially built villages — or ceremonial centres as they are called in Maya archaeology — that they might have lived in and to think of some way of extracting from

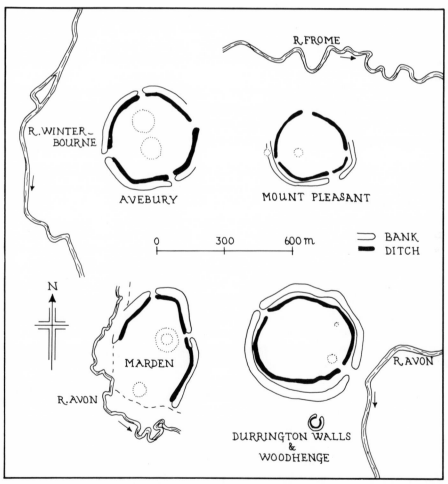

Fig. 24. Plans of the four large henges of southern England, showing their closeness to rivers: Avebury, Durrington Walls, Mount Pleasant and Marden

the economic and technological evidence from such sites information which would indicate whether these people were being supported with food and equipment by the rest of the rural population in their full-time non-agricultural pursuits. This is attempted for two important dwelling sites in chapters 7 and 9, but here we may confine ourselves to noting some specific evidence for the steady development of organisational ability in southern Britain in Neolithic times, mainly in the third millennium BC.

LONG BARROWS AND CAUSEWAYED CAMPS

The earliest Neolithic farmer colonists seem to have arrived in Britain at about 3500 bc, perhaps a little earlier in Ireland,[4] a date which is equivalent to about 4380 BC. Characteristic of the Early Neolithic peoples of the southern and eastern chalklands, whose archaeological debris is called the Windmill Hill culture,[5] is the sepulchral monument known as the long barrow, a huge heap of chalk raised over a number of skeletons and sometimes over a burnt wooden structure which seems to have housed them for a considerable period. Presumably these barrows were not built immediately after the colonists had landed in Britain but a few generations later when stable farming communities had established themselves. Many of them incorporate cores of stacked turves, showing that primeval forests had already given way to grassland nearby, doubtless because of systematic clearance by the Neolithic farmers and herdsmen. There are now at least twenty radiocarbon dates available for the barrows and they range from 3415 ± 180 bc (GX-1178) for Lambourn in Berkshire to 2307 ± 90 bc (BM-506a) for Beckhampton Road in Wiltshire. Skendleby in Yorkshire may in fact have been built even later in Beaker times, after 2000 bc, in spite of the earlier C-14 dates obtained.[6]

In size the barrows range in length from 100 ft to nearly 400 ft and though most are severely denuded by weathering and ploughing, estimates of the work involved in building them can be made from the size of the flanking ditches; this of course can be discovered accurately by excavation. A long barrow 400 ft long, flanked by two quarry ditches of the same length and perhaps 20 ft wide at the top, 10 ft at the bottom and 10 ft deep, would have contained about 120,000 cu ft of chalk. According to the results obtained from the experimental earthwork on Overton Down[7] an average rate of excavation in a chalk ditch for a three-man team (two digging and one carrying and dumping) working with Neolithic equipment is 5 cu ft (weighing about 5 cwt) for each man hour. At this rate our hypothetical barrow's ditches would have taken about 24,000 man hours to dig out, or assuming a ten hour day, 200 men for 12 days or 80 for a month. Part of the work of piling up the barrow has not been included nor has that involved in supervising the project or in housing and feeding the labour force (however, with a relatively small number of people from a restricted area it might not have been necessary to make any special arrangements for feeding). Clearly this is the kind of communal effort which a small Neolithic settlement or two or three neighbouring ones could expend without undue distress in the slacker seasons of the agricultural year.

The causewayed camps are irregular, ditched enclosures with many entrances, built by the people of the Windmill Hill culture, perhaps as tribal centres or for markets, social meetings and ceremonies.[8] Five of these camps have been dated by C-14 and the results range from 3110 ± 130 bc (BM-351) for Abingdon, Berkshire, to 2580 ± 150 bc (BM-74) for Windmill Hill in Wiltshire.[9] There is thus a clear overlap with the long barrows and also with the more standardised round henge monuments of the later Neolithic period to which the causewayed camps may be in part ancestral. The outer of the three concentric ditches at Windmill Hill is about 3,600 ft long, the middle one about 2,200 ft and the inner one about 800 ft, a total of 6,600 ft or 1.28 miles. However, the effective total should be reduced by perhaps a quarter, to perhaps 5,000 ft, to allow for the numerous causeways. If we assume that the average ditch dimensions at Windmill Hill were 11 ft wide at the top, 6 ft at the base and 5 ft deep[10] an approximate volume of chalk of 200,000 cu ft is involved and this could have taken, according to the experiment mentioned above, at least 40,000 man hours to dig out and partly pile up into the banks. Thus a gang of 200 men working for 200 days could have excavated the chalk at Windmill Hill, and this takes no account of some of the work of piling up banks, supervising or housing and feeding the labour force. In fact the formula $H = V(120 + 8L + 2F)/100$ has been evolved to take account of some of the more complex factors of such a project, such as the amount of lift of the chalk up out of the ditch and onto the bank.[11] In this H is the total work in man hours, V is the volume of solid chalk excavated from the ditches in cubic feet, while L and F are the vertical and horizontal distances in feet between the centroids (centres of area) of the cross-sections of the bank and the ditch respectively as they were originally constructed. Using this formula, and supposing L and F to be about 5 and 20 ft respectively (the former has to be an estimate because much of the bank has disappeared), we again obtain a figure of 40,000 man hours. This would be a minimum figure involving the actual work force only. Even so, the effort still seems of an order which could be contemplated by a local tribe of a few hundred people, perhaps working in stages over several years. For some of the enormous sites of the latter part of the Neolithic period a vastly greater expenditure of effort must have been involved, and this says something important about the way society in southern England was developing in the third millennium BC. Indeed, during the 29th century BC two major monuments were built, one the temple-observatory at Stonehenge and the other a gigantic mound of unknown purpose, which together strongly suggest that Neolithic Britain had by that time evolved into a state in which 'national' as opposed to local projects could be undertaken, one in which we see the first clear signs of the arrival or emergence of an élite class with the authority and prestige to organise huge engineering projects for esoteric reasons.

SILBURY HILL

The largest prehistoric artificial mound in Europe lies in northern Wiltshire about ¾ mile south of Avebury and 1¼ miles northwest by west of the Sanctuary. It is one of the second (northerly) group of major Neolithic monuments in Wessex, which in addition to the two mentioned also includes the two Kennet long barrows and the Windmill Hill causewayed camp. Silbury Hill is a chalk mound in the form of a truncated cone 130 ft high with a flat top 100 ft in diameter (it has often been remarked that the sarsen monument of Stonehenge would fit neatly on to this top). The diameter of the base of the mound is about 550 ft and it covers an area of just under 5½ acres. Around the base is a huge, irregularly cut quarry ditch, now largely silted up, which is up to 120 ft wide and which was as much as 21 ft deep originally. The original volume of this huge heap of chalk, including a considerable quantity which was thought to have slipped down into the ditch, was at first calculated at about 12½ million cu ft.[12] Later, during the excavations of 1968 and 1969, it was realised that the ditch silts were probably not derived from the mound, which seemed to have suffered little erosion, but from flooding. Thus the original volume of the Hill is likely to have been not much more than its present one of about 8,700,000 cu ft.[13] This may be compared with the approximate volume of chalk dug out of the great ditch of Avebury which was some 3,400,000 cu ft. On the basis of experimental studies,[14] the material in Silbury Hill could have been excavated by 1,000 men in about 174 days (assuming a prehistoric working day of ten hours). However, this figure takes no account of the much greater depths of the Silbury ditch, nor of the height of the mound and the time taken to construct it in a systematic manner, nor of supervisory staff or the large number of man hours which must have been expended in housing and feeding such a large labour force over many months. The most economical quantity of chalk which could be carried in a basket out of the ditch and tipped on to the bank at Overton Down was found to be about 30 lbs and it has been estimated that some 50 million such basket-loads would have been required to build Silbury Hill. Taking these various factors into consideration, it has been estimated that a labour force of 500 men working continuously for 15 years[15] or seasonally for two or three times longer would have been required to build the Hill.

Excavations have been made on Silbury Hill on six occasions, from the late eighteenth century onwards, the most recent being a horizontal tunnel at the base driven in 1968 and 1969; none of these shafts and tunnels have ever revealed a trace of a central burial of any kind. The most recent work confirmed and refined our knowledge of the structure of the internal mound gained from previous explorations and yielded an exceptionally valuable and reliable radiocarbon date for its construction.[16] The whole mound seems to have been built as a single operation, though in distinct stages. It seems that a circular area 65.6 ft in diameter was initially marked out with widely separated stakes and in the middle of this was built the first stage, a low circular mound some 16.4 ft in diameter and 2.6 ft high made of clay with flints: this material had presumably been obtained not from the ditch but from some alluvial deposit in the flood plain of the nearby valley. This mound was extended with stacked turf and soil outwards to the fence and the primary structure was completed with four more successive layers of alluvial material. Its final dimensions included a diameter of about 111.5 ft and an estimated height of 17.2 ft. Unfortunately the common centre of the various features of this primary mound had been destroyed by the shaft sunk from the top in 1776.

The structure of the rest of the Hill, the chalk part, has to be inferred from the section visible in the outer part of the most recent tunnel, and from the other trenches on the upper slopes and on the flat summit also excavated by Atkinson. It seems probable that the whole mound was built of separate, circular dumps of chalk to ensure a stable core, each of them contained by a revetment of blocks. Moreover, the clear terrace near the top of the sloping side has proved to be an original Neolithic feature and suggests that the whole Hill was built in flat stages as a stepped cone, all the steps except the topmost having finally been filled in. The builders achieved considerable accuracy in their construction. The first structures at the base were strictly circular and the centre of these was evidently projected upwards as the mound rose higher. The centres of the primary features and that of the flat top all lie within a circle less than 1 m in diameter.[17]

A further structural feature was discovered in the trench across the quarry ditch. The side nearest the Hill had been deliberately covered immediately after the excavation by chalk rubble held on the outside by stepped timber revetments, a device obviously intended to prevent the inner face of the ditch eroding and so undermining the slope of the Hill. It seems strange that such a device was necessary when the danger could have been avoided by siting the ditch a few yards further out, and the revetment may perhaps mean that the Hill was enlarged to a size beyond that originally planned for.

The date of Silbury Hill is now well established by a C-14 measurement. Earlier estimates of its chronological and cultural context, lacking anything definite to go on except that it was pre-Roman (a Roman road avoids the Hill), tended to rely on the assumption that it was a giant round barrow and probably linked with the great period of Bronze Age activity on Salisbury Plain (then thought contemporary with the Mycenaean age in Greece), the most splendid achievement of which was the third phase of Stonehenge, the sophisticated sarsen temple. The possibility existed that the chief who had ruled when Stonehenge III was built was laid to rest under this colossal tumulus. However, the excellent state of preservation of the cut turves forming the core of the primary mound made it possible to collect enough unburnt material — mainly hazel fragments — from the surface of these turves. These produce a date of 2145 ± 95 bc (I-4136), equivalent to a time span centred on about 2830 BC, which must, from the nature of the material, refer to the time the turves were cut and stacked. Since the Hill seems to have been built as a single operation, the date should be that of the whole mound and it compares surprisingly well with that of 2180 ± 105 bc (I-2328) — equivalent to 2850-2870 BC — for the digging of the ditch of Stonehenge I (chapter 5). In terms of the history of the urban civilisations of the Mediterranean and the Near East, Silbury Hill and Stonehenge I seem to be slightly older than the great pyramid-building age of Egypt, the IVth Dynasty, which is estimated to have flourished in the 27th century BC. The implications of this early date are discussed later. (A set of six C-14 dates done on the buried turf line ranged from 4045 to 2365 bc and showed that dating turves is not a reliable method.)

The purpose of Silbury Hill remains obscure: no trace of any burial was found in the primary mound, and none was reported when the shaft sunk in 1776 tore out the centre of it. The question of whether it was an astronomical observatory of some kind does not seem to have been investigated although the almost exact contemporaneity of this giant structure with the first phase of Stonehenge (for which an astronomical function seems highly probable) now strongly suggests that the two projects were in some way interlinked. Two possibilities spring to mind. In the first place the flat-topped Hill might have been a high observation point, analogous to a Mesopotamian ziggurat or a Maya temple-pyramid (and similarly securing useful elevation above a flat terrain), though whether any astronomically significant horizon marks are visible from the summit is not yet known. In the second place the summit might have supported an enormous and high post which could have served as a universal astronomical foresight — viewed against the horizon sky from a number of positions in the countryside round about — in the manner claimed for the great stone known as Le Grand Menhir Brisé at Locmariaquer in Brittany.[18] The central part of the platform, where a post would have stood, has been destroyed by the shaft sunk in 1776. In fact such an astronomical function for Silbury Hill does not seem very likely at present. It occupies a very low-lying position in relation to its immediate surroundings and no part of Salisbury Plain can be seen from it, or the other way round.[19] Thus the Hill may well have served quite a different social purpose, for example as a symbolic welding together of an emerging stratified society with the huge communal effort required. Its importance in social terms for prehistoric Britain is certainly very great.[20] These problems are kept in sight and reviewed again later.

AVEBURY

The great henge site with stone circles at Avebury in northern Wiltshire is one of the second major group of outstanding Neolithic and Early Bronze Age monuments in Wessex which also includes Silbury Hill, the West Kennet Avenue, the Kennet long barrows and the Sanctuary.[21] In many ways Avebury is the most impressive site in the whole of Wessex, although it is difficult to appreciate as a whole now because of the village built inside it. In the sheer quantity of work involved in the construction of its mighty bank and ditch it is surpassed only by Silbury Hill, but if one also takes into account the bringing to the site and erecting of the scores of massive sarsen monoliths forming the three stone circles, Avebury may have involved an even greater investment of physical effort than the Hill. It is all the more unfortunate that no exact dating for the inception of this colossal work is available; the last excavations were carried out by Alexander Keiller between 1934 and 1939 and no suitable organic material seems to have been obtained from below the bank, or from the more suitable context of the base of the ditch, which could now be radiocarbon dated.

The bank and ditch

The huge flat-bottomed ditch, now about 13 ft deep but found to have been dug originally down to 30 ft, encloses an approximately circular area about 400 yards in diameter; this area totals about 28½ acres or 0.04 square miles. There were at least three and probably four entrances into the enclosure, formed of undug causeways across the ditch and gaps in the huge bank outside it. This bank now stands about 15 ft high but must once have towered at least 50 ft above the base of the ditch: it is about three-quarters of a mile in circumference. The bank is faced with blocks of the Lower Chalk obtained from the base of the ditch; the total volume of solid chalk excavated from the ditch and piled into the bank must be of the order of 4,100,000 cu ft and it has been estimated that this was equivalent at this site to some 1,560,000 man hours of work.[22] Using the dimensions given by Wainwright[23] and the formula mentioned earlier, I obtained a figure of 1,540,000 man hours. Such a project might have been completed by a gang of 200 men working continuously for 780 days. With a project such as this both the supervision and the housing and feeding of the work force are clearly of first importance and one should probably add on a quarter of the total man hours to account for such activities (though this obviously does not affect the time taken to construct the site). Again nothing has been said about the vast effort which was involved in bringing about 150 large blocks of sarsen stone to the site and setting them up, and the planning and supervising of the whole project and its labour force must clearly have been of a much higher degree of sophistication and complexity than that involved in building a long barrow or a causewayed camp. It has been rightly said that, in terms of the likely resources of Neolithic society, buildings like Silbury Hill and Avebury probably required an effort equivalent to that involved in the Apollo space programme in twentieth century USA.[24]

The outer stone circle

Inside the ditch and about 30 ft from its edge stand the remains of the great stone circle, now sadly reduced from its former glory by deliberate destruction in past centuries.[25] There must have been between 90 and 100 huge sarsen stones in this circle, weighing many tons, but only 31 remain though the positions of 16 sockets were recovered by Keiller and marked by concrete posts. The circle seems to have been built at the same time that the ditch was dug; packing blocks of Lower Chalk, only obtainable from the lower part of the ditch, were used round the bases of some of the stones. This outer circle is not in fact circular but is composed of arcs with different radii which have some pronounced 'corners' between them; the edge of the ditch follows the shape of the circle closely. Because of the vast size of the outer circle geometrical constructions can be inferred for it with a considerable degree of confidence, and this has been done by Thom on the basis of a new survey more accurate than any previous one.[26] As he says, because of the unique nature of the shape of the circle, 'without a knowledge of the exact length of the megalithic yard and of the simpler [geometrical] designs [in other circles] it is doubtful if the construction could have been discovered.' An inspection of Thom's plan is required to appreciate the complex geometry involved, and it is certainly clear that the great majority of stones and sockets lie either right on or very close to the suggested construction. The basis of this construction is the elemental 3:4:5 Pythagorean triangle, formed of units of 25 MY (i.e. 75:100:125 MY) and most of the arcs on the west and south sides of the outer circle have a radius of 260 MY (104 MR) drawn from the three corners of the triangle. (The east side of the outer circle is too poorly preserved for any confidence to be felt about the details of its geometry.) One arc on the southwest is much flatter, having a radius of 750 MY (300 MR) which is drawn from a centre on one of the lines produced out to the northeast. This centre falls well outside the site, and if the geometry is correct, must mean that the outer circle was designed and the positions of the stones surveyed and marked before the bank and ditch were constructed; the bank in the northeast cuts right across this long radius.

When the proposed geometrical construction was carefully drawn out on tracing paper and superimposed on the large scale survey of Avebury the fit between the stones and sockets and the geometry was remarkably close. Impressive too is the fact that this geometry is founded on the basic 3:4:5 Pythagorean triangle, that the radii of the arcs are all in round numbers which divide neatly into megalithic rods, and that the yard used was assumed to have been 2.720 ft. If it had been taken, for example, as 2.73 ft, the shape would have been the same of course but the construction would have passed about 5 ft outside all the stones. Even the calculated lengths of the separate arcs of the outer circle are extremely close to whole numbers of megalithic rods (38.89, 46.97, 79.95, 51.87 and 60.04). Complex though it appears, it is difficult to doubt the solution for the southwest half of the site except by avoiding careful study of the details and their implications. Reasons for the peculiar design are also suggested.[27] The two inner circles appear to have diameters of 125 MY, or 50 rods, exactly the same as the Ring of Brodgar in Orkney (chapter 9). The circumference of such a circle is 392.75 MY or almost exactly 157 rods (actually 157.08). The northern circle is much less well preserved.

Archaeology

Because of the vast size of Avebury, and because of the high level of the intellectual, technical and practical skill of the people who designed the site, it is of first importance to know the date of its construction and how it fits with the chronology of Silbury Hill, the history of Stonehenge and the establishment of the giant henges at Durrington Walls and Marden (chapters 7 and 8). Unfortunately this information is not yet available; no material suitable for radiocarbon seems to be extant and the primary silts of the ditch when excavated by Keiller failed to yield any identifiable pottery. Beaker sherds higher up in the ditch silts were found as well as Late Neolithic Peterborough pottery, and the latter alone was found on the old ground surface under the bank. Peterborough ware is an evolved version of the Early Neolithic round-based bowls and has an approximate life span in southern England of between about 2700 and 1600 bc (c. 3400-2000 BC): Beakers belong to the period from about 2000 bc (2500 BC) onwards or a little later.[28] Thus Avebury may have been built shortly before the Beaker period and the beginning of the first metal age.

The Kennet Avenue and the Sanctuary

From the south entrance of Avebury — the inside of which is flanked by two of the largest stones of the outer circle — the sockets of a double row or avenue of standing stones have been traced for about a third of a mile to the southeast. This is one end of the Kennet Avenue some of which is still preserved[29] but much of which has been destroyed since William Stukeley described it, and the Sanctuary (below), in the 18th century. Originally this avenue must have consisted of about 200 stones set in pairs 80 ft apart longitudinally and 50 ft transversely. It followed a winding course for about 1½ miles to finish on Overton Hill, at another prehistoric site of some interest known as the Sanctuary.

This latter site, also described by Stukeley, stands on a small, level plateau less than 440 yards from the river Kennet; it was explored by the Cunningtons in 1930[30] and proved to be a circular site with close links with the timber buildings found at Woodhenge and, later, at Durrington Walls. Fresh assessments of the site by Piggott[31] and more recently by Musson[32] suggest that the circles of post-holes found are the remains of four successive wooden roofed buildings the latest of which was a massive structure some 68 ft in diameter and perhaps having a raised lantern. When this was in ruins it was replaced by a stone circle of sarsen slabs beside one of which was a Beaker burial contemporary with it.

Strong evidence that the round buildings had been roofed, and were not simple rings of posts, was found in the post-pipes noted in the post-holes by the Cunningtons; four of these were slanting outwards as if the posts had been forced out at an angle by the weight of a roof. Also a few of the molluscan remains found on the site were of species which live in fresh water and a reasonable explanation of their presence on top of a dry chalk hill is that they arrived with reeds brought from the river Kennet to thatch the roofs of the successive roundhouses.[33] An examination of the pottery from the Sanctuary showed that most of it was Middle Neolithic Peterborough ware, Beaker and Grooved ware and this suggests that the site was probably in use between about 2500 and 2000 or 1800 bc.[34] The total of animal bones found during the excavations — which covered the whole site — was not large and ox, pig, horse and dog were identified among them. Sheep seem to have been absent.

Clearly the whole complex of Avebury, the Kennet Avenue and the Sanctuary was of considerable ritual importance and Avebury indeed must have far surpassed Stonehenge I in size and splendour. More the pity is it that as yet we have little idea of the purpose of this gigantic structure and of the ceremonial road which led from it to the roundhouse or temple on Overton Hill.

THE DORSET CURSUS

The extraordinary linear enclosure known as the Dorset Cursus, named after the Roman word for a race-track, lies on Cranbourne Chase and consists of two parallel banks of chalk about 90 yards apart and flanked by outer quarry ditches.[35] The entire earthwork runs for 6.2 miles across hill and dale in a SW-NE direction. It actually consists of two separate sections of which the northeast one appears to have been added on to the other: the intermediate terminal is attached to the southwest section. It has been estimated that to make this remarkable structure, by far the largest of about twenty similar earthworks known in Britain, it was necessary to excavate and pile up between 6 and 7 million cu ft of solid chalk, about half the volume of Silbury Hill. This would have represented about 1,200,000 to 1,400,000 Neolithic man hours so one might suppose that this cursus could have been constructed by a gang of 500 men in between 240 and 280 days — a formidable project indeed.

No proper excavation has been done on the Dorset Cursus, but clues to its age are given by the several Neolithic long barrows which appear to be closely associated with the earthwork, notably at the northeast terminal at Pentridge. Such a barrow is actually enclosed by the Cursus at Gussage St Michael (no. III) and the north ditch is interrupted by another at Pentridge (no. IV). Groups of round barrows, presumably of Bronze Age date, are also numerous near the earthwork. The Cursus is therefore probably later than at least some long barrows, and a clue to its origins may be found in the excavations of the similar Greater Cursus north of Stonehenge.[36] There a sherd of Grooved ware was found in the primary silts of the ditch suggesting a Late Neolithic date for that site and, by analogy, perhaps for the Dorset Cursus also.

Possible astronomical use

Penny and Wood have shown that it is possible that useful astronomical alignments were incorporated in the Dorset Cursus and in neighbouring barrows.[37] Several distant long barrows are visible on the skyline when viewed from certain prominent parts of the Cursus or from other barrows nearby, and they appear to mark both solstitial and significant lunar declinations for the middle of the third millennium BC, a date which seems appropriate for a Late Neolithic structure. For example if one stands on the centre of the Wyke Down terminal (the northeast end of the south section of the Cursus) the long barrow called Gussage St Michael III is clearly visible on the southwest horizon about 1.86 miles away, right in the middle of the Cursus itself. When the site was new two white chalk banks would have pointed directly southwest to this barrow on the skyline. Indeed the reasonable suggestion is made that the fact that the Wyke Down terminal is sited just far enough down the slope on which it stands to make the Gussage barrow appear as a silhouette on the skyline was a deliberate arrangement on the part of the builders. In about 2500 BC the last flash of the setting sun on midwinter's day should have appeared at the notch formed by the left end of the barrow[38] and would have given a reasonably accurate indication of the solstice, to within about two days. Similarly the same long barrow when viewed from the centre of the Thickthorn terminal 1.7 miles to the southwest could have marked the rising moon at its lowest midsummer position $(-(\varepsilon - \imath))$. Five other similar alignments are postulated, some between barrow and barrow, and the number of suggestions as to where wooden sighting devices could have been placed on the Cursus if the astronomical interpretation is correct are capable of being checked. It is important to recognise that the Cursus itself was not necessary for marking the alignments; large posts would have been sufficient to mark the backsights. However a prominent system of banks and ditches would certainly be a good and permanent way of marking the ritual importance of the zone, and perhaps the only satisfactory one in an area lacking material for standing stones.

DISCUSSION

Thanks to radiocarbon dating, the two 29th century BC sites discussed earlier in this chapter, Silbury Hill and Stonehenge I, throw a flood of light on the society of southern England at that time and on the development of some segments of it. Considering first Silbury Hill, one must note that its very existence at this time must surely have had a profound social significance. Bringing together and keeping a large labour force at work on the project for many years must have involved a tremendous effort for a relatively small, predominantly rural population, as that of Neolithic Wessex presumably was. It seems improbable that in a non-urban environment there was a full-time labour force of any size available for this kind of work, so the men would presumably have had to have come from their villages to take part in the project. Moreover, in order not to disrupt the agricultural activity of the area around the Hill it also seems likely that work would have gone on mainly in the slacker periods of the peasant farmers' year (midsummer and winter), or that a few men only were spared from each village for a continuous but much longer project, or else that a few men were drawn from villages over a much wider area. In either case the scale of the work suggests the involvement of men from villages over a wide area.

Food and shelter for the work force must have been a formidable problem. Unless the Hill was built by only a few score of men over many years, the large labour force would have required many huts to live in, considerable quantities of surplus stored food to support them and a number of administrative and ancillary staff to organise these facilities. The existence of Silbury Hill seems clearly to imply that a well organised hierarchical society of some kind, with leaders able to collect and store large food surpluses and with the authority to command the prolonged help of thousands of tribesmen, must have existed in the 29th century BC. The Silbury Hill project was on a far larger scale than any of the earthworks and stone monuments — long barrows and cairns, causewayed camps and early henges — built in the earlier part of the Neolithic period and it suggests a 'national' rather than a local enterprise, and a correspondingly powerful religious or secular authority to organise it.

In relation to the likely human and technological resources of Neolithic Wessex,[39] Silbury Hill bears comparison with the slightly younger great pyramids of Early Bronze Age Egypt. Mendelssohn has recently offered a novel social explanation for the rash of giant pyramid building during the IVth Dynasty (c. 2700-2500 BC), basing it on the discovery, through analyses of the technical aspects of the structures themselves, that several are likely to have been under construction at any one time.[40] This contrasts with the older and more usual view that one at a time was built — each by the reigning pharaoh as his own tomb — and implies that pyramid building was a dominant economic factor in Old Kingdom Egypt. At least 70,000 workers, he suggests, were continuously employed and therefore absent from their villages for prolonged periods: they were housed, fed and organised by the government of the pharaoh. One inevitable result of these massive enterprises must have been an unprecedented amount of contact between thousands of villagers from all over Egypt with people from other areas and with the skilled specialists and administrators of the central government; this doubtless increased their feeling of being members of the nation of Egypt and undermined for ever the old tribal ties of the restricted life in the villages.

Mendelssohn is also rightly sceptical of the idea that this huge labour force was working under conditions of slavery, toiling for endless years under the overseer's lash, and he draws comparisons with similar events in modern China — a comparable authoritarian society with an as yet primitive technology and an immense labour force. Volunteers to build a new bridge or dam are never lacking because of the prestige attached to working on such projects, especially after their completion when the workers go back to their villages as local heroes.

Of course the Silbury Hill project was a tiny effort when compared to an Egyptian pyramid of the IVth Dynasty, but one may wonder whether it was on a similar scale in proportion to the relative size of the populations concerned and also whether its construction may have had a similar effect on the rural Neolithic population of Wessex. Perhaps the raising of the Hill was both the result of and a primary cause of the increasing integration of the tribes of southern England into a larger political and religious unit, and of the evolution of a more stratified society in which distinct classes were coming into being, formed of various kinds of full-time specialists and supported by central authority. This last picture is amplified by that presented by Stonehenge I.

The earliest Stonehenge has so many potentially deliberately arranged astronomical features that it is hard to accept, first, that observational astronomy did not play an important part in the motives of those who designed the site, and second, that these people were not members of a full-time élite group, a specialist class of wise men, astronomers, priests and so on who were supported in their activities by a surplus of food grown and reared locally and by surplus labour for the building of their sites when required. That the scale of astronomical activity in southern England in the third millennium BC may have been far greater than is suggested by Stonehenge is clearly implied by the discoveries made at the Dorset Cursus. It is true that the existence of such a class would be rendered more likely if one could point to special temple precincts — a form of prehistoric combination of monastery and college — where such communities could have lived. In comparable societies such as the Classical Maya or the early proto-urban cultures of Mesopotamia and Peru the priesthood seems to have lived and worked in ceremonial centres which contained impressive masonry temples and dwellings, centres which grew larger and more elaborate with the passage of time and as the power and wealth of the priestly class increased. Nothing clearly identifiable as an inhabited ceremonial centre is known in Britain in the 29th century BC though, as we shall see, there might well have been such places a few centuries later (chapter 7). Moreover a few sherds of the Grooved ware pottery which was found in abundance at these later sites were also found in the primary silts of the ditch of Stonehenge I, so it seems fair to infer that there was a close connection between the people who presumably designed the Stonehenge temple-observatory in the 29th century BC and those who used the ceremonial centres from the 25th century onwards.

We seem to be left with the inescapable conclusion that by about the 29th century BC an élite class had appeared in Wessex, either through a process of gradual development or through the arrival of a skilled people from elsewhere, and had reached a stage in which they commanded considerable prestige, power and authority. This authority was clearly not derived from wealth accumulated as a result of the metal trade — the inception of the Early Bronze Age was perhaps half a millennium in the future and its full flowering in the Wessex culture still further off — so the original cultural and economic setting suggested for the great mound of Silbury Hill no longer suffices. If the Hill stood alone it might still be possible to explain it as the enormous barrow of some paramount Middle Neolithic chieftain and to assert that it meant no more than that such a chief had emerged, perhaps as only a temporary phenomenon. Such an explanation is still possible despite the failure to find a grave of any kind under the Hill. However, the closeness of the C-14 dates for the Hill and for Stonehenge I strongly suggests that both were built at about the same time and as part of a particular stage in the development of Late Neolithic society. The two sites seem to symbolise the start of a new era in which theocratic rulers had established themselves to the extent that they were able to control men and supplies to a degree never before achieved in Britain. This in itself suggests that the esoteric knowledge that these people had accumulated — and the religious beliefs that they doubtless promulgated — were in the 29th century BC already sufficiently impressive and capable of practical use to have gained them that respect and authority. We may conclude that somehow the astronomical and magical expertise of these wise men had given them this power — or that they were able to practise their astronomical work as a result of power gained from some other skills — and that southern England may have been approaching that peculiar form of authoritarian, theocratic society which seems to have been the precursor of urbanisation in more favoured areas (chapter 10). This picture is supported and amplified by the much more detailed evidence for the activities of this hypothetical class in the 25th and following centuries BC, culminating in the construction of the great stone temples at Stonehenge.

The Sanctuary is important because it provides us with what is probably the earliest example yet known of a Neolithic round, roofed wooden building, though the first round house at Durrington Walls (before the great earthwork was built) might be contemporary with it. Whether the building was a special inhabited house or a temple of some kind, or even a combination of the two, is not clear from this site alone. The quantity of occupation material found does not seem to have been great, not comparable for example with that recovered from Durrington. However the clear links with Avebury by way of the Kennet Avenue emphasise that the Sanctuary was a very important and probably older ritual site of some kind and this is confirmed by the long history of its rebuilding and by the replacement of the decayed wooden structure by a stone circle in phase IV. The Sanctuary, and probably the earliest roundhouse at Durrington Walls, are surely providing us with the other half of the picture of Middle and Late Neolithic society presented by the massive earthworks discussed earlier. The earthworks illustrate the power and organising ability of the governing class of the time while the Sanctuary provides us with a clue to its theocratic nature. The increase in the number and size of the wooden buildings in the following Late Neolithic phase seems to confirm this and also to show that these buildings could have been the residences of an élite group.

7

Durrington Walls:
A Late Neolithic Ceremonial Centre

INTRODUCTION

Since 1966 no less than three of the four largest Late Neolithic henge monuments of southern Britain have been subjected to careful excavation, one of them, Durrington Walls, on a fairly large scale. The results of these investigations, carried out by Dr G. J. Wainwright on behalf of the Department of the Environment, have effectively revolutionised our understanding of the nature of that part of British prehistoric society which built and used them in the second half of the third millennium BC but hitherto they have, understandably, been interpreted fairly cautiously and essentially in terms of the framework of theory which existed prior to the impact of Thom's work. In fact the results from these three large henge sites could, in my view, have provided the crucially important, direct evidence for the existence of that specialist class of astronomer-priests and wise men in populous lowland Britain which is required by Thom's theories (themselves based mainly on the simple stone circles and standing stones of the highland zone) but which can only be indirectly inferred from those theories. The great henges could have been, as I hope to show, the exact counterparts of the Maya ceremonial centres of Central America — the residences, temples and training schools of the learned orders which undertook, doubtless among many other activities, the decades or even centuries of work at the standing stone observatories.

Before the work at Durrington Walls from 1966 to 1968, Marden in 1969 and Mount Pleasant in 1970, most excavated henges had produced few signs of domestic occupation in the form of middens containing large quantities of pottery, stone tools and animal bones. Stonehenge itself yielded a relatively small quantity of potsherds and antler picks but no middens were found[1] — while the henge at Dorchester on Thames yielded even less.[2] The ditch of the huge henge at Avebury was sectioned by Keiller, but little in the way of animal bones and sherds was recovered.[3] Woodhenge alone gave a substantial quantity of animal bones from the ditch, and this site is really part of Durrington Walls, being but 63 yards south of the bank there. Taking into account this plain absence of concentrations of domestic rubbish, of the non-functional, rapidly silting ditches *inside* the banks of the henges (contrasting with the external, defensive ditches of the Iron Age hill-forts) and also of the peculiar rings of burial pits or standing stones and the massive wooden constructions inside some of them, it is hardly surprising that these structures have been regarded as purely ceremonial and non-domestic, as 'temples' in fact.[4] However, the excavations at the giant henges have provided a somewhat different picture.

THE EXCAVATIONS

Before 1966, when the recent excavations began, the great henge near Durrington, Wiltshire, very little of which is now visible on the surface, had hardly been examined at all archaeologically. In 1952 some excavations across the bank confirmed the conclusions derived from the discoveries made from some earlier trenches — that there was a buried land surface under it about 3½ in thick on top of which was an occupation layer containing charcoal, flints and potsherds. The pottery was mainly Grooved ware with a few Beaker sherds and similar material had accumulated on top of the talus slope of the bank.[5] Two radiocarbon dates were obtained for charcoal from below the bank and proved to be 2625 ± 40 bc (Gro-901a) and 2635 ± 70 bc (Gro-901) and seemed inconsistent with the archaeological evidence at that time.[6] However, the subsequent discovery by Wainwright of Middle Neolithic bowl sherds under the bank suggests that the occupation layer there was a mixed horizon and that the dated charcoal belongs to a much earlier period than the henge itself.

The excavations of 1966-8 were carried out along the track of the realigned A345 road, on a strip of land some 833 yards long and varying in width from 20 to 43 yards.[7] This strip was cleared by machine down to the level of the chalk land surface of Late Neolithic times and in this were found exceptionally clear traces of two massive, round wooden buildings (referred to as the northern and southern circles) within the enclosed area as well as part of a causeway entrance including one end of the deep ditch which enclosed the site. Another feature of interest was a dark midden deposit immediately next to one of the round buildings.

The dating of the site

A number of radiocarbon dates were obtained which accurately dated the digging of the ditch and the construction of the second, larger phase of the southern circle. Several of the dated samples were animal bones and antler picks, organic samples which should relate very closely to the deposits in which they were found, even though an antler may have been dead for a year or two when it was collected for use at the site (most of the antlers found had been shed). The equivalent in calendar years for each date, based on the bristlecone pine tree-ring calibration,[8] is given in parentheses.

The average date for the digging of the ditch is about 2014 bc, equivalent to about 2570 BC, and that for the construction of the southern circle is 1930

TABLE 7

Radiocarbon dates for Durrington Walls

post-holes of the	BM-395 (antler)	1950 ± 90 bc	(2490-2540 BC)
southern circle	BM-396 (charcoal)	2000 ± 90 bc	(2560 BC)
	BM-397 (bones)	1900 ± 90 bc	(2340-2430 BC)
basal layers	BM-398 (charcoal)	1977 ± 90 bc	(2520-2540 BC)
of the ditch	BM-399 (bone)	2015 ± 90 bc	(2570 BC)
	BM-400 (antler)	2050 ± 90 bc	(2610 BC)
hearths higher up	BM-285 (charcoal)	1610 ± 120 bc	(2080 BC)
in the ditch silt	BM-286 (charcoal)	1680 ± 110 bc	(2110-2130 BC)

bc, equivalent to 2420-80 BC (with a slightly smaller standard deviation in both cases), so we may confidently assume that work on the site probably started in the 26th or 25th century BC. The two dated hearths were at a relatively low level in the ditch silts, so it is clear that the henge was in use at least until the 22nd or 21st century BC (the equivalent in real years of the later dates) and probably well beyond that time. The large number of dates obtained for specific events, their closeness in time, the well stratified contexts of the organic samples concerned, and the evident closeness of the time of death of the organisms concerned (equivalent to their radiocarbon age) to the time they were incorporated in the deposits from which they were recovered all mean that the date obtained for the building of Durrington Walls is likely to be accurate. The similar series of C-14 dates for the settlement at Skara Brae in the Orkneys and for the Grimes Graves flint mines in Norfolk are almost identical (chapters 8 and 9) and show clearly that the three sites, each of which yielded large quantities of Grooved ware, were more or less exactly contemporary.

The ditch and bank

The southern part of the broad excavated strip just included the terminal of the ditch at the causeway forming the southeasterly of the two opposed entrances into the site. The ditch proved to be 42 ft wide at the top and 22 ft wide at the base; the original width at the top was somewhat less, before weathering caused the upper parts of the steep sides to fall in. The depth was 18½ ft, the average cross-section 455 sq ft, and the total volume of chalk excavated from the ditch around its entire length of 1,280 yards must have been of the order of 1,750,000 cu ft. On the basis of the experimental earthwork on Overton Down and of Atkinson's formula this would have involved at least 880,000 man hours of work.[9] Thus a gang of 200 men, if working full time, could have constructed the bank and ditch in about 440 days or 1.2 years. As with other excavated henge ditches the layers of silt which had accumulated in it over the years showed clearly that the ditch was never cleaned out; the sequence of a coarse silt of clean chalk blocks at the base (layer 7), a finer clean chalk silt above that (layers 6 and 6A), a 'rest layer' on which was a hearth and further layers of darker silt higher up (layers 5 to 0), all suggest that the ditch was not defensive but was allowed to fill up steadily through the processes of natural weathering. The absence of post-holes for fences and gateways on the causeway confirms that the site was not a fort. It is clear, however, that the ditch remained close to its original depth for a long time — several centuries at least — after it had been dug and that there was therefore no need for any clearance of silt if it was needed as a barrier.

This information about the rate of silting of chalk-cut ditches in Late Neolithic times also has relevance for the interpretation of other sites like Stonehenge. The speed at which the primary, clean, coarse silt accumulates in chalk-cut ditches, under modern climatic conditions, was illustrated by the experimental earthwork on Overton Down; there it was found that initial silting of coarse, clean chalk blocks from the upper parts of the steep sides of the ditch took place very rapidly and that this primary rubble, followed by the second stage of finer but still quite clean chalk silt, had all accumulated to the stage where a temporary stable rest layer was formed within the space of a few years.[10] This kind of evidence was partly responsible for the short chronology of a century or two for the whole history of Stonehenge[11] which was suggested before the full significance of the C-14 dates from that site was available. However, at Durrington Walls one hearth in the ditch was close above layer 6 — the upper layer of rapid, clean silt — and was dated to 1610 ± 120 bc. The profile of the ditch was still markedly U-shaped at this time and the hearth concerned was about 2½ ft above the base of the ditch. The date strongly suggests that the 'rapid' primary silt in a chalk ditch took not just a few years to accumulate in Late Neolithic times but several centuries.

This might have important implications for the chronology of Stonehenge and other sites, particularly if the lesser rate of silting at that time was due to a milder climate (although it has to be remembered that a smaller ditch, such as that at Stonehenge, would fill up more rapidly anyway).

Potsherds were found scattered through most of the earlier levels of the ditch silt, but occupation refuse became denser near the terminal on the south side. Pottery, flints and animal bones were found in quantity there as well as thick layers of ashy soil and the excavator had the impression that the distribution of this material was consistent with its having been tossed into the end of the ditch by people entering or leaving the site across the causeway. The boundary between layers 6B and 7 (smaller, clean chalk rubble and large blocks of primary chalk respectively) was particularly rich in pottery, freshly struck flints and well preserved animal bones and pieces of antler. At one point on the undisturbed chalk floor of the ditch, 59 ft from the terminal, a group of 57 antler picks was found; many of them were worn and broken and had evidently been discarded in a heap by the diggers of the ditch when their task was completed. The C-14 dates for the digging of the ditch, averaging at 2014 bc (2570 BC), have already been described.

The bank was not well preserved in any part of the site and is indeed only traceable on aerial photographs for much of its length. Its width proved to be about 100 ft and its greatest preserved height 2½ ft: in most places it was only 6-12 in high. An exceptionally wide berm about 90 ft broad lay between the bank and the ditch. As already explained, the bank lay on top of a buried land surface with an occupation layer on top of it which contained a mixture of Grooved ware and Middle Neolithic pottery; evidently there had been an earlier site in the area dating to about 3220-3330 BC judging from the two C-14 dates for the pre-bank deposits already mentioned.

The southern roundhouse

The post-holes of two large, circular wooden structures were uncovered in the excavated strip and there can be little doubt that several more exist in the unexcavated parts of the enclosed area of the henge. Another huge, complex wooden building, surrounded by its own ditch, stood about 60 yards south of the main enclosure (Woodhenge, chapter 8). The remains of the southern circle (as it is named in the excavation report) were exceptionally well preserved for several reasons but mainly because, being sited on the bottom of a shallow, dry valley, an unusually thick layer of soil had gradually been washed and ploughed down the slope over the remains and had thus protected them. Because of this even the small mounds of chalk blocks which had been piled up around the bases of the posts as packing when they were erected often still remained above the level of the floor of the building; evidence on the floor for the way the building had been used was thus preserved undisturbed which in other circumstances (as with the northern roundhouse) would have been destroyed.

The circular building stood only 30 yards from the southern entrance and more or less directly in front of it; thus anyone entering the site across the causeway would have had to have skirted round the 40 yard diameter building either to the left or right. Wainwright distinguished two phases among the eleven concentric circles of post-holes and the rectangle of four massive posts near the centre which he found; the fact that all the posts had evidently decayed in position meant that the 'post-pipes' within the fill of the holes were identifiable and that the exact positions and diameters of the wooden posts themselves could be determined.

The phase 1 post-holes differed from those of phase 2 in that they all, except for those of the central rectangular setting, lacked ramps and were very narrow in proportion to the width of the posts. These earlier post-holes were diagnosed as such on the basis of some intersecting features, and their packing also differed from that of the later ones in being composed of rammed earth and chalk powder as opposed to the clean chalk blocks of the

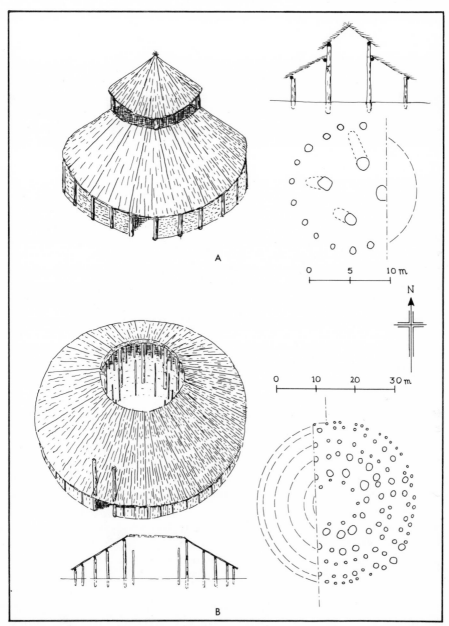

Fig. 25. Plan of the post-holes of the northern roundhouse and of the second phase of the southern roundhouse at Durrington Walls as revealed by excavation and reconstructions of the complete buildings after C. R. Musson

latter. The circles of posts could not be shown to be truly concentric, with a common centre, nor was there any evidence that they had been laid out using the megalithic yard as the unit of length.[12]

The first building consisted of four concentric rings of posts the largest of which was 75 ft in diameter, and this was flanked by a straight palisade on the east between the timber building and the south entrance of the henge itself. Taking into account the size and spacing of the posts in the several rings Musson suggested that the phase 1 structure was probably an annular building with a lean-to roof around an open court, sloping either inwards or outwards, which rested on the second and third rings of posts.[13]

The 'rectangle' in the centre of the open court would have held four free-standing posts surrounding, and possibly supporting a canopy over, some small, central circular feature about 7 ft in diameter. However, a complete conical roof over the whole building was not ruled out though the timbers seemed a little light to support the large superstructure which would then be required. The entrance was evidently in the southeast arc where there was a corresponding gap in the wooden palisade. The posts of this building had evidently decayed in position and had not been extracted.

In phase 2 the southern roundhouse was a much more massive circular building about 120 ft in diameter and equipped with six concentric rings of posts. The post-holes were wider and deeper and many had ramps leading down into them; a thin layer of humus had accumulated in the holes so they had evidently been left open for some time before the timbers were put into them. The posts had been packed with fresh chalk blocks which, it was assumed, had been obtained during the digging of the ditch: the implication would thus be that the construction of the second phase of the roundhouse took place at the same time as the excavation of the henge ditch. The three C-14 dates obtained for the phase 2 post-holes ranged from 2000 to 1900 bc and were more or less exactly contemporary with those obtained for antlers used in excavating the ditch (1977-2050 bc), so there is a definite possibility that the phase 1 building antedated the henge proper by a considerable length of time (this possibility is explored further below). However, the remains of its decayed uprights must still have been visible when the second roundhouse was erected because the rings of posts of the latter are more or less concentric with those of the former. Many antler picks, potsherds and flint tools were found in the packing of the post-holes; most of the pottery was Grooved ware but a few sherds of Beaker were also found.

The quantity of potsherds and flint and stone tools associated with phase 2 of the southern roundhouse was vastly greater than that with phase 1. For example, out of a total of 6,753 flint flakes and implements found all over the site during the excavations only 1 per cent were associated with the features of phase 1 but no less than 59 per cent with those of phase 2. Even more striking is the fact that 87 per cent of all the arrowheads found (mostly transverse) were associated with its second phase. Grooved ware sherds occurred in both phases but Beaker pottery (9 sherds) only in phase 2.

There was evidence that fragments of pottery did not reach their final resting places within the structure entirely by chance. Several examples were found of pieces of the same vessel lying next to different posts, and in such cases they must either have been deliberately placed there or fragments of the same pot must have been broken against different posts. Alternatively it is possible that broken pots were simply swept against the nearest posts to produce the same result.

Other features of the second southern roundhouse included two massive posts flanking the entrance on the southeast with a platform in front of it, two areas of rammed chalk flooring inside and a hearth near the centre of the building. The platform was up to 57 ft long from north to south and 29 ft from east to west and composed of chalk blocks immediately in front of the entrance and rolled flint gravel further north. Traces of intensive burning were found at the junction of these two areas while very large quantities of pottery, artefacts of flint and bone, and animal bones were found scattered round this burnt area. Most of the artefacts and food refuse found in the building came from this platform; the floor inside was relatively free of refuse though much was concentrated around the bases of the posts as already described.

There were two areas of rammed chalk flooring within the building, one immediately inside the doorway and the other 20 ft further in towards the centre. The hearth at the centre of the roundhouse consisted of a circular patch of reddish ash about 4 ft across. The posts of the second phase were also inferred to have decayed in position because the post-pipes were intact and material had evidently fallen down these hollows after the wood had rotted.

The sizes of the timber uprights used in the second southern roundhouse are impressive and could be calculated reasonably accurately from the exact dimensions preserved by the post-pipes in the centre of the sockets and from the spacing of the timbers themselves.[14] The fragments of charcoal found in the pipes showed that the posts were all of oak trunks. Assuming that all the wood was green oak, the two posts flanking the entrance were calculated in this way to have weighed about 3½ and 5 tons respectively, weights which are comparable to those of the bluestones at Stonehenge. More than 200 tons of timber should have been required for the roundhouse in phase 2 and the felling and trimming of this quantity of massive trees must have required the use of scores if not hundreds of flint and stone axes. However, very few such axes were found in the excavations and the inference is that the timbers were hauled and rolled to the site from a distance and already trimmed. The erection of the building must nevertheless have required a considerable amount of carpentry on the site, but the axes used have not been found. They may of course have been deposited, like the antler picks, in some part of the ditch as yet unexcavated.

An estimate for the minimum life of the building was obtained from the knowledge that oak now decays at the rate of about an inch of radius of heartwood every 15 years. On this basis the slimmest timbers of the phase 1 roundhouse should have had a minimum life of about 60 years and those of phase 2 of about 90 years. By contrast the thickest posts of the latter could have stood for 195 years. Bearing in mind that the structures were almost certainly roofed so that the lower parts of the posts were protected from the weather, and that the climate was very probably milder in Late Neolithic times, it seems reasonable to allow a life of two or even three centuries at least for these massive timber buildings. The later C-14 dates in the silting of the ditch could confirm this.

The midden

Just outside the northeast arc of the southern roundhouse was an elongated hollow measuring about 42 ft from north to south and 20 ft from east to west. It was partly surrounded by two arcs of stake holes and the north end had been cut into the slope of the shallow valley to a depth of 2 ft. Within the hollow, but not overlapping its edges, was a layer up to 1 ft thick of black ashy soil containing very large quantities of animal bones, potsherds and stone tools. A collection of small pieces of charcoal from various parts of the midden gave a C-14 date of 2320 ± 125 bc (NPL-192). The great majority of the 981 potsherds found were of Grooved ware, 3 were of unweathered Middle Neolithic bowls and 25 were of Beakers. It may be significant that these Beaker sherds comprised half the total of this ware found over the whole site. The hollow was interpreted as a deliberately constructed dumping area for midden material with a wooden screen partly concealing it from view, particularly from anyone going in or out of the roundhouse doorway 70 ft to the south.

The northern roundhouse

The post-holes for a second, circular timber building were found 130 yards north of the southern one, higher up on the northern crest of the dry valley and in a position where greater erosion had taken place. As a result only the bases of many of the post-holes were preserved, the floor level of the building had vanished and few 'post-pipes' remained in the fill of the post-holes. There is a possibility that there were two phases in this building also, but this could not be verified stratigraphically. The first building may have been about 39 ft in diameter and have consisted of a double circle of fairly slender posts; there may have been an avenue of posts or stakes leading up to it from the SSE.

The second phase of the building was much clearer. The massive timber structure consisted of an outer ring of posts 47 ft in diameter, and judging from the few 'post-pipes' preserved, the timbers of this ring were 15 in in diameter at their bases. The centre of the building was supported on four massive timbers, which had been erected with the aid of ramps, standing on a square with sides of 16-17 ft and also on the perimeter of a circle 21 ft in diameter. The post-butts of these timbers were 23 in in diameter. The only finds made in this building were in the upper parts of the fill of the post-holes and the assumption, as with the southern roundhouse, is that part of the deposits of potsherds and other artefacts placed at the bases of the posts when the building was standing and in use ultimately fell into the post sockets after the timbers had decayed. A façade of posts flanked the building on the west side (towards the main entrance of the henge) and a post-lined avenue or path approached it from that direction and penetrated the façade.

The question of whether the second phase of the northern roundhouse was once a roofed building some 47 ft in diameter was reviewed by Musson[15] who concluded that it could easily have been roofed and that the four central posts could have supported a 'lantern' or raised central section of roof, which would have let some light and air in at the top and let out any smoke (fig. 25). The only doubt thrown on this interpretation was that the four central posts resembled the central setting of phase 1 of the southern roundhouse, and since the latter was clearly composed of posts too flimsy to support the central part of a conical wooden roof, this might imply that the four central posts of the northern building were also non-functional. However since these latter clearly held massive timbers of just the kind and size required for a high, conical roof it seems a little unnecessary to seek for more complex explanations without more evidence. (In fact the northern roundhouse at Durrington Walls strikingly resembles the Iron Age wooden house at Little Woodbury, Wiltshire, which was just over 48 ft in diameter and also had four massive central posts arranged in a square with sides of 9-10 ft.[16] No doubt has ever been expressed about this being a roofed building.) The northern roundhouse could well have been much larger if its outer wall rested on a ring of posts of which only an arc remains and which has been tentatively allocated to an earlier phase. In this case the diameter of the building would have been about 70 ft and the central posts would, it seems, still have been massive enough to support the higher and heavier roof required.[17] The calculated load-bearing capability of the uprights is far in excess of the estimated roof weight.[18]

Material culture and economy

The question of the primary function of the large henge sites, and of the wooden buildings within them, is intimately bound up with the nature of the finds made and this problem is reviewed again later. Here it is sufficient briefly to describe the nature of the finds, their frequency and the sort of deposits in which they occurred. Enough has been said already to show that the quantities of domestic rubbish found — broken pottery, stone tools, animal bones and layers of ash and dark earth — were very great and contrasted sharply with the scarcity of such material at other henge sites, except Woodhenge (below).

The great majority of the thousands of fragments of pottery recovered were of Grooved ware (fig. 33), but in spite of the large quantities of sherds it was possible to reconstruct only a handful of complete pots; most of the vessels were represented by only a small part of the originals. About 50 sherds were of Beaker pottery and a few were fragments of Middle Neolithic bowls probably from the pre-henge phase of occupation. The origins and nature of Grooved ware are discussed separately in chapter 10.

About 12,000 struck flint flakes were found of which 333 (2.8%) were implements. The great majority of these tools (62%) were scrapers but transverse arrowheads were also fairly common (17%). Other items were all rare and, as noted earlier, flint and stone axes were almost totally absent in spite of the large quantities of cut wood which had clearly been brought to the site and worked there. There were 40 bone implements, mostly pins and awls, while the 440 antler tools were all picks. Only 29 of the 316 fairly complete such picks, or 9%, were cut from dead or killed animals; the rest had been shed and must have been systematically collected in the forests. The distribution of the antler picks was curious; 17½% (77) were found on the bottom of the ditch in the two areas excavated, 80% (354) in the southern roundhouse and only 2% in the northern roundhouse. The antler picks were far more numerous than at comparable henge sites and long barrows and this suggested to the excavator that at Durrington Walls they may have been deposited deliberately.

Of the food brought to the site only the remains of the meat have survived; no saddle querns for grinding grain were found in the excavations nor were any charred cereal grains discovered (no impressions of cereal grains have ever been noted on a sherd of Grooved ware, either, a fact commented on later). Animal bones were extremely plentiful and well preserved and allowed a detailed picture of the meat brought to the site to be built up. It has already been noted that very large quantities of animal bones were found in the terminal of the ditch, around the southern roundhouse and in the midden. Out of a total of about 8,500 bones (representing a minimum of 320 animals) 50% came from the southern roundhouse, 45% from the primary levels of the ditch, 3% from the midden

TABLE 8

The totals of individuals of various species identified among the animal bones from Durrington Walls (*assumed not to be edible)

domestic animals		*wild animals*			
pig	228 (63.4%)	aurochs	3 (0.8%)	red deer	14 (3.9%)
cattle	97 (27.0%)	roe deer	2 (0.6%)	*badger	1 (0.3%)
goat	1 (0.3%)	*horse	3 (0.8%)	*pine marten	1 (0.3%)
sheep	7 (2.0%)	*beaver	1 (0.3%)	*fox	2 (0.6%)

(total 360 (100%))

and 1% from the northern roundhouse. No difference in the percentages of each species present in these groups, nor in the bones recovered from under the bank (1%), was noted. Including 830 bones (from at least 44 animals) found under the bank in the 1952 excavations, the total of individual animals found at the site is given in Table 8.

The ratio between edible domestic and wild animals found at this site is 91% to 5½%, a striking contrast to the situation on some domestic sites in the Atlantic zone of Scotland (chapter 9) but comparable to the Iron Age and later sites in southern England and Wales, and to that on one very informative Hebridean Iron Age site (chapter 9). The only comparable contemporary Late Neolithic domestic site is Skara Brae in the Orkney Islands, but the differences between the local environments of the Northern Isles and Wiltshire are probably sufficiently great to make close comparisons between the bone assemblages of the two sites difficult, though some tentative conclusions may be drawn (chapter 10). The final occupation at the Windmill Hill causewayed camp is likely to be more relevant and is discussed in the final chapter.

Several other interesting features were noted in the Durrington Walls bones. Even though pigs and cattle clearly formed the staple meat diet of the users of the henge, very few skulls of these animals were found; in other words it is unlikely that flocks and herds were kept close at hand but very likely that useful parts of already slaughtered beasts were brought to the site. Among the cattle mature animals were in the majority but among the pigs immature individuals (less than a year old) were most frequent. Zeuner points out that the pig is a very useful animal, being long-lived, maturing in a year, capable of producing up to two litters each year and providing much meat and fat when killed.[19] These facts are probably sufficient by themselves to explain the frequency of bones of young pigs at the site without invoking any more elaborate theories about the selection of immature beasts for the table. The many herds of pigs which must have lived in Wessex in Late Neolithic times must show that there was plenty of oak woodland for them to root in and also that the society of the time was firmly settled in villages. Pigs, unlike sheep, are extremely difficult to drive successfully from one place to another.

In the excavator's opinion the evidence of the animal bones supports the diagnosis of the site as primarily a ritual one. The absence of animal skulls could mean that meat was brought to the site already cut up, and the alternatives envisaged to explain this were that this was either for 'feasts' or 'offerings'. The zoologist who studied the bones goes further in his specialist report and, after commenting on the good state of preservation of the animal remains and on the very large number of entire, almost perfect pig bones, says 'On a ritual site, however, the bones are more likely to have been those of animals killed for ritual purposes.' But skulls should be present in this case so their absence, 'it is tentatively suggested, may perhaps be evidence that the act of slaughtering was not in itself important from the ritual point of view'.[20] A re-reading of the remarks in chapter 1 about the nature of direct deduction from archaeological evidence might be appropriate at this point and the question of whether such conclusions are the only ones which can be drawn from the evidence or are even legitimate is reviewed in the next section.

DISCUSSION

To review the remarkable wealth of evidence recovered from this, the first of the Late Neolithic giant henges to have been systematically excavated, is to bring up in acute form the problems inherent in grafting social interpretations onto archaeological data which were discussed in the opening chapter. We see clearly in the excavation report, and in the various other comments and discussions on Durrington Walls, how British archaeologists, perhaps unconsciously, have hitherto been setting arbitrary limits to the kinds of interpretations of such sites which are considered possible, limits which are not, and cannot be, derived solely from the archaeological facts themselves but must be largely dictated by what are thought to be probable explanations on the basis of accepted theory and of preferred analogies with the material cultures of known societies (chapter 1). Durrington Walls presents a problem because it belongs to a class of sites — the henge monuments — which there have long been good reasons for thinking had primarily non-domestic functions. Most of these 'ritual' sites lacked domestic refuse and were embellished with many features, such as circles of standing stones or timber, or grave pits, for which no obvious explanations in terms of domestic functions suggested themselves. Yet Durrington produced huge wooden buildings, very probably roofed, and masses of occupation refuse — in fact all the usual archaeological signs that a permanent population lived within an enclosed area or precinct. The result has been a variety of sometimes tortuous explanations in terms of 'feasts', 'ritual slaughtering', 'offerings', temporarily used 'council houses' and so on, all designed to preserve the ritual function of a henge while somehow explaining the large quantities of domestic-looking refuse found.[21]

Yet there is a third social explanation which has never been considered in detail, though the excavator suggested it before the detailed report appeared and hinted at it on the last page of that report.[22] In fact in his latest review of the problem of the giant henges Wainwright spells out in some detail why a ritual and a domestic function for them ought to be combined, though without saying exactly how.[23] This third explanation in my view combines all the evidence neatly, finds good analogies in known recent and ancient societies, and sees no contradiction in a special 'ritual' enclosure having clear and abundant signs of a permanent population. It is that the great henges of Wessex were inhabited ceremonial centres on the

Maya pattern in and near which lived a permanent population of non-agricultural specialists such as priests, astronomers, wise men, poets and all their attendant craftsmen and servants (as well, no doubt, as their womenfolk) — professional classes which were supported by tributes of food and labour by the peasant population. The only major difference from Maya sites, apart from the latter having been built in stone, would be that whereas the temple-pyramids occur within the ceremonial centres in Central America,[24] in Wessex the temples and purely ritual sites were apparently quite separate. We may review again the evidence from Durrington Walls with this third social hypothesis in mind.

The history of the site

It is clearly important first to reconstruct as accurately as possible the chronology and sequence of structures and the development of the occupation of the site. The first problem that arises concerns the possibility that there were one or more wooden roundhouses on the site before the ditch was dug and the enclosed ground thereby converted into a formal henge. If the freshly dug chalk blocks which were used to pack the posts of the second southern roundhouse were excavated from the ditch near by, it should follow that ditch and second roundhouse were under excavation and construction respectively at the same time, as the radiocarbon dates strongly suggest, and that therefore the first roundhouse was earlier. Moreover, the latter should have been built many years earlier since its posts were evidently allowed to decay slowly. It can hardly be a coincidence that the nearby midden gave a C-14 date of 2320 ± 125 bc and contained Grooved ware as well as three sherds of Middle Neolithic bowls (but also Beaker), or that the occupation layer preserved under the bank of the henge gave the same two types of pottery and even earlier C-14 dates in the 27th century bc. In the absence of a convenient ditch into which to drop rubbish it seems natural that the inhabitants of the first southern roundhouse should make a midden hollow nearby and screen it off with a fence. The presence of fragments of the same Grooved ware vessels in the midden and in post-hole 45 of the second southern roundhouse which appear to link the two features together in time,[25] need not conflict with the deductions made above since the midden hollow could well have remained in use during part of the period of occupation of the second roundhouse. The Beaker sherds in the midden also suggest this.

An objection to the idea of the history of the site as a ceremonial centre having started at about 2400 bc (c. 3000 BC) is the general reluctance among archaeologists specialising in this field to extend Grooved ware back to that time.[26] However sherds of Grooved ware were found in the ditch at Stonehenge, the cutting of which has been dated to well before that at Durrington Walls (to the 22nd century bc, chapter 5), and the origins of the ware and of the great 'ceremonial' round wooden buildings could easily go back before that. If this view is not accepted it becomes necessary arbitrarily to separate out the Grooved ware from Middle Neolithic sherds occurring together in deposits dated early by radiocarbon when the only reason for denying the sort of direct archaeological associations which are accepted as a matter of course on other sites is the preconceived belief about the firmly Late Neolithic date of Grooved ware. It must be significant that no Beaker sherds — whose earliest appearance in the British Isles does seem to be well dated to 1900-1800 bc[27] — were found in those deposits sealed below the bank at Durrington Walls which were excavated by modern techniques. Even if the two C-14 dates in the 27th century bc, obtained for charcoal from below the bank, are thought to be too early for Grooved ware it seems difficult to dismiss the 24th century bc one from the midden in the same way, and the start of 'ceremonial' activity on the site in that century, or slightly earlier, cannot be ruled out (see p. 222 below).

Viewed in this way the history of Durrington Walls seems to fall neatly into at least three phases. Phase 1 was in Middle Neolithic times, and the site was presumably an open one consisting of one or more large wooden roundhouses the users of which deposited refuse in the midden. The site would then be analogous to, and contemporary with, the early stages of the Sanctuary. It is possible that this part of the site was abandoned for a while as the first southern roundhouse seems to have been allowed to disintegrate. In phase 2 in the 20th century bc (26th BC), in the Late Neolithic/Beaker period, the site was greatly enlarged and enclosed with a huge ditch and bank; more massive wooden roundhouses were erected, probably all over the enclosed area, and there may be smaller dwellings still to be discovered. A phase 3 might be distinguished by the erection in the nineteenth century bc of Woodhenge, a very complex and geometrically sophisticated wooden roundhouse outside the main centre, and occupation of the main site continued for a few centuries more, into the Early Bronze Age. When the second southern roundhouse eventually decayed and fell into disuse (perhaps being replaced by another as yet undiscovered one nearby) its remains were left undisturbed — a striking tribute to the sanctity of the site since, judging from the slow rate of erosion at that time, many centuries must have elapsed before the remains were gradually covered up.

The function of the roundhouses

The nature of the site naturally hinges on the question of whether the 'circles' were roofed buildings or simple sets of concentric rings of posts analogous to stone circles. Unless a wooden building is burnt down, so that the charred remains of its walls and roof are found on the floor where they fell, there can of course be no direct proof that such a set of concentric wooden uprights was in fact roofed. However, consideration of the problem by a professional architect led him to the conclusion that not only was there no evidence against the two circles at Durrington Walls having been roofed but that the size, spacing and general arrangement of the timbers were consistent with the hypothesis that they had once supported fairly massive, conical superstructures.[28] It is probably true to say that were it not for the 'ritual' context of the buildings (within the bank and ditch of a henge monument) there would never have been much doubt about the matter. The central hearth, the clearly defined doorways (some with avenues of stakes directed towards them) and the extensive deposits of domestic refuse outside the circles are all features consistent with the view that at Durrington Walls we are dealing with the remains of two very large, round, wooden roofed buildings. The excavator accepted this view and drew an interesting analogy with the traces of a huge wooden roundhouse found at the Irene Mound site in Georgia, USA which was evidently used by the Creek Indians in the eighteenth century AD.[29]

The activities of these Creek Indians were observed in these large timber houses in the eighteenth century by contemporary Europeans.[30] The buildings were used as council houses, for special meetings and ceremonies during which the ritual drinking of cassine played an important role. The pottery drinking vessels for the sacred liquid were smashed after the ceremonies were completed and thrown onto a nearby midden. Next to the wall of the roundhouse, which consisted of six concentric rings of posts, each set in a bedding trench, the excavators of Irene Mound found a midden in which there was nothing but large fragments of pottery vessels. The similarity with the southern roundhouse at Durrington and its associated midden seemed very striking to Wainwright, though he rightly resisted the temptation to transfer the special social functions of the eighteenth century AD Creek Indian site to the 26th century BC southern English one, in spite of the obvious similarities between the two sets of material remains.[31]

The probability that the southern roundhouse was a council house, or a building for public ceremonies of some kind, seemed high to Wainwright, however. The discovery of pieces of the same vessel against different posts could certainly mean that the ceremonial smashing of drinking vessels had occurred, but it could equally easily be explained by supposing that the scattered fragments of accidentally broken pots were simply kicked out of the way against the nearest posts. The contents of the midden, and of the heaps of refuse lying on the external platform and in the terminal of the ditch, were strikingly dissimilar to those found at the Irene Mound site in that they contained large quantities of ash and food refuse as well as broken pottery. This must surely mean that meals of pork and beef were regularly cooked and eaten on the site; presumably the meat was boiled since the bones are described as being excellently preserved and charring or cracking by fire is not mentioned. Such a midden is entirely consistent with the hypothesis favoured here, that the giant henges were the permanently inhabited centres of a specialist class, but its nature does not seem to fit so well with the theory that the site and its roundhouses were only used occasionally for 'offerings', 'feasts', council meetings or unspecified ceremonies.

The persistent attempts to see the domestic refuse at Durrington Walls as somehow 'ritual' in nature, and therefore not simple domestic rubbish, are in my view not well founded and involve contradictions between the different aspects of the total evidence from the site which they cannot resolve satisfactorily. There can obviously be no *direct* way of deducing the social motives behind the dumping of potsherds and food refuse in a midden (chapter 1), and unless there are very strong reasons for thinking differently it is surely best to choose the simplest hypothesis available. In the case of this site, the 'ritual' explanations for the refuse never really stand up to close examination when compared with simpler, domestic hypotheses. Instead of providing independent evidence that the site was a purely ceremonial one, they in fact derive from that theory *a priori*. The clearest example of this process is seen in the specialist comments on the animal bone refuse already referred to. The social deductions made from the observed absence of skulls do not arise directly from the facts, as we saw in chapter 1, but have to be imposed on them. They have inevitably been produced by the belief that the site was primarily a ritual one and was not lived in permanently and the further speculation that 'the act of slaughtering was not in itself important from the ritual point of view' can be valid only if the original deductions were incontrovertible. However, if a different social interpretation of the site seems more likely, then the dry bones also have to be interpreted differently. Of course the zoologist concerned was only accepting the interpretation of the site given to him. The absence of skulls almost certainly does mean that the animals were slaughtered away from the site (unless the heads were dumped in a part of the ditch as yet unexcavated) and suggests strongly that the meat was brought to it already cut up. Yet an equally plausible interpretation of this phenomenon is that the cut meat was brought in to feed the permanent population of the henge, either as tribute or for sale or barter. The ash deposits, potsherds, broken tools and black earth layers (which must have been formed by being impregnated with charcoal or organic human refuse — bones alone will not turn a midden black) all fit excellently with this interpretation.

Another 'ceremonial' aspect of Durrington Walls might be seen in the great quantities of fresh animal bones, bone refuse, potsherds, flints and ash that had been tossed into the terminal of the ditch. One could if one wished invoke a 'ritual' explanation for this and see the material as 'offerings' made by people entering or leaving the sacred enclosures. However, since the southern roundhouse is so close to the ditch terminal a simpler explanation would be that its inhabitants used the end of the great ditch as a convenient rubbish pit — a pleasanter way of disposing of domestic refuse than digging a special pit just outside the house as was done in the first phase of occupation. The presence of ash layers in the terminal surely proves this as ash seems an unlikely 'offering'. This interpretation also seems to be borne out by the discoveries at the allied giant henge at Mount Pleasant in Dorset (chapter 8). There the wooden roundhouse was some 70 yards from the nearest entrance and had its own surrounding ditch which was full of rubbish. There was little refuse in the main ditch terminal, obviously because it was too far away from the house. No 'ritual' deposits were made here!

Implications of the material culture

Other aspects of the material culture could be said to support the hypothesis of permanent domestic habitation of the henge by a non-agricultural élite class. The complete absence of grain and saddle querns seems extraordinary in a settled Neolithic society whose forebears had been cultivating grain on the chalk downs for perhaps 1,500 years,[32] but it would be explicable in terms of a community supported by tribute if the grain was brought to the site already ground into flour, or even already baked into loaves. Admittedly this is negative evidence which might be interpreted differently, and one cannot but recall the similar apparent complete absence of querns and grain from Skara Brae (chapter 9) which used to be one of the most notable features of the site until 1973 when new excavations revealed masses of grain at the base of the midden there.[33] It seems quite fantastic to believe that in Late Neolithic times there was no cereal growing in Wessex, the granary of Iron Age Britain, particularly when a sample of barley dating to 1564 ± 120 bc (2040 BC) is known from the Ness of Gruting house in Shetland (BM-441). It seems even more fantastic to suppose that the inhabitants of this major centre were denied grain when it was being grown all around on the downs. The complete absence of grain impressions on Grooved ware need not be held to prove the absence of grain growing since the ware need not have been made in the same place as the flour.

Flint-working took place at Durrington Walls as the debris of thousands of struck flakes confirms, and the fact that the vast majority of the implements made were scrapers clearly points to domestic occupation. Scrapers are usually thought to have been used for preparing skins, and no doubt many furs were needed for blankets, bedding, hangings, screens and so on. Even more significant could be the solitary spindle whorl found — the first from Neolithic Britain — since it must surely show that another domestic craft, the spinning of thread, was practised on the site and it also implies that weaving of cloth, presumably carried out by women, also took place there. It seems appropriate that the first evidence for woven clothes in Neolithic Britain should come from a ceremonial centre inhabited by an upper class. The many transverse arrowheads found were presumably used for hunting and seem at variance with the small number of game bones found in the middens, but again they are not difficult to explain in terms of a permanently inhabited site.

It must also be recognised that a site does not have to be *either* ritual *or* domestic: it can be both. If one assumes that an élite class of wise men and their followers and wives lived at Durrington Walls there is every reason to suppose that, in addition to actual living quarters for these people, there were probably other buildings with other ceremonial functions, where novices were taught, instruction in the higher levels of the *disciplina* given, special religious ceremonies for initiates and 'graduates' performed, 'research' carried out and so on. The various phenomena inferred to be 'ritual' could be explained with such assumptions without difficulty. Indeed a classic example of how problems vanish when the data is viewed in a slightly different way — that is when 'ceremonial' is not automatically assumed to be incompatible with 'domestic' — will be seen in some of the discussion about Woodhenge. A building does not have to be non-functional simply because it may have been laid out as a form of mathematical experiment:[34] there is no reason at all why the posts of the Woodhenge roundhouse should not have supported a massive roofed building *and* have been skilfully positioned according to some sophisticated geometrical scheme; the brochs seem to show just this combination of practical and esoteric skills (chapter 3 above).

A final point needing discussion is that the midden was claimed to be some kind of ceremonial depository of pots and 'offerings' because so few sherds could be reconstructed into whole vessels.[35] However, ordinary Iron Age domestic sites show exactly the same phenomenon even when conditions are ideal for the preservation of all the pieces of broken pots — inside a massive stone broch for example — and when shattered vessels are found in such places only parts of them can be rebuilt.[36] Similarly the heating of the platform outside the doorway into the southern roundhouse, and the quantities of bones scattered nearby, could be more simply explained as the remains of the cooking (boiling?) done outside the building for communal meals which were eaten inside were it not for the assumption that such domestic activities were unlikely in a henge.

In summary, the evidence from Durrington Walls is, in my opinion, much more easily explained by assuming that the site had a permanent population of non-farming specialists who lived off a surplus of food provided by the surrounding peasant population than by supposing that the evident 'ceremonial' nature of the site and its wooden buildings meant that permanent habitation was improbable and that therefore the domestic refuse has to be explained in ritual terms. The contradiction between 'ritual' site and 'domestic' refuse which keeps emerging is resolved by the explanation advanced here, which combines the simplest explanation of the two classes of phenomena. Such inhabited ceremonial centres surely provide exactly the evidence for classes of skilled specialists — wise men, magicians, astronomers, priests, poets, jurists and engineers with all their families, retainers and attendant craftsmen and technicians — which the Thom theories imply existed in Late Neolithic Britain. The contrast between conditions at these sites and those at other contemporary Neolithic settlements like Windmill Hill reinforces this hypothesis and is discussed in the final chapter.

8

Other Ceremonial Centres
in Southern England

It was in 1925 that traces of rings of large pits were first seen from the air as dark crop marks inside what had hitherto been regarded as a large disc barrow near the village of Durrington, Wiltshire, and excavations by the Cunningtons in 1926 and 1927 revealed that massive timbers had once stood within the bank and internal ditch.[1] The site was named Woodhenge because of the supposed similarities with Stonehenge and until 1940 it was believed that the structure had been an open one with rings of simple, upright timbers, perhaps embellished with wooden lintels. Woodhenge stands only 60 yards south of the south entrance of Durrington Walls and less than 300 yards west of the river Avon.

The site and the excavations

The bank proved to be only poorly preserved, but a buried land surface containing potsherds and other artefacts was found under it. Between this and the internal ditch was a berm 4-5 ft wide. The ditch itself was discovered to be 6-7 ft deep with a flat bottom 12-16 ft broad; it contained four distinct layers of fill separated by three old turf-lines representing periods of stability. At the bottom was the usual clean, coarse silt of lumps of chalk; this was surmounted by a finer, darker silt on top of which was the lowest turf-line. Only Late Neolithic and Early Bronze Age pottery (together with animal bones) was found in these two lowest levels. Two radiocarbon dates of 1867 ± 74 bc (BM-677) and 1805 ± 54 bc (BM-678) were recently obtained for an antler lying on the base of the ditch and a bone in the primary ditch silt respectively and they appear to date the construction of the site.[2] The equivalent calendar date of the average of these two is 2190-2290 BC.

In the next layer of silt above, probably due to cultivation, there were Romano-British sherds and on top of this was the second turf-line. This was covered by a second layer of ploughsoil of unknown date on which the third turf-line formed. The final and uppermost layer of ploughsoil was due to activity which began about AD 1845-55.

The single entrance to the site was in the NNE and consisted of the usual causeway across the ditch and corresponding gap in the bank; distinct gaps in the three outer rings of posts occur opposite this entrance (fig. 26). This causeway and much of the interior of the site had been scraped and abraded by the plough so that the prehistoric ground surface had been largely destroyed, together with any artefacts lying on it. The six rings of post-holes are not circular but more oval in shape; each long axis is about 10½ ft longer than the corresponding short one (the geometry of the rings is discussed later). They are lettered A-F from the outside to the centre and the A ring of 60 post-holes is seen to be the most irregular and the C ring to have contained the most massive posts. There seems to be an arithmetical relationship between the numbers of the posts in each ring as well as between the sizes of the rings themselves: from A to F the rings have 60, 32, 16, 18, 18 and 12 post-holes respectively. The C ring holes have an average depth of 5 ft 8 in, and all have ramps leading down into them mostly from the south (all the holes were probably 12-18 in deeper originally before the chalk floor level was eroded by ploughing). The present average depths of the other holes, from A to F, are 2 ft 10 in, 3 ft 10 in, 2 ft 10 in, 3 ft 4 in and 3 ft 4in respectively.

The Cunningtons detected the darker 'post-pipes' in the rammed chalk fill of some of the post-holes (others had been completely excavated before the possibility of timber uprights was envisaged). The posts thus traced proved to be about 12 in in diameter in the smaller holes and 3 ft in the largest. These post-sockets were filled in after the completion of the excavations in 1927, the position of the holes being marked on the ground surface by a mound of earth surmounted by a large flint.[3] The low concrete pillars which now mark the positions of these post-holes, and which Thom had to use as the basis for his survey (fig. 26), were evidently not inserted until later.[4] There is therefore a possibility that geometrical constructions based on the concrete pillars are not absolutely reliable.

A long stone-hole, probably for a sarsen upright, was found on ring B near the south and had clearly been cut at a later time than the adjacent post-hole B9; the Cunningtons drew a tentative analogy with the recumbent stones of the circles of Aberdeenshire (chapter 2). At the centre of the site, and on its NE-SW axis, was a burial pit in which was the crouched skeleton of a child, about 3½ years old according to Sir Arthur Keith; its skull clearly appeared to have been split in half before burial. There is an outlying monolith called the Cuckoo stone about a quarter of a mile to the west and on an azimuth of 266¼° from the centre of the site.

A considerable quantity of broken pottery and animal bones was found on the site even though the floor had been destroyed by ploughing. These remains occurred mainly in the primary silting of the ditch, with some under the bank and in several of the post-holes. Nearly all the pottery was Grooved ware, and an interesting and potentially important feature of these sherds was that some of them were tempered with fragments of marine shells. It follows that either the shells, or more probably the pottery itself, was brought from the coast to Woodhenge.

Of the fragmentary animal bones found no quantities are given in the

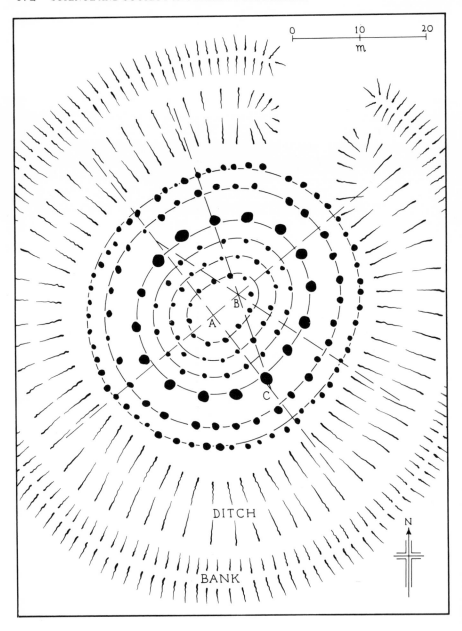

Fig. 26. Plan of the post-holes found at Woodhenge with, superimposed, the geometrical construction suggested by A. Thom. The latter is based on two opposed right-angled triangles of 6, 17½ and 18½ **MY** (12-35-37 in half yards) from the outer angles of which arcs are drawn. These arcs connect segments of six circles, drawn from the centre points, so that the six oval rings so drawn have perimeters of 40, 60, 80, 100 and 140 megalithic yards

specialist report but wild animals like *bos primigenius,* red deer, roe deer, fox and cat and a few other small creatures are mentioned. Most of the bones were of domestic animals and the majority of these were of ox though, as at Durrington Walls, no skulls were found. The animals next most frequently represented, pigs and sheep, were rare. Deer antlers were found, some of which showed the wear on the tines characteristic of use as picks; most of them had been collected after shedding but a few had fragments of skulls attached and had therefore been taken from killed animals. Flint tools included leaf-shaped, hollow-based and lop-sided arrowheads as well as scrapers, and a flake from the cutting edge of a polished greenstone axe was also found.

Orientation and geometry

It was clear to the Cunningtons when they examined the site that the post-holes were arranged in concentric rings in a systematic way. They noted that the midsummer sun rose on an azimuth of 50½° at the site and that this line formed the long axis of the post-hole ovals and passed through the central burial. Indeed, when the posts were standing in their holes, anyone positioned at the centre of the site would have been able to look to the northeast along a narrow, clear avenue between the posts and to see this sunrise. A similar clear line evidently extends just south of west towards the Cuckoo stone. There is also a clearly open line to the north-west from the centre on an azimuth of 315° which could point to the midsummer sunset (fig. 26); a gap in the A ring at this point seems to confirm the existence of such a line.

The Cunningtons observed an interesting relationship between the lengths of the long axes of the concentric ovals, which they determined by working out as 9.6 ft the average distance between the holes of one ring and those of the next (except between rings B and C when it was 1½ times greater, or 14.5 ft). Assuming such a separation, they obtained long diameters of, from A to F, 144, 125, 96.0, 76.8, 57.6 and 38.4 ft respectively. If the unit of length employed was assumed to be 11½ instead of 12 in these dimensions become 150, 130, 100, 80, 60 and 40 'Woodhenge feet', a methodical relationship which could scarcely, they felt, be attributable to chance. They surmised that a prehistoric foot equivalent to 11½ modern inches was used in laying out the site.[5]

Forty years later Alexander Thom offered a more detailed interpretation of the geometrical construction of Woodhenge, basing it on a new, accurate survey of the concrete pillars marking the positions of the post-holes.[6] He too found that a symmetrical figure of concentric rings could be drawn through the pillars with their common long axis pointing to the positions of the first appearance of the sun at midsummer calculated for about 1800 BC at the site (azimuth 49.2°). The suggested geometrical figure (fig. 26) is based on two opposed right-angled triangles with sides of 6, 17½ and 18½ megalithic yards: in units of half yards this is the sixth in the sequence of perfect Pythagorean triangles, that is $12^2 + 35^2 = 37^2$. The ends of the 'ovals' are here seen to be segments of true circles with their centres at either end of the common short base of the triangles and these are joined with arcs of larger circles drawn from the tips of the two opposed triangles. Yet none of the radii of the various rings which thus appear are in whole numbers of megalithic yards, a fact which might seem to reduce the plausibility of this geometrical solution in spite of its good fit with the concrete markers.

However the *perimeters* of the egg-shaped rings drawn in this way prove to have a very clear arithmetical relationship, recalling the Cunningtons' inferences forty years earlier. The exact perimeters in MY are, from rings A to F, 161.0, 138.2, 104.2, 79.9, 61.3 and 39.4 respectively, and these could be regarded as good approximations to 160, 140, 100, 80, 60 and 40 MY. Ring C is the least accurate in this respect, its perimeter being some 4% too large from the 'ideal' of 100 MY, but if it is assumed that these very large posts were intended to touch the egg-shaped ring with their *inside* edges only, the perimeter would be almost exactly 100 MY. Thom surmised that the geometry may have been intended to create a set of 'circles' with their π values (relation of radii to circumferences) as close as possible to 3 and simultaneously to have the perimeters as near as possible to multiples of 20 MY. If this is a correct interpretation of the geometry underlying Woodhenge it must be regarded as an impressive intellectual achievement on the part of the architect.

Discussion

The earliest interpretation of Woodhenge was that it was built as an open temple or sanctuary, perhaps, like Stonehenge, with lintels joining the tops of some of the rings of posts. Piggott was the first to suggest that the posts may have supported a huge, roofed building and favoured the idea that it was an annular structure with an open central court.[7] Musson has recently reviewed the problem again and accepts this idea.[8] Ring C held the most massive timber uprights, with ramps leading down into the holes, and is well interpreted as the support for a ridge roof for this ring-shaped structure, requiring the tallest and strongest posts. The roof could have sloped down on either side of this ridge and the other post-holes are in fact smaller. The outermost ring A is the most irregular of the six and recalls the outermost set of posts of the southern roundhouse at nearby Durrington Walls, interpreted there as the uprights of the outer wall of the building. The open central court of the Woodhenge building would have been some 107 ft across along its major axis, providing an extensive round 'cloister' open to the sky. One minor drawback to this view might be the absence of any water containers or channels to take away the rain which would have fallen into the middle of this open building, and also drained off the inner half of the ridge roof, but it is possible that the destruction of the old

Neolithic ground surface has also destroyed any drainage gullies that may have existed.

The relatively large quantity of food and other refuse found at Woodhenge puts the site firmly in the same class as Durrington Walls, an apparently domestic 'ceremonial' structure (henge monument), and seems to make its interpretation as the foundations of a huge roofed wooden building more probable. The same arguments which apply to Durrington Walls, and favour that site having been a permanently inhabited enclosure containing roofed buildings, apply also to Woodhenge, on the grounds of the similarity of the two sites' features, their close physical proximity and their known contemporaneity. Nor need there be any contradiction between the concept that Woodhenge was a roofed building and the elaborate geometry inferred for its ground plan. Wainwright[9] implies that Thom's interpretation is less likely if Woodhenge was a roofed structure, but there is no reason why a large building should not have been designed and constructed on elaborate geometrical principles just as easily as an open sanctuary or temple. Indeed the Iron Age brochs of Scotland seem to be examples of just such buildings (chapter 3). Also there is no doubt that the midsummer sunrise — and any other celestial phenomenon designed to be seen from inside Woodhenge — would have looked more impressive if the first rays from the orb at dawn had shone into the heart of a dark, roofed building through slits in its outside wall than if they had simply shone into a structure open to the sky.

Woodhenge thus appears to have been a massive, annular roofed wooden building which could well have been used as a residence or ceremonial structure by the members of a learned order. The central open space recalls the cloisters of medieval monasteries, an area open to the sky and sun yet completely cut off from the world outside, suitable for meditation and learned thought. Woodhenge must be closely connected with the Durrington Walls ceremonial centre in every way; in fact it should probably not be considered as a separate site at all but as an integral part of the giant henge. The greater geometrical sophistication of its design, together with its position a short distance outside the southern entrance to the main site, and the fact that it had its own surrounding ditch and the slightly younger C-14 date for its construction, could well mean that Woodhenge was added to Durrington Walls a century or two after the latter had been enlarged to its final size and at a time when geometrical and perhaps astronomical knowledge had become more advanced. It may not be too fanciful to see Woodhenge as a special building, outside the main centre and perhaps serving a special function. Perhaps it was the residence of the high priest-astronomer, or an advanced college for the more learned and talented members of the order. If it is accepted that the view of the two adjacent sites as permanently inhabited ceremonial centres containing roofed buildings is plausible, then all these possibilities become real.

The special nature of Woodhenge is emphasised again by what

happened after the building disintegrated. The existence of post-pipes in the fill of the sockets presumably means that the roof-supporting pillars decayed where they were and that the structure fell gradually into ruin after it became unsafe (though the roof could perhaps have been taken off first). The recumbent sarsen monolith placed on the south side of ring B, evidently after the posts had rotted, suggests a desire to commemorate the site in some way and recalls the more elaborate memorials at the Sanctuary and Mount Pleasant (described below).

MOUNT PLEASANT, DORSET

The site and the excavations

The third of the giant henges of southern England to be excavated was Mount Pleasant in 1970;[10] at the time of writing the detailed excavation report is not yet available. The site stands on a low hill, well away from the great concentrations of sites on Salisbury Plain; it lies about 40 miles southwest of Stonehenge, just east of the modern town of Dorchester and only a few miles from the sea. The henge is an approximately egg-shaped enclosure defined by a bank and internal ditch, both interrupted by four entrances. It measures about 315 yards from east to west and 285 yards from north to south, enclosing an area of some 14½ acres. The bank was found to be severely eroded but it was some 63 ft wide in places. The areas excavated were the west entrance, the palisade trench just within this, and a timber roundhouse within the enclosure and about 65 yards back from the entrance. Both the last two features had previously been observed on air photographs.

The ditch was irregular in depth, varying from 6.5 to 9.8 ft; it seemed not to have been completed and ridges between the separately dug sections were observed. A few antler picks were on the floor and a flat bronze axe and a sherd of Grooved ware came from the primary silts. Radiocarbon dates from two of these picks, evidently used to dig out the ditch, gave remarkably consistent results at 1784 ± 41 bc (BM-645) and 1778 ± 59 bc (BM-646): the equivalent in real years would be about 2170 BC.[11]

The trench for the wooden palisade ran parallel to the ditch at the west and east entrances and probably enclosed the whole of the hilltop on which the site stands. Excavation of a section on the west showed that it was a continuous trench with vertical sides, 7.5 ft deep and 2.5 ft wide. The post-pipes of many timbers 1-1.3 ft in diameter were found in the deposits filling it and it must originally have contained a truly massive stockade perhaps standing 16 ft above the ground; this would have formed a second barrier to the enclosed area of the henge, concentric with the ditch. Radiocarbon dates of 1687 ± 63 bc (BM-662) and 1695 ± 43 bc (BM-665) were obtained for the construction of this feature (about 2120-40 BC), and the stockade was therefore very probably built slightly later than the digging of the main ditch; it seems to have completely barred off the entrances through the latter.

The wooden circular structure, surrounded by its own ditch with a single entrance gap on the north side, consisted of five concentric rings of post-holes, the largest of which was 125 ft in diameter. The posts were arranged symmetrically, with wider radial 'corridors' dividing the building into four equal quadrants, each of which contains the same number of post-holes (41 or 42). The corridors on the north and south have parallel sides, the two on the east and west widen slightly towards the exterior. The prehistoric floor level had been destroyed by ploughing so that only the bases of the post-holes remained as dark circular markings in the chalk. Radiocarbon dates for material from the primary silts of the ditch dating the construction of the site included 1961 ± 89 bc (BM-663), 1991 ± 72 bc (BM-666) and 2038 ± 84 bc (BM-667); Grooved ware was associated with the strata thus dated (the average of these dates is equivalent to about 2560 BC).

Presumably after the wooden building had decayed an open-sided square of standing sarsen stones was built at its centre, a 'cove' of three such stones on the west periphery and a single stone on the north edge. The square had sides of exactly 21.3 ft according to Wainwright: 8 MY are equivalent to 21.76 ft, or about 5½ in more.

The surrounding ditch was up to 5.6 ft deep and contained quantities of bones and artefacts, presumably confirming that the structure within was an inhabited roundhouse. The primary silts contained Grooved ware with no Beaker sherds, fresh flint flakes and implements, animal bones and antler picks. The three C-14 dates from this level have already been mentioned. On top of this layer was a 'level of rest', formed in a period of temporary stability, and lying on this was a layer of fragments and chips of sarsen stones and many mauls (hammerstones), evidently associated with the importation, dressing and erection of the standing stones. Charcoal from a hearth immediately above this layer gave a date of 1680 ± 60 bc (BM-668), equivalent to a real year date of about 2110-2130 BC. Higher up in the ditch was another hearth, associated with sherds of collared urns and food vessels, and this gave a date of 1324 ± 51 bc (BM-669), equivalent to about 1640 BC.

Discussion

Inevitably little information can be given in an interim report about the types and quantities of animal bones found, since this information usually comes from a specialist helper, but it does appear that the conditions around the Mount Pleasant roundhouse were very similar to those encountered at Woodhenge, and that both structures could well have been large, inhabited roofed wooden buildings around which domestic refuse accumulated. There is a marked difference from Durrington Walls in the absence of much refuse from the ditch terminals, but that might be easily explained by the relative distances of the roundhouses at each site from the causeway across the main perimeter ditch. At Durrington Walls the southern roundhouse was only a little over 20 yards from the ditch terminals, and at Marden even less, so that some domestic refuse could easily have been tossed into them at these sites. At Mount Pleasant, however, the great roundhouse was 65 yards from the same spot; in addition it was probably built some time before the main ditch. We have already noted that the absence of much refuse in the main ditch terminals at Mount Pleasant casts a great deal of doubt on the oft-repeated hypothesis that people going in and out of these huge ceremonial sites threw pottery and pieces of meat into the ditch terminals as 'offerings' as they entered the temple precincts: it seems much more likely that, if an inhabited roundhouse was close by, refuse was continuously being thrown into these convenient deep depressions.

Two of the implications of the dating of the Mount Pleasant roundhouse to the 21st or 20th century bc are particularly interesting. In the first place it was clearly built before the excavation of the great precinct ditch of the henge and well before the stockade was erected: if the radiocarbon dates are translated into real year dates the roundhouse could be older than the main ditch by perhaps three or four centuries. It would seem therefore that the possibility which was suspected at Durrington Walls is confirmed: that some of the giant henges began as round, ditched wooden buildings on open ground which were later enclosed (presumably after a sufficient number of them had been built). In the second place the parallel with Woodhenge is seen to be close; both houses were built on unenclosed ground and both have their own smaller ditches closely surrounding the wooden building. By its radiocarbon dates the ditched roundhouse at Mount Pleasant, a relatively simple, circular structure, is clearly earlier than Woodhenge with its more complex geometrical construction and this seems to support the view that a knowledge of sophisticated geometry was evolving gradually throughout the Late Neolithic period. The closeness of the dates of the construction of the Mount Pleasant roundhouse to those of the second southern house at Durrington Walls is remarkable; it does seem that these great wooden buildings began to be erected in the Wessex region at a definable point in time, around 2000 bc (c. 2550 BC), and perhaps for a specific reason.

Of particular interest too is the further clear example at Mount Pleasant of a large wooden building falling into decay and being 'commemorated' with an arrangement of standing stones — in this case an open-sided square, a cove and a single, isolated stone. Furthermore the radiocarbon dates indicate clearly that at almost exactly the same time that this happened, a truly massive stockade was constructed, apparently completely barring off the interior of the henge. Why the presumably redundant henge should have been so completely sealed off in this way must of course remain a mystery, but the evidence from Mount Pleasant, when combined with that from Durrington Walls and the Sanctuary, confirms that settings of standing stones in that part of the world often mark the position of the vanished special wooden buildings of a slightly earlier period. Whether the numerous stone circles up and down the country originated in this way, or whether the circle-building traditions were imported to Wessex from elsewhere and used there for this purpose, is a separate problem.

MARDEN, WILTSHIRE

The second of the giant henges of southern England to be excavated by Wainwright, in 1969, was Marden, situated in the vale of Pewsey some ten miles north of Durrington Walls and on the same river Avon.[12] The site is an irregular enclosure, defined on its northeast half by the usual broad bank with an internal ditch, with two causewayed entrances on the north and east, and on the southwest half by the slope down to the flood plain of the river Avon which runs close by (fig. 24). A geophysical survey of the area showed that the ends of the bank and ditch had not been cut off by the river but were deliberately constructed, rounded terminals; evidently the Avon served as part of the boundary of the precinct of the henge, doubtless when it was somewhat closer to the site than it is now. The area thus enclosed totals some 35 acres, the distance across it from north to south being about 580 yards and from east to west some 394 yards. The excavations took place on and just within the north entrance and causeway and the site of a simple wooden roundhouse was discovered.

Below the bank a buried soil was found with a layer of charcoal, flints and Early and Middle Neolithic potsherds in it. A radiocarbon date from this layer of 2654 ± 59 bc (BM-560:3380 BC) compares well with one of 2760 ± 150 bc (BM-204) for charcoal from the nearby causewayed camp of Knap Hill. Evidently, like Durrington the site was inhabited, or at least used, some centuries before the henge was built.

The main ditch, dug through drift into the greensand below, was relatively wide and shallow, doubtless because of the less stable nature of the subsoils from which it was excavated. It was about 52 ft wide and 6.5 ft deep in the centre and part of its basal layer was waterlogged, the water table being but 9.5 ft below the surface. A deposit of primary silts had accumulated at the base of each side and antlers, animal bones and charcoal fragments were found in it; the charcoal gave a date of 1988 ± 48 bc (BM-557:2560 BC) but samples of antler and bone gave later dates and were thought to have been contaminated by the waterlogged conditions. A thin stratum of charcoal, bones, antler picks, flints and potsherds lay immediately on these early silts and directly on the floor of the ditch elsewhere; joining fragments of three vessels were found in this layer and in the silt below, confirming that the deposits had been laid down in fairly quick succession. On top of the stratum of artefacts was an almost sterile, thick layer of soft, grey-brown clay. A crouched skeleton of a young woman, perhaps between 17 and 24 years old, was found on the artefact layer.

The post-holes of a small timber roundhouse were found 15 yards south of the entrance, but because of erosion only the bases of these sockets were preserved. Among a scatter of post-holes, both within and outside the assumed area of the house, 21 could be fitted onto a circle about 34.5 ft in diameter and 15 of these had the impression of a timber upright in them. From these post-pipes it could be seen that the standing timbers ranged in thickness from 4 in to 1 ft, apparently quite strong enough to support a roofed structure of the diameter mentioned. There were also three post-holes in a triangle near the centre of the ring which might have supported the apex of the roof.

Many flints, totalling 40% of all those found in the excavations, were found in and around these post-holes. The base of a shallow pit was found nearby, containing a scatter of charcoal and some indeterminate sherds, which might have been the remains of a midden deposit like that outside the southern roundhouse at Durrington Walls. These various features suggest that the circle of posts supported a simple, round roofed building, rather similar to the second and third buildings at the Sanctuary. No internal roof supports should have been needed for such a building, but they could have existed. The potsherds recovered from the site were all of Grooved ware and the rest of the material culture was the familiar assemblage of flint flakes, cores, scrapers and points and antler picks. The animal bones included the remains of the following (minimum) numbers of individuals of these species: 8 cattle, 8 pig, 2 sheep, 1 horse, 1 red deer and 1 possible wild aurochs.

Discussion

Only a minute proportion of the enclosed area of the great henge at Marden has been explored, so one can get little idea of how many roundhouses there may have been on the site or of whether any of them were the large, complex buildings found at the two other large henges already described. Presumably the scatter of artefacts and bones in the ditch terminals of the north entrance could be midden material thrown out from the nearby small roundhouse, but it is interesting both that the layers immediately above the midden scatter were sterile and that no Beaker pottery was recovered. That there was a distinct interval between the construction of the great Late Neolithic henges and the arrival of the Beaker people is shown clearly by the finds and stratigraphy at Durrington Walls and Mount Pleasant, so it is possible that Marden — or at least the northern part of it — was not used for very long after the ditch was dug.

The situation and design of the henge are themselves of great interest and in its use of a river to form one side of the boundary of the enclosed area Marden strongly resembles the Early Christian monastic sites of northern Britain and Ireland nearly three millennia later. Sites like Old Melrose in Roxburghshire and Clonmacnois in Co. Offaly consist of an area of ground next to a river, demarcated by that river and by a bank and ditch running down to it at two points. The wood and turf residences of the monastic community as well as a small chapel or church were within the enclosed area (traces of stone buildings are rare in this pre-Norman period). Several contemporary sources, eg Adomnan's *Life of Columba* (probably written in the 690s), describe the enclosed area and 'refer to something called *vallum* or *vallum monasterii*. In Britain this is to be interpreted as meaning (jointly) an earthen bank and an outer quarry ditch, surrounding and enclosing a monastery, and constituting a spiritual and legal, though hardly a militarily defensible, boundary between the monastic establishment and the world outside it.'[13] The parallels with the larger henge monuments, and especially with Marden, seem striking in several ways and will be referred to again later (chapter 10).

FLINT MINES

The date and manner of use of the Neolithic flint mines and axe factories in Britain may not, at first sight, seem very relevant to the problem of the nature of the society which used the giant henges of southern England and the stone circles of the highland zone. However, the two types of tools which were used in vast quantities to build the great enclosures, and the huge wooden buildings inside them, were deer antlers for excavating the chalk and flint and stone axes to cut and trim the thousands of trees needed for the numerous roundhouses and palisades. It is reasonable to suppose that a sudden upsurge in activity at the flint mines, and perhaps also at the axe factories, took place in Late Neolithic times as part of the ramifications of the events in Wessex. Obviously there is not much hope of finding out how the antlers were collected — though the sheer quantity which must have been needed, as well as the rarity of deer bones on Wessex Neolithic sites, suggests that a nation-wide operation to collect them from the forests may have been organised — but the sites of the mines and factories are known and are being increasingly subjected to systematic investigations and radiocarbon dating.

On the whole the few dates available for activity at the stone axe factory sites appear to be some centuries earlier than the major phase of large henge building in Late Neolithic times. For example a C-14 date of 2730 ± 135 bc (BM-281) was obtained for a working floor of chips and axe rough-outs at the Great Langdale factory site in Westmorland, and two dates of 2510 ± 90 bc and 2250 ± 90 bc (UB-371, 372) are available for a chipping floor in peat at the Killin factory site in Perthshire.[14] The flint mines in the chalklands of southeast England were also used throughout the Neolithic period.[15] For these the dated material is usually the antler picks which were used to dig out the shafts and galleries and which are found abandoned in the mines in large numbers: these radiocarbon dates should relate closely to the use of the mines. The Church Hill mine in Sussex has a date of 3390 ± 150 bc (BM-181) and that at Blackpatch, also in Sussex, one of 3140 ± 130 bc (BM-290). The other Sussex mines at Harrow Hill and Cissbury have dates in the first half of the third millennium bc and it seems clear that mining for flint started in the area first colonised by the Neolithic farmers, and very soon after this settlement began.

Grimes Graves

The biggest complex of prehistoric flint mines is undoubtedly that known as Grimes Graves, near Thetford in Norfolk; the scores of filled-in shafts and open workings, visible from the air as shallow depressions, cover about 93 acres.[16] Various excavations have been carried out at the site over the years and a series of C-14 dates were obtained during the 1960s for material obtained much earlier from several shafts by Greenwell and Armstrong.[17] These ranged from 2340 ± 150 bc (BM-97) to 1600 ± 150 bc (BM-276) and suggested a Late Neolithic and Early Bronze Age date for the complex. The details of flint mining do not concern us here; it is sufficient to note that, in the case of the deep mines, vertical shafts were driven down to a depth of up to 45 ft through two seams of inferior flint to reach the third and deepest seam of high quality black flint which was evidently best for implements. Horizontal galleries were driven in along above the seam from the base of the shaft and blocks of flint were levered out with the same antler picks which were used for removing the chalk. When a mine was worked out, or when the galleries had become too long for safety, the working was abandoned and the shaft filled with chalk rubble. On the surface around the shafts the nodules of flint were roughly shaped into axes and vast quantities of flint flakes are found on these working floors. Open-cast mining was practised where the flint seam came nearer the surface, lower down the hill.

Systematic excavations by the staff of the British Museum and the Department of the Environment have been taking place at Grimes Graves since 1972 and the preliminary results, made known in a special exhibition at the Museum in the first half of 1975, have dramatically increased our knowledge of the site and its users and have put the mining complex firmly in its context in relation to the Late Neolithic developments in the Wessex area already described. Only a brief account can be given here, based on a leaflet printed for the exhibition.[18] An unexplored, undisturbed deep mine shaft was selected for thorough investigation and a programme of surface exploration was designed to trace the full extent of the mines, to study the flint-knapping techniques of the miners and to locate their settlements. Some 600 tons of rubble were removed from the shaft and a large number of antler picks were found in the empty galleries radiating from the bottom of this. Some 17 C-14 dates were obtained from these picks and they evidently ranged between the mid 21st and the early 18th centuries bc. One can reasonably assume that any one mine was not in use for more than a few years and that, since antler picks were plentiful and had a limited useful life, all the picks in one mine ought to be of about the same age. This means that the dates probably represent a scatter of measurements of what is effectively the same event and that it is legitimate to combine them. The mean date is in the middle of the 20th century bc and it has a much smaller standard deviation than the 17 individual measurements, something like ± 15 years if the separate sigma values are about ± 60 years.[19] If these dates are the final ones they would show that this shaft was worked in the 20th century bc, or in the late 26th or early 25th BC. Another shaft at Grimes Graves was excavated in 1971 and four consistent dates on charcoal were obtained for the start of the back-filling of the mine-shaft, marking the end of its use. Grooved ware was associated with this event and doubtless with the earlier digging of the mine. The mean date is 1837 ± 31 bc.[19] This extra precision is one of the advantages gained from performing a whole set of radiocarbon determinations, instead of just a couple, on ideal material.

However, the main point is that we can now see that this deep flint mine was being dug and exploited at exactly the same time that the great wooden roundhouses were being erected at Durrington Walls and Mount Pleasant and that Skara Brae was being lived in in Orkney (chapter 9). Grooved ware found in quantity associated with this mine and with the working floors on the surface nearby confirms in a most striking way the close connection between the two geographically separate series of events. That links between the two areas were established in Early Neolithic times is clearly shown by the distribution of long barrows and pottery finds,[20] and the new discoveries have shown dramatically what a wide effect the development of the giant henges of Wessex had on Late Neolithic society. It seems clear that intensified exploitation of the mines was needed to produce the thousands of axes required to fell and trim the hundreds of oak trees needed for the new buildings, and that the class of people who were organising the ceremonial centres also organised the mining. In the next chapter we shall see that their activities extended much further afield, even as far as the Orkney Isles.

9

Expansion to Orkney

INTRODUCTION

It seems paradoxical that one should have to go as far afield from Wessex as the Orkney Islands before finding settlement sites and 'ritual' structures as informative and well preserved as those of southern England — sites which are moreover closely linked with the ceremonial centres of the south both by their shared material culture and by their exact contemporaneity as witnessed by radiocarbon dates — yet this is the case. Orkney is rich in archaeological remains of many periods[1] but it is outstanding in possessing in Skara Brae the only well preserved stone settlement in Britain of Late Neolithic times, and in the sites of Ring of Brodgar and Stenness two of the finest stone circles and 'ritual' sites in the country.

That there were close cultural links of some kind between Orkney and southern England at this period has long been recognised[2] and the term 'Rinyo-Clacton' was eventually coined to describe the similar pottery (now called Grooved ware again) of these two widely separated regions.[3] Yet it has always been difficult to explain this rather clear archaeological link in social terms, particularly when the occupants of the sites concerned are assumed to be humble peasants. It is even more difficult if the current climate of archaeological theory is unfavourable towards diffusionist theories of any kind, as it is at present, and indeed the doctrine of independent development has been applied to the Orkney pottery concerned to get over this difficulty.[4] Yet the possibility that a nationwide learned order existed in Britain in Late Neolithic times could have a profound impact on the problem of the 'Rinyo-Clacton culture' and its pottery, and it might well provide a social explanation for this strange archaeological phenomenon.

SKARA BRAE: DISCOVERY AND EXCAVATION

At the Bay of Skaill, on the west coast of the mainland of Orkney, is a group of prehistoric stone dwellings which is remarkable in being both well preserved and almost unique. Since its discovery in about 1850 Skara Brae has been considered to be a settlement of the prehistoric peasant population of Orkney and its inhabitants have been tacitly assumed to be in no wise out of the ordinary. The peculiarities of its buildings have always been

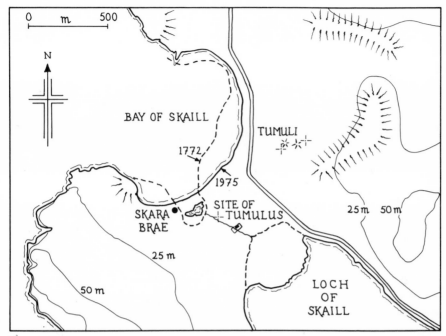

Fig. 27. The Bay of Skaill, Orkney, with the shore line and other features mapped in the late 18th century compared with the present topography; location of Skara Brae marked. *Crown copyright reserved*

explained by supposing, first, that they simply represent the translation into stone in tree-less Orkney of furniture which would elsewhere be made of wood (an unanswerable argument since no wooden furniture from elsewhere has been discovered), and second, that the undoubtedly high quality of the drystone masonry which appears in Skara Brae, as in many other ancient Orkney structures of all periods, derives from the quality of the easily split, laminated sandstone available there. Yet there are features of Skara Brae which, in the light of the working hypothesis being considered, seem capable of re-interpretation.

The structures

The basic facts about the structures of Skara Brae and the material culture associated with them are well known and have often been described.[5] The site stands among sand dunes close to the sea at the south corner of the Bay of Skaill and the settlement consists of six large stone houses, or huts as they are usually called, and two smaller ones. All the buildings are of drystone masonry, many built against one another, and all are linked together with a network of lintelled stone passageways so that the whole forms a single warren-like complex of dwellings. Several of the huts were cleared out in the nineteenth century with no regard to stratigraphical observation[6] but the

Fig. 28. Plan of the main village at Skara Brae, after V. G. Childe

excavations of Professor V. G. Childe in 1928 and 1929 remedied this.[7] He showed that a substantial midden deposit had accumulated on top of the passageways and the hut walls; thus the settlement was, except for the roofs of the huts, buried under its own midden and must have been well protected from cold and draughts.

The stone dwellings themselves are remarkably sophisticated; until the earlier site at Knap of Howar, also in Orkney, was revealed nothing like them was known from the Neolithic or Bronze Age periods except at one other much more ruined Orkney site, at Braes of Rinyo on Rousay Island.[8] At Rinyo Childe found another village of identical dwellings to those at Skara Brae and also the vital clue for dating, missing at the former site. This was a C Beaker of the Early Bronze Age which was stratified in a late level in the village, and it should give a date perhaps in the seventeenth century bc according to the typology of Clarke.[9] Previously, without this clue, Childe had estimated that Skara Brae might belong to the Late Bronze or Early Iron Age[10] and be a village of native Picts (what would now be called 'proto-Picts'[11]). The earlier dating was strikingly confirmed and given greater precision in 1973 by several C-14 dates from samples taken from the top to the base of the Skara Brae midden in new excavations by Drs D. V. Clarke and Anna Ritchie.

The first dates clustered closely together and suggested that 'the settlement was occupied for a relatively short period, perhaps two or three

TABLE 9
Radiocarbon dates for Skara Brae (1973 excavations)

(1) from the main village occupation (the dated samples were taken from the whole range of the midden deposits, the first mentioned being from the top and the others lower down, in sequence):

	calibrated date
1800 ± 110 bc (Birm 433)	2210-2440 BC
2070 ± 110 bc (Birm 434)	2620 BC
1920 ± 100 bc (Birm 435)	2350-2480 BC
2090 ± 110 bc (Birm 436)	2630-2680 BC
1830 ± 110 bc (Birm 437)	2190-2290 BC
2190 ± 120 bc (Birm 438)	2860-2900 BC
2000 ± 100 bc (Birm 477)	2560 BC
1900 ± 140 bc (Birm 478)	2340-2460 BC

(2) from the earliest midden (all on bone):

2400 ± 130 bc (Birm 636)	3150 BC
2480 ± 100 bc (Birm 637)	3180 BC
2480 ± 120 bc (Birm 638)	3180 BC
2450 ± 100 bc (Birm 639)	3160 BC

centuries around 2000 bc'.[12] Subsequently earlier dates were obtained for the base of the deposits, showing that the site had been established as early as the 25th century bc.[13]

The dwellings at Skara Brae are simple in design, being essentially single nearly square chambers or huts with rounded corners; the largest measures 21 by 20 ft and the smallest 14 by 13 ft. The walls still stand up to 7.9 ft high and the internal furnishings are remarkably well preserved, thanks both to the quality of the stone available for building and also to the fact that the whole village was buried under a sand dune at the end of its occupation. Hut 7 is the best preserved and perhaps one of the earliest; it was built directly on the old land surface (though there is a possibility that it was dug down to the depth through midden material).[14] This dwelling was undisturbed before it was excavated by Childe and its contents provided most of the detailed information about life in the village before the excavations of 1972-3.

The hut has the characteristic paved entrance with a hole for the securing wooden drawbar built into the wall; in this case, however, the bar was controlled from a chamber entered only from the outside passageway, not from inside the hut as with all the other examples preserved at the site. In the centre of the floor is the almost square stone paved and kerbed hearth with a cubical stone block next to it serving as a seat. On each side of the hearth, and built against the side walls, are the two box beds formed of large stone slabs on edge which, one supposes, would have been filled with heather or something similar when in use. On the top edge of the end slab of the right bed are the remains of a series of incised marks which form a distinct pattern but much of it has been worn away. Immediately to the left of the entrance (coming in) is a raised dais or working platform and opposite this, against the rear wall, is the famous 'dresser' consisting of two flat, stone shelves supported by three pillar legs. Stone tanks, two stone mortars and a drainage sump are set into the sandy floor and a small intra-mural cell of unknown function opens from the south corner. Some of the similar cells in other huts have drains leading away from them, and were presumably latrines, but this one does not. The crouched skeletons of two old women were found in cists under the wall of this hut; they may have been foundation burials.

Most of the eight huts of the final (phase III) village were built on top of the same midden deposit which covered their walls and there were the ruined foundations of earlier stone huts (phase II) under these walls. Even these earlier huts were themselves lying on midden material which rested on the old land surface, and the corner of a typical Skara Brae hearth was encountered in this phase I level. There was a sand layer of unequal thickness under this first midden but the site was obviously free of massive dunes at this early stage. The pottery and artefacts found in all these levels, including those of the re-occupation of the abandoned village (phase IV), were of the same kind and Childe doubted that the site had been occupied from beginning to end for more than a few generations, a conclusion which seems to have been strikingly confirmed by the C-14 dates already mentioned.

Economy

The inhabitants of Skara Brae were thought by Childe to have been herdsmen since only shellfish remains and animal bones were found in the midden deposits and inside the huts. No traces of cereal grains, or of corn grinding equipment, were noted and this seems to have been confirmed by the excavations of 1972 and 1973 during which extensive and systematic water sieving of the midden deposits failed to reveal a trace of cultivated plants except at the very bottom (below). Nor does fishing seem to have been important. At Rinyo also no traces of agriculture were found and from the lack of gloss on the many flint blades found (sickles with flint blades show a characteristic gloss on the edge) and the absence of saddle querns Childe concluded that none was practised.[15] Nevertheless, in spite of this belief, held apparently without question since 1931, some evidence of the availability of grain might be seen in hut 1 in the form of what looks like a large saddle quern, complete with rubber, on the floor beside the 'dresser'.[16] It could be a trough quern similar to those found in the 'courtyard house' village at Jarlshof in Shetland.[17] Hut 1 was excavated in the nineteenth century and it is not clear whether 'quern' and 'rubber' were in fact found together, although they are so exhibited at the site now.

At the very end of the 1973 excavations at Skara Brae carbonised cereal grains were found in abundance at the base of the midden, a circumstance which makes their absence from the upper levels all the more striking.

Grooved ware

The most striking aspect of the material culture of Skara Brae and Rinyo, and one which has never received an adequate explanation as opposed to a description, is the presence of Late Neolithic Grooved ware at both sites, closely similar to the contemporary pottery found in East Anglia and the Wessex area. When Childe first described the finds from Skara Brae this identity of form and decoration between the pottery of such widely separated regions had not been noted and he was able to conclude that the culture of Skara Brae largely lacked extraneous features and to suggest a date of about the fifth century BC at the earliest for the site.[18] However, in 1936 the close links between the pottery of these two widely separated areas were recognised:[19] the pottery was thought to justify the creation of northern and southern zones of what was subsequently called the Rinyo-Clacton culture, and Skara Brae was accordingly assumed to be of Late Neolithic or Early Bronze Age date (Grooved ware having been found on the submerged land surface at Clacton, Essex, with nothing else later than B Beakers).[20] This dating was confirmed by the discovery of a C Beaker in a secondary level at Rinyo.[21]

Three forms of Grooved ware were found at Skara Brae and Rinyo. Skara Brae A had only patterns in relief and was found in all the levels at that site; ware B, with incised and relief patterns, and ware C, with incised patterns only, turned up only in the first two phases at Skara Brae, not in the main village occupation of phase III. On the other hand, in the two phases distinguished in the Rinyo village, class A sherds were found only in the second one, with the C Beaker, whereas B and C sherds were in the first phase levels as well (there was a deposit at Rinyo earlier than the village but this gave only plain, earlier Neolithic pottery). Thus at both Orkney sites the Grooved ware ornamented with relief patterns was alone in the latest levels, and this division is usually emphasised by calling the two earlier styles (with incised and incised-with-relief decoration) Rinyo I and the relief-ornamented style Rinyo II. The closest similarities with the Grooved ware of the southern province are seen in the Rinyo I style with its emphasis on grooved decoration; relief ornament is rare in the south. As we have seen, Grooved ware is closely associated with the large ceremonial centres of the south and was found in great quantity at Durrington Walls (fig. 33). This situation is what one might expect if there was an early phase of contact between Orkney and the south which was followed by a period when the Skara Brae and Rinyo settlements, or at least their potters, were more isolated.

A recent study of the Rinyo-Clacton culture considered the question of the origins of the Rinyo sub-style of Grooved ware.[22] The authors rejected the ideas that it was an independent northern development which by chance acquired similar formal and decorative traits to the Grooved ware of the south because of similar 'influences', and that both the earlier Orkney Neolithic, incision-decorated Unstan ware and the Beaker pottery contributed to it.[23] The flat-based Rinyo ware shows the same complete contrast with earlier local Neolithic pottery as do the three southern sub-styles and it also shows close similarities with the Grooved ware of the south. The dominance of relief ornament in Rinyo II suggested closer links with the Durrington Walls sub-style than with the other two. Comparisons between the motifs on the Rinyo sherds, notably the well known 'spiral lozenge', and the art styles of the Boyne passage graves are favoured (fig. 33) and are indeed clearer in Orkney than in the south (chapter 10).

Of course this analysis was undertaken before radiocarbon evidence was available for the exact contemporaneity of Durrington Walls and Skara Brae. Also, in common with all other archaeological studies up until now, it does not take into account the significance of the independent evidence for nation-wide social contacts inherent in the conclusions of Thom. Further comments on this theme follow later.

Stone and bone implements

The flint implements found at the two Orkney sites included many standard working tools such as polished-edged knives, an axe and scrapers. Among the stone tools found were axes and adzes, a 'hatchet' of flagstone and mortars and pounders. Some of the mortars look rather like trough querns. There were also perforated mace-heads and some peculiar spiked, decorated objects which may be ceremonial maces. Spiked stone balls occurred and other carved spherical objects which resemble the numerous carved stone balls which have been found unassociated in northeast Scotland. Bone and antler tools were numerous and included chisels, perforated heavy adzes, points and awls as well as scapulae used as shovels. The similarities between some of these bone tools and those of the Mesolithic cultures of northern Europe was noted.[24] There were also many ornamented bone pins, some of which can be closely paralleled in Late Neolithic sites in southern England and others of which resemble pins found in the Iberian chambered tombs.

The equipment of two huts

Hut 7 was explored systematically by Childe, and it seems to have been abandoned suddenly by its occupants judging from the many whole artefacts found apparently left where they had last been in use. The floor was strewn with food refuse — fragments of animal bones and shells — and this rubbish had occasionally been covered by paving slabs. The complete skull of a calf was in the left hand bed together with a fine tusk pendant, several pins and beads, a Skaill stone knife and a broken pot with a slate lid. In the right bed lay a bone shovel and other pins and beads. Several tools, including seven flint flakes, two pairs of bone adzes, a stone axe and a carved stone ball, lay on the floor between the beds and the central hearth while a great monolithic stone slab, presumably a roof support, had fallen and crushed a pot near the hearth. A whalebone basin was near the right bed. On the raised dais near the entrance was another whalebone basin, a stone mortar and two large pots which had contained bones. In the left corner of the hut a small whalebone dish full of red pigment was embedded in the floor while in the mural cell there was a pot and a collection of beads and pendants. A large pot had stood on the 'dresser' and another between the limpet boxes in the right rear corner.

Hut 8 was set apart from the others and was the only one which seemed not to have been a dwelling. It was equipped with a hearth but had no beds of the usual type and no 'dresser'. Instead there was a large recess in each side wall where the bed would have been and a doorway in the rear wall led to an annexe or small room outside the hut proper but only reached from it. In this annexe was a packed layer of burnt stones, possibly the base of a kiln or oven or perhaps a collection of pot boilers used for cooking. There were very few domestic artefacts in hut 8 but the whole floor was littered with the debris of a flint knapper's work in the form of cores, flakes and scrapers. Several of the stones of the hut bore scratched and engraved designs.

Catastrophe and re-occupation

The excavation of hut 7 showed clearly that the occupation of this house, and presumably of the whole village, had ended abruptly. The equipment was found, buried in the intrusive sand fill, where it had been left by the occupants. That these people had rushed out in a hurry was plainly shown by Childe's discovery of a cluster of bone beads from a necklace in the doorway and by a scatter of several more down the passage. He surmised that the owner of the necklace had broken it while squeezing hastily through the door and that the remaining beads had dropped off as she fled down the passage.[25] On the surface of the covering midden too were found many pots, apparently broken where they had been standing, and many entire tools, neither worn nor broken. It seemed that the inhabitants had been accustomed to live and work on the top of the mound covering the village in fine weather and had abandoned their equipment there when the disaster struck.

Childe deduced that no hostile raid had occurred because all the tools and ornaments were in place. He decided that a great storm, similar to the ones which originally exposed the site in about 1850 and damaged it again in 1924, had blown up and that this had moved the sand dunes towards the village causing the inhabitants to leave suddenly. Skara Brae was then partially buried in sand. The fall of the stone roof pillar in hut 7 supports the idea that the disaster was sudden.

However it seems that the inhabitants came back and continued to live in some of the half-filled huts (another argument perhaps against the idea of a hostile raid). Childe found clear evidence of this re-occupation in hut 7 in the form of four habitation levels in the sandy infill. The first of these was represented by a stone hearth of normal Skara Brae type, laid 3 ft above the floor and associated with a stratum of ash, shells and antler fragments up to a foot thick. The three other layers were higher up, the uppermost being 5½ ft above the original floor. Clean sand lay on this to a depth of 1 ft and on this was a mass of rubble fallen from the hut walls which filled the interior (no rubble was reported as lying on the original floor). Childe noted that the food debris of these later occupants of Skara Brae differed markedly from the diet available before the disaster; deer bones and shellfish remains were dominant in the phase IV levels whereas in the earlier midden deposits bones of sheep and cattle were abundant and those of deer very rare.[26] He also eventually concluded that it was not just a matter of hut 7 being abandoned by itself but that the whole village suffered at the same time. Similar traces of re-occupation, including a female burial, were reported from hut 1 in the nineteenth century.[27]

SKARA BRAE: A RE-ASSESSMENT

The clear archaeological links between the inhabitants of Skara Brae and Rinyo and those of the great ceremonial centres of southern England, seen in the occurrence at both sites of Grooved ware and in the exact contemporaneity of the two groups of sites now revealed by the C-14 dates, is surely sufficient reason to suspect that there is more to the Orkney settlements than the simple stone dwellings of peasant herdsmen. When one considers that it is possible to make a good case that the southern ceremonial centres were the headquarters, residences and training schools of a Late Neolithic learned order of astronomer-priests and wise men whose works are visible throughout the country in the stone circles and standing stones, a comparable re-assessment of the significance of Skara Brae becomes inevitable. There are many features of the site itself which are open to re-interpretation.

The nature of the village

One feature of the village has never been commented on: the striking contrast between the architectural sophistication and elaboration of the stone dwellings — unmatched in prehistoric Europe — and the supposed impoverishment of the inhabitants, ignorant as they are supposed to have been of agriculture and eking out a 'living under miserable conditions on a sea coast'.[28] The standard theory, accepted unquestioningly because no alternative has been offered, is that this was the normal (miserable?) dwelling of a Neolithic peasant translated, with its furniture, into stone thanks to the unique qualities of the locally available building material.[29] But in the light of the rapidly increasing evidence for the presence of an élite class of wise men throughout the country at that time, an alternative hypothesis comes to mind which might explain the evidence better. Could Skara Brae and Rinyo have been the residences of some of these wise men and their families who were engaged in astronomical, ceremonial and magical work in the Orkney Islands? In other words, could Skara Brae and Rinyo have been the Late Neolithic equivalents of an Orkney Early Christian monastic site like Deerness[30] or a Maya priest's stone residence in British Honduras?[31] Could they, like both these analogous structures, be groups of rare stone buildings among a rural population which was mainly housed in wooden or turf-walled huts with thatched or turved roofs? However, the question must be framed in direct archaeological terms. What we want to know, first, is whether Skara Brae is plausible as a standard peasant's dwelling, and second, whether it could be interpreted better if it is assumed that its inhabitants were not primarily engaged in agriculture and herding but were supported by the local peasant population.

Many features of the two Orkney sites and the finds recovered from them could be said to fall more neatly into place on the assumption that we are dealing with the residences of a non-agricultural upper class. In the first place there is simply nothing else like them known and this alone should be enough at least to cast some doubt on the peasant dwelling hypothesis (the Neolithic dwellings at Knap of Howar are different in design[32]). There are 55 Neolithic chambered cairns on the islands of Orkney[33] and about 100 Iron Age brochs.[34] Both these groups of buildings may reasonably be attributed to the activities of minorities of some kind with control over large labour forces, so there must surely have been a correspondingly large rural population in Orkney earlier in the Neolithic period, totalling some thousands at the very least. Yet we have only three small settlements for them, housing a few score of people at the most! It may be objected of course that the brochs and chambered tombs are massive structures the remains of which are obvious above ground, and that flimsier domestic dwellings, even of stone, are more easily wrecked and their remains buried out of sight. A better analogy might be with the earth-houses or souterrains of Orkney — Iron Age underground chambers with passage-like entrances communicating with the surface by a single inconspicuous shaft. In the case of structures like these it is not surprising that relatively few are known since little masonry occurs near the surface; yet even so there are 21 known and recorded souterrains in Orkney and the great majority of them are much smaller than Skara Brae.[35]

Another analogy might be drawn with the wheelhouses of the Western

Isles, even though it is by no means clear whether these Iron Age round dwellings were built for the mass of the rural population or were the mansions of an upper class of a Celtic aristocracy: the latter is a clear possibility.[36] Most of the wheelhouses are in North and South Uist, Benbecula and Barra and they stand by themselves; most are dug-out structures partly sunk into the ground. Many wheelhouses have been discovered over the years; a total of about 12 which have been explored in one way or another can be listed[37] and Lethbridge claimed, after some years of fieldwork, to know of 22 wheelhouse sites in South Uist and Barra alone.[38] It is true that there was probably a larger population in Atlantic Scotland in the Iron Age than in Late Neolithic times, but the fact still remains that there are far fewer brochs and chambered cairns in the Long Island south of Harris (and fewer still in Harris and Lewis) than there are in the Orkneys. The total of known and suspected brochs in this Hebridean zone is 17 (11 more in Harris and Lewis) and of chambered cairns about 34.[39] The value of this analogy is reduced because not a great number of wheelhouse and allied dwellings are known from Orkney (about 6) but the comparison with the souterrains certainly suggests that Skara Brae and Rinyo are something very unusual indeed.

The sophisticated architecture of Skara Brae has in fact always been suggesting this, and the contrast between, on the one hand, the splendour of these Neolithic dwellings, with their sub-floor drains, well designed chambers (some with internal privies) and complex of interconnecting covered passages, and on the other the supposed impoverishment of the inhabitants, is striking indeed. By the standards of Neolithic Scotland, and England too for that matter, Skara Brae was surely a palatial structure, almost as far removed from the dwellings of the rural population as was a Roman villa in Wessex some two millennia later. The filthy state of the rooms, commented on by Childe, need present no obstacle to the theory that they were the residences of a small élite; only a few centuries ago the domestic habits of European upper classes were deplorable by modern standards.

There are one or two other features about the site, apart from the quality of the structures, which seem a little odd if it was a simple peasant community. For example hut 7 has a unique arrangement for barring the door from *outside* the room, not from within as with the other huts: this chamber could then have been used as a prison and anyone inside would have had no means of getting out except through the roof. Obviously it is impossible 4,500 years later to determine why hut 7 was designed in this way, particularly as it was equipped with the normal domestic furniture and was in use, presumably as a dwelling, at the time of the final catastrophe. Yet its unusual door-bar might just be comprehensible in terms of a small community of religious and wise men. Such a room might have been used for vigils, or for penance, or for concentrated study at some stage.

It may also be relevant too that hut 7 contains the only stone carving from the village that looks at all like an inscription.[40] It runs along the edge of the front slab of the right bed and most of the lines have been worn away, presumably by the use of the slab as a bench: they are preserved only where protected by the upright post slabs at the ends. This could suggest that the carving was made before the stone was used for the bed and that hut 7 might originally have had a different function with which the externally controlled drawbar was connected. The carving consists of a series of transverse lines across the edge of the stone at approximately equal intervals and of rough St Andrew's crosses carved within the divisions so made. It resembles the calendars the author remembers making as a boy — a series of squares representing days, in a ladder pattern leading up to some important event, which were crossed off with diagonal strokes or crosses. It is surely not beyond the bounds of possibility, particularly in view of the astronomical activities which are now suspected to have been carried on, that this carving is the remains of a calendric record or tally connected with the occurrence of ceremonial and celestial events (which were probably not distinguished at that time).

The economy of Skara Brae

The peculiar absence of evidence for the growing or consumption of cereals at Skara Brae, until the excavations of 1973, has always been thought striking and an important pointer to the nature of the community which lived in the village. It could, however, be easily explicable if the village was the residence of a group of priests and wise men, and their families, which depended on tribute or on bought or bartered produce to maintain itself. Bags of grain — or flour or actual loaves of bread if there really are no querns there — could have been brought to the site together with supplies of meat. Now that the new excavations have in fact revealed abundant traces of carbonised cereal grains at the base of the midden,[41] it becomes doubly difficult to assume that the inhabitants of Skara Brae were simple herdsmen ignorant of agriculture, and the hypothesis of a non-farming and non-herding élite seems to be strengthened. The discovery of grain also provides a sharp lesson that the maxim that 'absence of evidence is not evidence of absence' is an important one for archaeologists to remember.

The evidence of the animal bone remains provides us with a better opportunity to assess the nature of the inhabitants of the village, although unfortunately no exact data is available on the bones recovered from the earlier excavations: no doubt this will be remedied by the new work. Analyses of the parts of the animals represented should reveal whether live flocks were kept nearby (in which case fragments of all parts of the skeletons should appear) or whether only edible cut joints were brought to the site. If the latter situation prevailed it would suggest strongly that the community was being supplied with meat butchered elsewhere, either as tribute or gifts. Professor Childe, discussing the animal bones found during his excavations at Skara Brae, noted that those found in the middens which had accumulated during the life of the main village were almost entirely of sheep and cattle, sheep being by far the commonest; bones of wild animals were extremely rare.[42] This dominance of domestic animals contrasted sharply with the situation in the deposits which accumulated after the catastrophic abandonment of the village.

Dietary evidence for specialist classes

It can be shown that the existence of non-farming specialists can be reflected in the proportions of the various kinds of animal bones found in the middens of an Iron Age site, and this evidence is very relevant to the situation at Skara Brae. The excavation of the broch of Dun Mor Vaul on the island of Tiree, Argyllshire, in 1962-4 uncovered a long series of stratified deposits extending from the late sixth or fifth century BC probably down to the end of the third century AD and a detailed analysis of the animal bones recovered was carried out by Barbara Noddle.[43] The following table illustrates her results in summary form; the percentages of animal bones of various species found in the deposits of the six major phases of the site's occupation are shown together with a summary which distinguishes simply between the percentages of bones of wild and domestic animals in each phase. The phases represent: the pre-broch settlement (I), the building of the broch (II), its primary occupation as a fort (IIIa), its use as a dwelling, probably by a single family (IIIb), its use as a dwelling in the same way but after the demolition of the walls (IV), and an occupation on top of the abandoned ruins (V).

TABLE 10

Frequency of animal bones in six phases at Dun Mor Vaul

total bones	approx date	phase	Domestic %			Wild %				
			sheep	cattle	all domestic	roe deer	red deer	pig	bird	all wild
84	500-300 BC	I	31	18	49	32	13	2	4	51
445	c. 50 BC	II	66	18	84	3	10	2	1	16
237	50 BC-AD 200	IIIa	35	30	65	14	15	5	1	35
80	AD 200-250	IIIb	25	29	54	5	21	11	9	46
466	AD 250-300	IV	26	29	55	6	22	2	15	45
245	c. 300-320	V	14	14	28	2	25	4	41	72

Several aspects of this table require comment. In terms of the overall proportions between wild and domestic animal bones the major site phases fall clearly into two groups. The deposits which were the middens of a normal, mixed-farming domestic site (or, in the case of IIIa, of the peasant

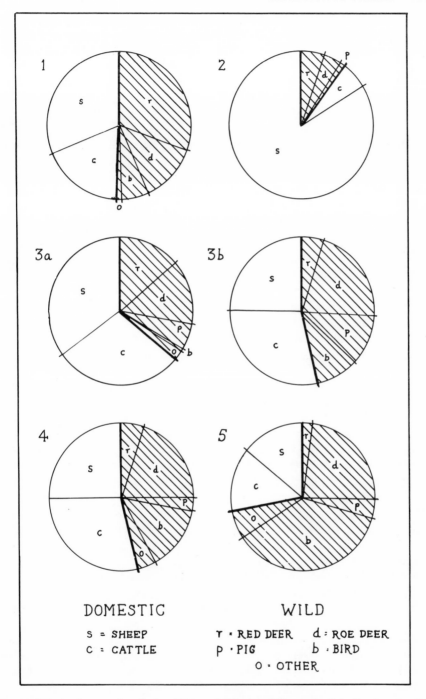

Fig. 29. Relative frequencies of animal bones of different edible species found in six successive deposits at the Iron Age site of Dun Mor Vaul, Tiree, Inner Hebrides

population taking temporary refuge at intervals inside the broch) show a fairly similar division between the domestic and wild animals eaten. The pre-broch phase I and phases IIIa, IIIb and IV show a roughly 50:50 division between the two groups. (Although there is a somewhat higher proportion of domestic bones in phase IIIa (65%), this is perhaps to be explained by the conditions of that period. It was presumably not so easy to hunt game while taking refuge in a broch and the wild bones in these layers should represent the game already caught when the emergency began.) On the other hand phases II and V are entirely distinct, showing a far higher proportion of domestic and wild animals respectively, and these two episodes require further comment.

The phase II deposits are unique at the site and nothing like them has been found in any of the other 50 or so brochs so far excavated. The layers which were clearly associated with the construction of the broch consisted of two groups; first, several deposits of clay-like material inserted as floor packing into uneven rock clefts in the intra-mural gallery to produce an approximately level surface, and second, one large deposit of successive layers of laminated clay which had been laid down directly on the rubble foundation underlying the broch wall in a specially designed, wider section of the wall gallery. This section formed a small lintelled cell or room which had been intensively inhabited for a short period at a very early stage in the history of the site; masses of large sherds and fresh-looking animal bones were found in these floor deposits which had presumably been renewed by adding a fresh layer of clay when the accumulations of sherds and bones became too inconvenient underfoot. For various reasons it seems highly likely that this section of the gallery was lived in by one or two people when the broch was actually being constructed (a process which might have taken about seven months if a gang of about 60 men was available and working continuously[41]), and that they were the supervisors of the project — professional broch-builders perhaps. During construction the central court would have been open to the sky and full of building stones, but the ground level wall gallery, once it had been lintelled over, would have served as an excellent shelter. When the broch was completed, the central court would have been much more attractive, of course, and extensive floor deposits of phase IIIa were in fact found there — and there are clear signs that the gallery was then abandoned as a residence.[45]

Table 10 shows an exceptionally high proportion (84%) of domestic animal bones in the phase II deposits, but in fact the figure is even higher than this because several other strata were included in phase II in this table and may have been slightly earlier. If we take only .the bones which were found in the unequivocal construction deposits in the mural gallery described, we get a slightly different picture (fig. 29). In this case it seems likely that the number of bones is more relevant to the present discussion than the minimum number of animals they represent since whole animals are unlikely to have been brought to the site to feed the supervisors; joints of meat are far more probable. The great preponderance of sheep bones is most striking — they form 87% of all the bones found, a far higher figure than on any other part of the site — and it combines well with the rather clear evidence of the non-agricultural nature of the people consuming the food of which these bones are the debris. The obvious explanation is that the broch engineer (and his assistant or wife?) who was hired to supervise the construction of the tower was provided with mutton and beef by the local chief during the several months he was on the job. This inference about the nature of the occupation was made from the deposits excavated at the site and long before the information about the animal bones was compiled, so the unusual proportions of the animal bones may be said to lend convincing support to the broch engineer hypothesis.

Phase II at Dun Mor Vaul is strikingly similar to the main occupation of Skara Brae two millennia earlier, where the proportion of domestic animal remains in the midden deposits of the main village occupation, particularly sheep, was again extraordinarily high. It seems reasonable to assume that a population of ordinary Neolithic peasants, herding domestic sheep and cattle, would supplement its diet of mutton and beef with as much game as possible, both for the sake of variety and to avoid killing valuable livestock unnecessarily. It is true that if Skara Brae and Rinyo are left aside we do not yet have a late Neolithic domestic site in Orkney which can be confidently identified as the dwellings of the agricultural population, so it is not yet possible to make the direct comparison between the diet of a possible élite group and that of ordinary peasant farmers living in the same area that was possible at Dun Mor Vaul. However, it does seem reasonable to assume that Tiree and Orkney were in the same broad economic zone in prehistoric times, and that the Vaul evidence is highly relevant to problems of the nature of the population of Skara Brae — more so perhaps than the material from contemporary Durrington Walls where the bones show that pig was the animal most frequently eaten (chapter 7). This relevance seems to be confirmed by the similarities in what happened at the two Atlantic Scottish sites after the main stone buildings were abandoned.

Catastrophe and re-occupation

Certain features of the catastrophe that brought to an end the main occupation of Skara Brae may be relevant to the problem of the nature of the primary function of the village, and are also of interest in their own right. The disaster which tore off the roofs of the huts, partly filled them with clean sand and caused the occupants to bolt outside at a moment's notice has been thought to be a violent storm which set the dunes moving, and there is the evidence of the instantaneous abandonment of hut 7 described earlier. But do these two sets of facts fit the hypothesis? They can, except for a small element of doubt which could arise from the rather clear picture of someone fleeing out of the house in such a haste that a valued necklace was broken and scattered. Were it not for the intact artefacts and the undeniable immediately following sandstorm, this could be more plausibly explained by an enemy attack. Even if such a thing did not occur one might guess that a steadily rising windstorm would not necessarily produce such a sudden terror; efforts would surely have been made to lash down the roofs (the only part of the structures vulnerable to such storms) and to hold them down from the outside. This task could well have been abandoned as hopeless until the storm died down, but surely not necessarily in a panic. Also there must have been time in the early stages of such a storm to store valuables in the lintelled passageways, which were still intact under their stone roofs when they were excavated and would have provided excellent shelter for the villagers. Then there is the fact that the village was not entirely buried; a layer of only 3 ft of sand was lying in hut 7 when the first re-occupation took place (below) and this hardly suggests a huge dune overwhelming the site.

One flees suddenly from a stone building for two good reasons: either because of the approach of a murderous enemy or for fear that the stone walls will fall in on one. The former danger, though still a possibility, seems unlikely because of the intact condition of the interior of the hut, and the latter fear in a pre-artillery age is most likely to be produced by the roaring and trembling of an approaching earthquake and by knowledge of the effects that this could have. We may note that the stone roof pillar fell flat before any sand blew in — perhaps as if shaken down by a tremor — but we must also note that no part of the drystone walls fell in at this stage, so that if there was an earth tremor, it was more frightening than destructive. Certainly a windstorm must have raged at the time, or soon after, to fill the dwellings partly with sand.

The nature of the disaster at Skara Brae is commented on here simply to illustrate how explanations other than the traditional ones can come to mind when the evidence is re-examined. Nothing definite can be inferred from a single site about the scale of natural disasters, but the evidence from such sites can suggest lines of research to pursue with the aim of reconstructing the broader picture of what happened at the time, if there is one.

Further instructive inferences can be made if the evidence for the re-occupation of hut 7 at Skara Brae, after the alarming storm (?) had passed, is examined again. The first hearth of the re-occupation period (phase IV), made in the standard village form, was laid on a thickness of about 3 ft of clean sand which had presumably blown in through the wrecked roof. It seems unlikely that any of this sand had previously been dug out: if it had been, why was the relatively simple task of removing the last yard not completed and the chamber thus restored to its original condition, incidentally recovering in the process many presumably useful artefacts? The failure to clear the structurally sound hut 7 (and presumably the rest of the village also) is hard to understand if only a storm had caused the trouble, and it is even more inexplicable when one considers that at least one major reconstruction of the stone dwellings had been undertaken by an earlier generation. The change in diet in the post-disaster period from an abundance of mutton and beef to shellfish and hunted venison is equally striking and suggests that the disaster did more than tear the roofs off a few huts and half fill them with sand. Either the flocks of sheep and cattle belonging to the village were destroyed or stolen or — the interpretation favoured here — the tribute and gifts brought to the priestly residents of Skara Brae suddenly ceased, perhaps for similar reasons.

One gets a rather vivid picture of a suddenly impoverished community, lacking the will or skill to clear their intact stone dwellings of sand properly and having to subsist on hunted venison and shellfish. Alternatively of course, and in spite of the carefully made hearth, the original inhabitants could have departed and the half-filled ruins been taken over by a band of hunters and food gatherers. In either case the decline in culture after the disaster is extremely marked and suggests the collapse of more than a few roofs; if the interpretation of the nature of the village offered here is right, then a whole social organisation supporting an élite group had also collapsed. The lack of purposeful effort in the final stages of life in the village brings out by contrast the unusually high standard of living enjoyed by the people of the last phase (III) of the main village occupation, and tends to confirm that it was something more than a community of peasant herdsmen.

We may look again at the rather clear evidence of the animal bones from the Iron Age site on Tiree, referred to earlier. At Dun Mor Vaul phase IV was the last period when the site was a flourishing farm where barley was grown, domestic animals kept and a variety of other activities such as spinning, weaving, iron working and bronze casting practised. There is a suggestion that a hostile raid took place at the end of phase IV; occupation of the broch abruptly ceased, a silver finger-ring was hidden in a crack in the wall, the reduced broch fell rapidly into ruin and turf grew over the outer court, once the scene of many domestic activities. However, the rubble filling the open mural gallery (but not that in the broch interior) contained many native sherds of the kind used on Tiree for the previous seven or eight centuries at least; the new pottery that had appeared on the site with the broch builders perhaps three centuries earlier had largely disappeared. It seems that a few people, presumably natives or impoverished rulers, continued to live for a while on the ruined site.

As at Skara Brae the diet of these post-disaster inhabitants at Vaul provides a sharp contrast with that of the preceding periods; no querns were found in these late levels and no less than 72% of the bones found were of wild animals. An exceptionally high proportion of these were of birds (41%) while sheep bones were the fewest in the whole history of the site. The drastic impoverishment of the phase V survivors at Vaul is thus reflected as clearly in their diet as in their destroyed settlement and their probably massacred leaders. The skill and will to build or repair a massive drystone structure had evidently gone and with it the ability to organise a flourishing farming community. As seems to have happened at Skara Brae, the social organisation of the broch and post-broch periods had evidently disintegrated and was never restored — in both cases perhaps because the organisers had vanished in some disaster. Yet the impression is of a greater decline at Skara Brae; whereas the phase V people at Vaul had some domestic animals, the post-catastrophe occupants of ruined Skara Brae evidently had hardly any and were reduced entirely to living off game and shellfish.

Residences and temples

It should be clear that there are now at least as many, if not more, reasons for interpreting Skara Brae as the architecturally unusual residences of a specialist élite group supported by the agricultural population as there are for thinking of it as the stone version of a normal village of rural peasant herdsmen of the Late Neolithic period. In fact several features of the site could be said to be explained better by this new interpretation. A better analogy is obtained by comparing Skara Brae and Rinyo with the monastic sites of the Early Christian period in the era before the arrival in Scotland of the elaborate Romanesque architectural tradition, rather than with the wheelhouse farms of the post-broch Iron Age. If the historical records for such monastic settlements were not available, and if we did not know what Early Christian chapels and churches looked like and were unaware that a new religion had appeared in the centuries following the fall of the Roman Empire, it would not be easy to identify for example the Deerness site, or the Brough of Birsay as it was in Pictish times, as other than defended settlements, perhaps with one larger, rectangular, stone chief's house. Of course the historical records about the establishment of such monastic communities never allowed such an interpretation to be considered seriously by scholars. Skara Brae, on the other hand, is truly prehistoric and the understandable archaeological practice of deducing only the bare minimum from the evidence was naturally applied. Now, however, we have some equivalent external evidence, albeit non-documentary, for the existence of learned orders of religious and wise men in Late Neolithic times, and Skara Brae and Rinyo should — particularly in view of their undeniable close archaeological links with the great ceremonial centres of Wiltshire — take their places as the equivalents in 2000 bc of Deerness and Brough of Birsay — as the superior residences of these orders. No doubt the inhabitants included both people from southern England, evidenced by the Grooved ware (which seems to have its closest resemblances with that of the south when it first appears), and local people, as shown by the presence of artefacts of undeniably local origin.

Indeed there may be greater resemblances between Skara Brae and the

Early Christian monastic sites — not to mention the giant henges of Wessex — than has been hitherto suggested even here. There may be a possibility that the village was built within a henge monument of the Marden type, that it was partly surrounded by a bank-and-ditch boundary which curved round to the seashore on both sides (fig. 24). Such a feature has never been looked for under the sand and the possibility of its existence is something that should be considered and investigated. Presumably, since the village itself rests on the old ground surface, any such bank and ditch would also be buried under the surrounding dunes and the latter at least would be well preserved. Until such a feature is sought for and found it must be admitted that the possibility of its existence is there, particularly in view of the close ceramic links with the Wiltshire henges already referred to and of the exact contemporaneity of the two groups of sites.

It is interesting to look at a plan of the area next to the Bay of Skaill, a short distance northeast of the prehistoric village, which was made in 1772 by F. H. Walden; it is now in the British Museum and a photograph of it was recently published.[46] This appears to show a rampart in two adjacent lengths (the narrow gap between them might be an entrance) on the north side of the outlet river from the Loch of Skaill to the sea and with a possible further fragment of rampart on the south side of this river and just beyond the village (fig. 27). Various presumably prehistoric graves in stone cists were seen in the enclosed area in the late eighteenth century and some were explored by Joseph Banks and George Low.[47] Skara Brae is, as noted, a short distance further southwest along the shore from these 'ramparts', which, in any case, seem rather large to be artificial. In fact a detailed comparison between the 1772 map and the recent contoured 6 inch map of the area by the Ordnance Survey suggests that Walden's hatched 'ramparts' are representations of the low hills nearby and are not traces of earthworks.[48] The possibility that Skara Brae was within a ditched enclosure like Durrington Walls of course remains.

There is one sharp distinction, however, which must be drawn between Skara Brae and the Early Christian monastic sites with which analogies have been drawn: no structure remotely resembling a church or temple has been identified either at the Skaill site or at Rinyo. However, beside the Loch of Stenness, some 5 miles due southeast of Skara Brae, stands the Ring of Brodgar, one of the largest circular henge monuments outside Wiltshire and one which contains one of the biggest stone circles known.

THE RING OF BRODGAR

Archaeology

The Ring of Brodgar stands on sloping ground on the isthmus between Loch of Stenness and Loch of Harray, on the mainland of Orkney (grid ref.

HY 294133). The remaining standing stones — long thin slabs of neatly split Old Red sandstone — are a conspicuous landmark. In 1971 and 1972 the site was surveyed and analysed afresh[49] and the description in the following sections relies mainly on this new work.

The site is a class II henge with two opposed entrances, consisting of causeways across the ditch, in the northwest and southeast but it lacks a bank. The diameter of the base of the circular ditch is about 408 ft (150 MY) and that of the enclosed stone circle some 367 ft. The average width of the berm is about 10 ft and the ditch itself is some 29½ ft wide and 6 ft deep: it encloses about 2½ acres. A total of 37 stones remain in position to be measured, either still standing or re-erected or traceable as stumps. There are fallen slabs from some of the rest and the original total was probably 60 stones.[50] However, a considerable amount of re-erection of the stones seems to have been undertaken by the Office of Works after it had taken over the site in about 1840.[51] A plan of the site made in 1772 shows only 14 stones still upright[52] but now there are 27, though only 21 of these are higher than 5 ft. The great sandstone slabs may have been dragged 6 miles from the ancient quarry at Vestra Fiold where similar slabs can still be seen, detached but never used.[53]

Geometry and orientation

The average thickness of the stone slabs is about 9 in, and since they are aligned along the circumference of the circle with their flat sides facing the centre, it was possible to determine with great accuracy the degree of precision with which the Ring had been laid out. The stumps and standing stones were found to be positioned at intervals of almost exactly 6°, starting from true north; the amount of variation from multiples of 6° at the centre of the face of each slab was usually no more than 9' of arc and this shows rather clearly that not only was a N-S line laid out to that sort of accuracy (about 1/6th of a degree) before the circle was laid out, but also that the designers of the Ring were capable of the accurate subdivision of the circumference into 60 parts.

The stones themselves were found, with two exceptions, to have been erected extremely close to the circumference of a true circle with a mean diameter of 340.02 ft ± 0.60. Most of the stones are within 2 ft of this circle, but stones 7 and 8 are substantially off, being 6 ft and 4 ft 7 in inside it respectively. In fact it is clear from Walden's survey of 1772 that these two stones were then prostrate,[54] so their modern positions need not be the same as their original ones. If stones 7 and 8 are excluded from the measurements the mean diameter of the ring becomes 340.66 ft ± 0.44. This independent survey and analysis thus produced a 'best fit' circle for the Ring with a diameter close to 125 of the megalithic yards of 2.72 ft (0.829 m) (totalling 340.00 ft) inferred from the statistical analysis of the dimensions of scores of stone circles on the mainland of Scotland and in

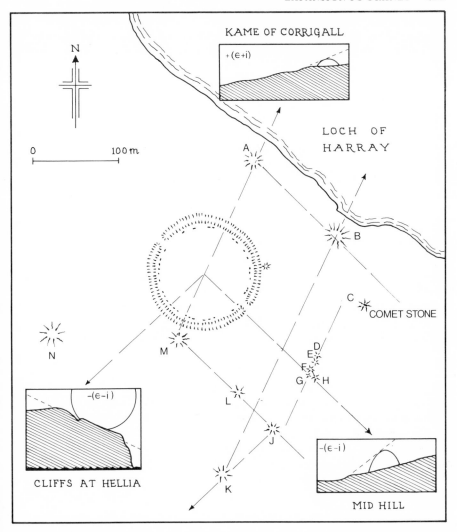

Fig. 30. Plan of the Ring of Brodgar stone circle, Orkney, with some suggested astronomical alignments, after A. Thom

England (chapter 2). Thom believes that the diameter of 125 MY was chosen because it is equivalent to 50 megalithic rods (2½ MY), a unit which he has inferred to have been extensively used at Carnac in Brittany.[55] Moreover the circumference of a circle 50 rods in diameter is 157.08 rods, and evidence from other sites has led Thom to suppose that the diameters of true circles, and the geometry of other shapes, were often chosen to make the resulting perimeters whole numbers of megalithic rods (see Woodhenge, chapter 8). We may assume that the circle builders were ignorant of the formula $2\pi r$ for calculating circumferences and that they must therefore have discovered the right radii by trial and error, by measuring round the perimeters of the drawn figures (marked with pegs). In the case of the Ring of Brodgar the result of measuring along the chords between wooden pegs 6° apart (before the stones were set up of course) would be a total of 157.01 MR, indistinguishable on the ground with the tools then available (and probably with those available to archaeologists now!) either from the desired 157 MR or from the true circumference of 157.08 MR. The ring's dimensions are exactly the same as those of the southern circle at Avebury (chapter 6).

The geometry of the Ring of Brodgar is of particular importance in view of the thinness of the stone slabs, the precision of their setting, and of the fact that the results give a surprisingly exact and independent confirmation of the value of the megalithic yard. It is particularly interesting that this value can be obtained here on an exactly set out site by dividing the diameter of the calculated 'best fit' circle by a round whole number of megalithic yards or rods, a method which, applied elsewhere, has led to the suspicion that the length of the measuring sticks for the megalithic yard actually varied a little over an inch or two across the British Isles (chapter 2).

Possible astronomical uses

The Ring, however, is not of interest solely for its precise geometry and orientation towards true north; its location is such that it could have been the central part of a series of important astronomical observation points.[56] There are a number of small outlying mounds and cairns in the vicinity of the Ring, as well as some nearby standing stones (including the Comet stone 200 yards to the east), which seem to fit well the assumption that the designers of the site were much concerned with tracking the movements of the moon with the help of various natural marks on the visible horizon. An overall impression of the plausibility of this interpretation is obtained from Thom's fig. 4[57] which shows the Ring and its neighbouring cairns (fig. 30).

As was described in chapter 4, the vagaries of the moon's movements have a conventional shorthand to describe them (fig. 17). Epsilon (ε) represents the obliquity of the ecliptic (equivalent to the declination of the sun at the solstices and to the tilt of the earth's axis); iota (ι) represents the 5.15° fluctuation of the moon's position on either side of ε (which arises because of the tilt of the lunar orbit in relation to that of the earth and which has a cycle of 18.6 years), while delta (Δ) represents the 9 minute wobble on either side of all the other movements with a cycle of 175.31 days. The s represents the moon's apparent radius (semi-diameter) of 15.5'. In this terminology $-s$ (i.e. minus s) indicates that the moon's *upper* limb is at the notch concerned at the southerly (low) standstills and its *lower* limb at the northerly (high) standstills, while $+s$ indicates the reverse: upper limb at northerly and lower limb at southerly standstills. If no s is present it is assumed that the chosen sight-line was aimed at the centre of the moon's disc.

For example an observer standing on the three small cairns M, L and J south of the Ring can look to the southwest where the vertical cliff at the western end of Hoy island (Hellia Holm) can be seen 5.15 miles away. There is a small notch in the slope leading to the cliff and the setting moon with its lower edge exactly in the base of this notch has three significant declinations when seen from these three cairns. From cairn M, the one closest to the Ring, the moon in this position would have had a declination of $-19°\ 00'.2$, very close to $-(\varepsilon - \imath + s)$, the southerly minor standstill, when the obliquity of the ecliptic was $23°\ 54'$. From cairn L, further to the left when looking at the notch, it has a declination of $-(\varepsilon - \imath + s - \Delta)$, that is the southerly minor standstill with the 9' 'wobble' at its minimum. From cairn J, still further to the left, the declination is $-(\varepsilon - \imath)$, the southerly minor standstill itself detected by using the centre of the lunar disc. These alignments could thus have been used to watch the moon every 18.61 years when its monthly swing (change in declination) was at a minimum and could have had the added possibility of detecting the superimposed 9 minute wobble ($\pm \Delta$), with its cycle of 173.3 days, a knowledge of which can provide a valuable clue to the prediction of eclipses.[58]

Similarly there is a notch visible 3.74 miles southeast of the Ring, on Mid Hill, in which the rising moon at its southerly minor standstill ($-(\varepsilon - \imath)$) should have been visible — also in such a way that the 9' wobble could have been detected — from the three positions A, C and M. The flat slab of the Comet stone is orientated towards this notch (thus making it a more reliable indicated alignment) which has a declination of $-(\varepsilon - \imath + s - \Delta)$ when seen from it. The third possible foresight is Kame of Corrigall, 5.12 miles away to the NNE and at which the rising of the moon at the major northerly standstill ($+(\varepsilon + \imath)$), including the 9' wobble, should have been visible from the two points R and J (fig. 30). No signs have been noted at the Ring of Brodgar of the fan-shaped extrapolation grids which would have been needed to work out the maximum declinations from the observations of the relatively rapidly moving moon which were actually made in the notches.[59]

10
Late Neolithic Society: Crisis and Response

In the previous chapters I have tried to show that the archaeological evidence surviving from the Britain of 3000-1500 BC will support two major explanatory social hypotheses of kinds not hitherto considered seriously, if at all, by prehistorians. The first hypothesis depends almost entirely on the work of Alexander Thom together with a little similar work by other hands and one excavation designed to test his specific interpretation of one site. It supposes that considerable achievements were made at that time in 'intellectual' matters, namely elements of what was later called Euclidean geometry, of field surveying and exact measurement to a high degree of skill, and of observational astronomy of a systematic and advanced kind. A corollary of this is here taken to be that such achievements are only credible in a stratified Neolithic society, one which was organised to allow specialised groups to pursue these activities for the whole of their time, supported by mass labour when necessary and always by surplus food. The second major hypothesis follows from this and is that Middle and Late Neolithic society, in southern Britain certainly and probably elsewhere, was indeed organised in this way and that groups of wise men — perhaps a theocratic élite — lived a life apart in special ceremonial centres or monasteries which can be identified both by their unusual nature and also by specific evidence from artefacts and food refuse.

THE MAYA CIVILISATION

The analogy preferred here is with the Classic Maya civilisation of Central America, despite its many apparent differences in detail, and a few words about this remarkable culture are appropriate at this point.[1] The origins of the Maya people seem to lie in the highland areas of southwest Guatemala, but by about the middle of the first millennium BC they had entered the densely forested riverine lowlands of the Petén district of Guatemala and the riverless bush country to the north in what is now the Yucatan province of Mexico. It seems that the challenging environment of the dense tropical rain forest resulted in this racially homogeneous though linguistically diverse Neolithic village people evolving a hierarchical social order in which élite groups of priests and warriors emerged. These upper classes eventually came to live in special ceremonial centres which were not cities in the true sense — since only the governing classes and their retainers and followers appear to have lived there — but were rather elaborate combinations of palaces, temples and aristocratic residences. In these ceremonial centres were concentrated all the civilised aspects of Classical Maya life — a complex religion, advanced astronomical, calendrical and mathematical knowledge, fine architecture and sculpture, painted pottery and murals and all the rest. Excavation in major ceremonial centres like Uaxactun (pronounced 'Wash-ak-toon') and Tikal, both in Guatemala, have shown clearly how the ceremonial centres grew in size and splendour, presumably as the power and prestige of the governing classes grew also.[2]

For example in the Proto-Classic period (c. AD 150-300) the buildings seem to have been of wood, although they were already mounted on masonry platforms having flights of steps and sloping faces. Later stone walls appear and finally the characteristic vaulted roof of the Maya, like an inverted V in section. Towards the end of the Classic period huge steep-sided pyramid-temples over 200 ft high were being constructed at Tikal. In the late ninth or early tenth century the entire elaborate social order in the southern (riverine) part of the Maya lowland area collapsed for reasons which are not fully understood and the great ceremonial centres reverted to the jungle. This collapse clearly illustrates how fragile the Maya civilisation was and how it depended on a relatively small number of people engaged in administrative, religious, martial and esoteric intellectual activities. When these people lost their authority — which happened suddenly at at least one site[3] — there was little left but the rural peasant population whose sparse descendants can be seen in the area today.

As far as the material culture of the Classic Maya civilisation is concerned, of course it differs radically at first sight from anything visible in Neolithic Britain. However the form taken by the *specific* elements of this, and indeed any, culture must obviously depend on the local environment and on the natural resources available: the *fundamentals* of the Classical Maya and Late Neolithic British material cultures and social organisations could have been very similar. For example, both were created by Neolithic groups, depending on stone, flint and chert for polished and chipped axes, spear points and other tools. Maize agriculture in the tropics obviously requires a different set of skills and techniques from the cultivation of wheat and barley in southern England: the former also requires fewer man hours of work per year and thereby releases its cultivators more often for public works. Yet the general similarities in the two peasant village ways of life are striking. Saddle querns were used to grind grain, round-based pottery vessels to cook and store food, and the populations lived mainly in thatched wooden huts in dispersed settlements (a fair assumption for Neolithic Britain). One sharp contrast is the lack of domestic animals in Mayaland in Classic times.

The specific features of the material remains of the civilised superstructure of the Maya clearly derive from the natural resources available. The impressive plastered masonry temple and palace buildings on their high pyramidal substructures were built because much of the land of the Maya rests on limestone which furnished building blocks for the structures and, when burnt and powdered, white mortar and plaster for binding and coating them. The Central American limestone (like that of Malta) apparently has the property of being relatively soft when first exposed, so that it can be cut and dressed to shape with stone tools, and of then hardening fairly rapidly on contact with the air. The same property allowed the Maya to carve elaborate façades on the roofs of their buildings and to sculpt their monumental standing stones or *stelae* (for setting up in front of the pyramid temples) with elaborate inscriptions and scenes. The *stelae* were also laboriously cut from harder rocks like granite. The Classic Maya pottery is of exceptionally high quality, partly because of the nature of the clay, partly because of the high temperatures achieved in the kilns and partly because of the primitive form of potter's wheel which was in use. This *k'abal* consisted of a cylindrical wooden block rotated on a smooth board which was propelled by the soles of the potter's feet and it imparted remarkable symmetry to the vessels. Materials for paints were available which could produce a variety of fine polychrome wares.

All these characteristics at first sight make the Classic Maya culture seem remote in every sense of the word from that of Late Neolithic Wessex, yet the essentials could well have been similar in both areas. They include the presence of small, non-agricultural élites engaged in esoteric intellectual and religious activities, living in special sites supported by the rural population and patronising in their turn a variety of specialised craftsmen and other professionals. The evidence for the intellectual achievement of this hypothetical British élite class of astronomer-priests and wise men was reviewed in Part 1 and found to be abundant. The inference could be that a similar kind of stratified, semi-civilised society existed here, and it is indeed easy enough to draw general and sweeping analogies with the Mayan situation. The geographically isolated state of Neolithic Britain might have provided the right isolated and protected environment in which such a fragile social superstructure could have come into being (the Maya seem to have evolved their advanced culture in relative isolation in their jungle-clad lowlands).[4] The astronomical and geometrical expertise of Late Neolithic Britain parallels in a remarkable way the greater achievement of the Maya, though we lack any surviving inscriptions here. Stonehenge and the stone circles could be the architecturally cruder — yet ceremonially perhaps just as complex — equivalents of the Maya temples, while the great henges of Wessex could be the equivalents in earthwork and wood of the stone ceremonial centres of Central America, and so on. Even the influx of warlike Mexican intruders at the end of the Classic period might find a parallel in the intrusion of the possibly Indo-European and martial Beaker people here!

However, if archaeological theory is to be regarded as remotely scientific

— and if this particular hypothesis by analogy is ever to be looked upon as more than an ingenious and entertaining speculation — some specific and testable implications of this general analogy with the Maya have to be defined. The material reviewed in chapters 7-10 does demonstrate fairly clearly that some form of society existed in Neolithic Britain which could plan and carry out formidable engineering projects, and this in itself could easily be explained by the Mayan analogy, but also by others.[5] Durrington Walls, Mount Pleasant and Marden could easily have been permanently inhabited sites, but were they the monastery-like enclosures of an intellectual élite as argued in chapters 8 and 9 or were they the much less refined Neolithic prototypes of the defended settlements and hill-forts of a later period?[6] Short of finding in a site like Durrington Walls or Skara Brae a stone plaque incised with a Pythagorean geometrical theorem or a solar calendar, it is hard to think of any specific evidence which would show that the former view is clearly correct. Nevertheless clues are available that the people who lived in the great henges were a group apart, a civilised élite of priests and wise men, and this is in addition to the circumstantial evidence in favour of the idea provided by the intellectually advanced activities revealed in the stone circles and standing stones (such activities imply that a learned order existed, and where better for this to have evolved and trained than on Salisbury Plain, near the two greatest temple-observatories of all?). Some of these clues were discussed in the context of the animal bones found at Skara Brae while others have not yet been mentioned. It is time to review this evidence again and, in the process, to suggest some tests for the hypothesis and some future avenues of investigation.

POTTERY AND SOCIAL CLASS

Maya pottery

Another characteristic feature of the Classic Maya civilisation was that the theocratic élite which inhabited and used the great masonry ceremonial centres evidently had the services of professional potters who produced a variety of finely painted vessels for its use. It has been observed that the lower down the social scale a Maya family was the more flimsy its dwelling and the less painted pottery it had.[7] At the ceremonial centre of Xunantunich in British Honduras,[8] inhabited in the latter part of the first millennium AD, this could be observed in a striking way (fig. 31). Of three distinct deposits of domestic refuse found, one was in a proper rubbish pit in front of the stone-vaulted masonry residence of someone who was presumably a member of the Classic period governing class, another was in a rubbish tip outside a contemporary peasant wooden hut in the bush beyond the precincts of the ceremonial centre, while the third was an extensive tip in and in front of the ruins of the stone residence mentioned, which had accumulated after it had been taken over by peasants following the collapse of the Classic culture. Each of these deposits yielded hundreds of sherds and showed the same overall proportions between 'service' and 'luxury' vessels, about 75 per cent to 25 per cent respectively (the service vessels were black-slipped and plain storage jars and black-slipped bowls while the luxury vessels were a variety of table and ritual pots, either polychrome or Red ware).

In the case of the aristocratic family half of its complement of luxury pottery was composed of fine polychrome vessels and the other half of Red

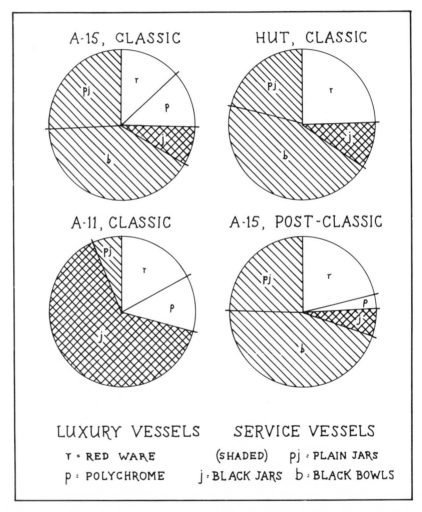

Fig. 31. Relative frequency of domestic and luxury pottery in four deposits at the Maya site of Xunantunich, Belize. A-15 was a priestly residence, re-occupied in ruins in post-Classic times, the Hut was a peasant dwelling of late Classic times, and A-11 was a palace building which had collapsed with pottery still on its floor

ware, but in the other two rubbish tips almost the whole of the quarter of luxury pottery was Red ware. Painted pottery was clearly confined to the upper classes and was probably made at the ceremonial centres by professional potters. The fourth deposit shown in fig. 31 is from the latest floor inside a collapsed masonry 'palace' building in the ceremonial centre itself; this is a form of structure which seems to be neither a pyramid-temple nor a residence but which was probably a place where the priesthood worked, studied and trained.[9] The distinctiveness of the function of this building is neatly reflected in the sharp differences between its pottery equipment and that of the domestic buildings.

A close correlation between pottery and social class can also be seen at the Hebridean Iron Age broch of Dun Mor Vaul on Tiree (fig. 32) the site sequence of which has already been outlined.[10] There the dark everted rim ware appears on the site for the first time with the broch builders, probably in the first century BC: in the pre-broch levels, going back to about 500 BC, the light coloured Vaul ware, decorated with incised lines, is alone present and must be the pottery of the aboriginal inhabitants of the island. In the following five major phases of the site's occupation there are several dramatic changes in the proportions of these two wares — Vaul and everted rim — and these can all be neatly explained by the social hypotheses built up from the structural and stratigraphic information in a way set out in detail in the excavation report.[11] There is little doubt that at this site the everted rim pottery was the preferred ware of the probably intrusive ruling class and that the Vaul ware was that of the native peasant population: when members of the ruling group were most numerous on the site the everted rim ware was also, and vice versa.

Grooved ware

If the great henges of Wessex were the permanently inhabited ceremonial centres of a Late Neolithic theocratic governing class, then one might expect the members of that class to have a fine pottery, specially made for them by professionals and perhaps quite distinct from the round-based bowls of the Neolithic farmers in the countryside around. Grooved ware is the obvious candidate for such a special pottery — having been found in large quantities at Durrington Walls, Woodhenge, Marden and Mount Pleasant — and it is worth looking again at the problem of this pottery and its origins with this hypothesis in mind.

One important kind of evidence is unfortunately not yet available: although some work has been done on the mineral content of the clay of which the Grooved ware at Durrington Walls is made, no comparative studies of clay sources or of the origins of the tempering material seem to have been carried out.[12] Thus we do not know yet whether the pottery was made by professional potters at one or more specific localities and traded to the ceremonial centres or whether it was made at the centres themselves.

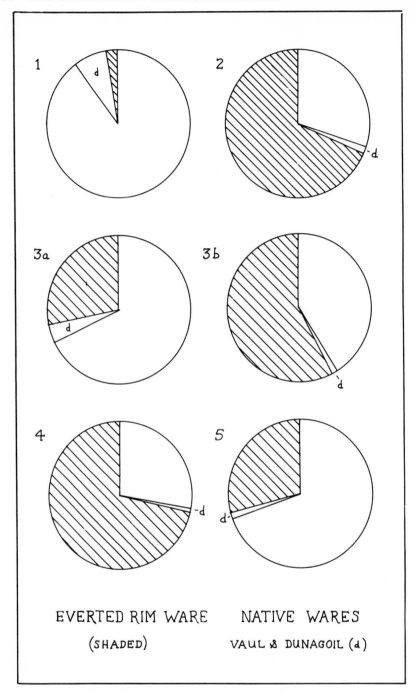

Fig. 32. Relative frequency of native and broch pottery in six successive occupation deposits at Dun Mor Vaul, Tiree

Such microscopic studies have transformed our knowledge of the manufacture and marketing of some Iron Age pottery[13] and ought to be applied to Grooved ware in the same way. The observation that sherds of Grooved ware found at Woodhenge were made from clay containing marine shells, if correct, should be relevant to this problem and could mean that the pottery, or at least the clay from which it was made, was imported from a coastal region.

The origins of Grooved ware have never been clear.[14] Both the flat bases of the vessels (fig. 33) and the striking, mainly incised geometrical decoration set it apart from the round-based bowls of the native Neolithic cultures on which any ornament (as with the Peterborough style) tends to be composed of thick cord impressions. The intrusive flat-based Beaker pottery certainly appears too late to inspire Grooved ware, which goes back at least to 2180 ± 105 bc at Stonehenge: at Durrington Walls and the other large henge sites this priority of Grooved ware is demonstrated stratigraphically.[15] This relatively abrupt appearance of Grooved ware, the distinctiveness of the shapes of the vessels and of their decoration, and the lack of plausible prototypes either outside or within England and Scotland, as well as the close association of the pottery with important ceremonial sites, all suggest that it was a specially made fine pottery for a special group of people.

Very striking in this context is the observation that no sherds of Grooved ware have yet been found bearing the impressions of cereal grains.[16] Prehistoric pottery made in a domestic context usually picked up the odd cereal grain while the clay was still damp and a microscopic study of the resulting impressions left after the vessel had been fired can provide valuable information about the crops grown at the time.[17] The fact that no such impressions have been found on Grooved ware almost certainly means that it was made in a non-domestic context, that is by professional potters in workshops which were probably in or near the ceremonial centres.

It seems more than possible that Grooved ware was actually invented for an élite group of some kind, and two further characteristics of the ware may be said to support this idea. The first is the flat base of all the pots, which contrasts completely with the uniformly round-bottomed bowls of the native Neolithic wares. Round-based bowls have to be hung over a fire (or in a store) or stood in loose, dry sand or earth. If knocked accidentally they can be tilted but are unlikely to tip right over and spill their contents: often they should rock back to near an upright position. Small flat-based pots stood on the ground, however, would be much more prone to being knocked right over and the flat base clearly suggests that they were designed to stand on wooden furniture such as tables and shelves. One could scarcely have a clearer illustration than this of the different living style of the users of Grooved ware: far from living in simple wooden huts with pottery standing around on the floor, we can surely envisage an élite group in special large wooden buildings in a demarcated *temenos* or special enclosure, doubtless well equipped with hangings and wooden furniture and enjoying a much higher standard of living than the rural peasantry around about. The flat shelves are of course preserved in stone at Skara Brae, and we can surely

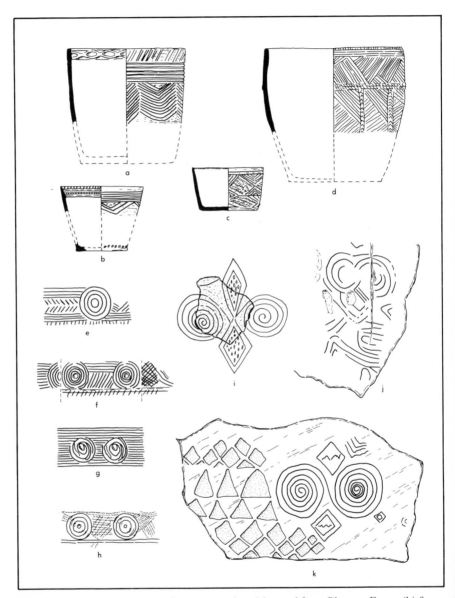

Fig. 33. Grooved ware, shape and ornamentation: (a) vessel from Clacton, Essex; (b) from Pishobury, East Anglia; (c) from Greeting St Mary, East Anglia; (d) from Durrington Walls, Wiltshire; (e-h) curvilinear motifs on sherds from Durrington Walls; (i) sherd with spiral-and-lozenge motif from Skara Brae, Orkney; (j) similar motifs carved on stones at the passage grave of Barclodiad y Gawres in North Wales; and (k) New Grange, Ireland

assume that the skilled carpenters who built the great roundhouses at Durrington Walls also constructed furniture and fittings to go inside them.

Another clue to the nature and origins of Grooved ware is seen in its decoration (fig. 33). The majority of the incised and cord-impressed motifs are geometrical patterns — filled triangles, herringbone designs and a variety of parallel lines.[18] A few, however, have curvilinear ornament, such as concentric circles and spirals, which recall the cup-and-ring rock carvings of the highland zone, and there is a distinct possibility that this decoration has its origin in the art of the passage graves of the river Boyne in Ireland.[19] A sherd from Durrington Walls shows decoration very similar to that pecked onto the stone 'basin' found inside the Knowth passage grave in Co. Meath and even more remarkable is the unique sherd from Skara Brae with the 'lozenge and spiral' motif (fig. 33). The same motif is seen on kerbstone no. 67 at the New Grange passage grave,[20] and stones on the related passage graves at Barclodiad y Gawres and Bryn Celli Ddu in Wales have similar designs, though not quite so well executed (fig. 33). Certainly the art of the Boyne tombs also includes many other motifs, many of them simple geometrical designs of the same general character as those found on Grooved ware.[21] It is of course true that the Irish Boyne passage graves belong to a somewhat earlier period than the great period of Grooved ware in Britain, New Grange having been built at about 2500 bc, but that need not be an obstacle to deriving the pottery decoration from that on the great Irish cairns. The carved stones in and around the latter must have remained visible for many centuries after they were set in place and thus vividly preserved their artistic traditions fresh in the minds of the people of the area.

If the hypothesis is correct that Grooved ware was the special pottery made by professionals for a Late Neolithic theocratic governing class and its retainers, then the features of that pottery cannot help suggesting something about the origins — or at least about the cultural connections — of that class. These links with the passage grave builders of eastern Ireland with their tradition of elaborately decorative rock carving, their concern with astronomical phenomena (as at New Grange[22]) and their habit of setting free-standing stone circles round the cairns (only found in the Boyne area), may all be giving vital clues to the origin of the whole phenomenon of Late Neolithic science and ceremonial in southern England, and by implication in Britain as a whole. The apparently sudden appearance of the Grooved ware in Wessex, East Anglia and Orkney with no plausible local ancestors could reflect the equally sudden arrival of skilled theocrats, priests and wise men, with their craftsmen and retainers, from Ireland who could have brought about the transformation in southern English Neolithic society. The absence of Grooved ware from Ireland need be no obstacle to this view: it could be an entirely new pottery invented in Wessex for the newcomers and reflecting their own tastes, needs and standards, and recalling in its ornament the finely decorated temple-tombs of the

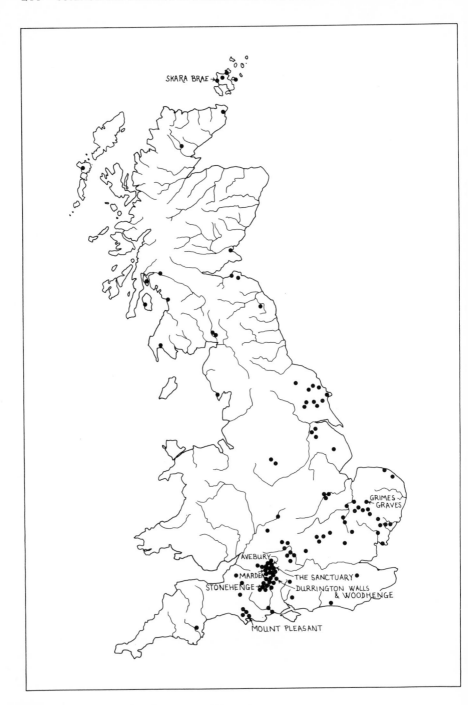

Fig. 34. Map of the distribution of Grooved ware, after Wainwright and Longworth

homeland. A similar phenomenon is seen in the Clettraval sub-style of Hebridean Iron Age everted rim ware; this is a locally invented pottery which combines several traditions and which was preferred by the socially dominant broch-builders.

If this is the explanation for the origin and occurrence of Grooved ware, then its appearance at sites like the Grimes Graves flint mines, Skara Brae and a variety of other sites mainly in Wessex and East Anglia[23] should mean that members of this dominant social group or their retainers or employees were present at these sites. Conversely it is equally clear that the great majority of the explored henge and stone circle sites in other parts of the more highland country — united with each other and with Wessex as they seem to be by a·shared tradition of accurate measurement and geometry as well as by considerable skill in observational astronomy — have not produced Grooved ware.[24] The implications of this phenomenon are as important as those of the abundance of the pottery at sites like Durrington Walls, though it must be added that no potential habitation sites of the period comparable to Durrington Walls have yet been discovered in the highland regions (except Skara Brae and Rinyo of course) and that artefacts of all kinds are rare on stone circle sites.

After the final draft of this book was completed Mr Aubrey Burl drew my attention to some recent finds of Grooved ware which are relevant to the arguments presented above about the origins and nature of this pottery. Firstly, and perhaps most important, sherds of Grooved ware have been identified in Ireland[25] and one of the Irish sites concerned is the stone circle/henge monument of Lios by Lough Gur in Co. Limerick. Grooved ware has also been found at the stone circle of Balbirnie, Fife[26] while a bowl of the same pottery was recently recovered from the primary silts of one of the ditch terminals of the Stenness henge/circle in Orkney, only five miles from Skara Brae. A radiocarbon date for charcoal from the base of the ditch dated the construction of the site to the 24th century bc and another dated the pot to the 23rd century: they neatly confirm the argument about the Middle Neolithic origin of Grooved ware put forward on p. 164.[27] As we have seen, C-14 dates for the earliest period of occupation of Skara Brae fell into the 25th century bc (the 32nd BC) and show that this settlement was already established when Stenness was built (p. 189).

ANIMAL BONES AND ARISTOCRACIES

Some indication of the potential importance of animal bone refuse in identifying specialised groups within Neolithic society has already been given and we have noted that, in the Atlantic zone of Scotland, the normal diet of farming communities in Iron Age times seems to have included about 50 per cent domestic beasts (sheep and cattle) and 50 per cent game (mainly deer). Sheep and cattle are about equally respresented in the former group (fig. 29) while pigs were extremely rare and probably wild. The presence of a non-farming specialist (probably a professional broch builder) at Dun Mor Vaul was suspected from the situation and appearance of his living quarters and easily detectable from his diet: he was given almost nothing but mutton to eat. Though Skara Brae was inhabited some 2,000 years or more before Dun Mor Vaul it seems reasonable to suppose that the almost total dominance of sheep and cattle bones in the midden of the main village occupation reflects a similar situation as did the broch-builder's midden on Tiree — that a special, non-farming group was being supplied with mutton and beef by the surrounding population. The sudden disappearance of this meat and the change to an almost total reliance on game in the post-destruction period seems to confirm this view.

The situation in Wessex cannot be compared in detail with that in Orkney or Tiree for a number of reasons. The environment was different; sheep and goats were not numerous in the southern province and large herds of domestic pigs were kept there, in contrast to the north. Deer seem to have been scarce also. However the same principle of comparing the diet of a suspected élite, non-farming group with that of farming communities could be applied here also if the appropriate sites have been explored. A basis for comparison is offered by the information from the animal bones recovered from the Windmill Hill causewayed camp, 1½ miles northwest of Avebury and only 15 miles north of Durrington Walls, recently published.[28] Three distinct midden deposits with many animal bones were found, which probably span a period from about 3000 to 1500 bc. The pre-enclosure occupation must be at the beginning of this time span and has a C-14 date of 2960 ± 150 bc (BM-73). The material from the primary levels of the ditches has a date of 2580 ± 150 bc (BM-74) while a Late Neolithic occupation was identified higher up which must be approximately contemporary with the main use of Durrington Walls. This last level gave a date of 1550 ± 150 bc (BM-75). Table 11 shows the percentages of bones of the various edible species and also those from Durrington Walls again (the latter have to be shown as minimum numbers of animals represented, not as individual bones).

Windmill Hill causewayed camp was clearly not an ordinary domestic site so it is perhaps not giving us the ideal information to compare with Durrington Walls. However, although it seems not to have been a permanent settlement, there are as yet no reasons to suppose that the people who lived there at intervals were not members of the ordinary rural population, so we may hope that their diet would be closer to that of a farming family at home than that of the inhabitants of Durrington. There is evidence from the pottery that people came to the site from some distance, from the Frome/Bath region twenty miles away.[29] Also burials of whole animals like young pigs suggest sacrifices of some kind, and the concentration of stone axes from distant localities in and near the causewayed camp confirms that it was an important centre of some kind.[30]

TABLE 11

Percentages of identified bones of edible animals (*or minimum number of individuals) from two Neolithic habitation sites

	cattle	sheep/ goat	pig	roe deer	red deer	wild ox	horse	total bones	
Windmill Hill									
pre-enclosure	67.5%	11.9%	16.3%	—	3.8%	—	—	133	99.5%
primary levels	58.7%	24.2%	14.9%	—	1.8%	—	—	496	99.6%
Late Neo. levels	56.2%	13.1%	22.6%	—	1.8%	5.6%	—	53	99.3%
Durrington Walls*	27.4%	1.9%	63.8%	0.6%	4.5%	1.0%	1.0%	8,500	100.2%

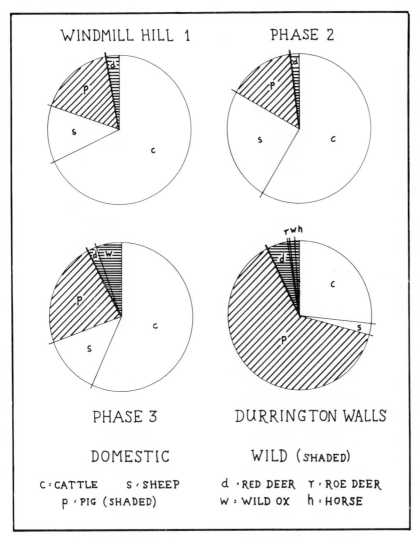

Fig. 35. Proportions of edible animal bones in deposits of the three successive phases at Windmill Hill and at Durrington Walls

The domestic nature of most of the refuse is clear enough: numerous fragments of rubbers and quernstones for grinding grain were found (in marked contrast to Durrington Walls) and these, together with the quantities of potsherds and bones, clearly show that families were living on the site at times. Thus the food debris is likely to be similar to that which would be found outside a Neolithic hut, if one could be located.

The diet of these people remained very similar throughout the long period of use of the site, perhaps nearly two millennia in calendar years, and contrasts strongly with that of the inhabitants of Durrington Walls in several ways. Sheep were eaten much more often at the causewayed camp but cattle provided the main part of the diet, especially in the earliest period. Pig was eaten in about the same quantities as sheep. At Durrington, however, enormous quantities of pork were eaten — more than three times as much as even in Late Neolithic times at the causewayed camp (assuming that the percentages can be compared fairly accurately) when pig was most frequent. By contrast the inhabitants of Durrington ate only about half as much beef and hardly any mutton at all. These contrasts in style of accommodation, preferred pottery and dietary habits between the occupants of Windmill Hill and Durrington Walls in Late Neolithic times appear to confirm in a very striking way that the people in the latter site were something altogether different from the general rural population of Wessex. The total absence of quernstones from Durrington recalls the situation at Skara Brae and suggests that flour or loaves were brought to the site from elsewhere (or ground in a part of the henge as yet unexplored).

The fact that the only spindle whorl so far known from Neolithic Britain was found at Durrington Walls,[31] whereas antler combs, presumably for dressing skins, are known from the Windmill Hill 'native' Neolithic sites,[32] reinforces the contrast again. We may legitimately suggest that the inhabitants of the giant henges wore woven clothes whereas most of the rural population was dressed in skins. One could hardly imagine a more striking way for our élite group of astronomer-priests to distinguish itself as an upper class than by being clothed not in the usual skin and leather suits but in long robes or cloaks, perhaps similar to the clothes worn by the Bronze Age chieftains of Denmark a few centuries later and found preserved in the oak coffin burials.[33] One recalls the cloaked Druids of Iron Age times with their long staffs and the white-robed priests and monks of the Early Christian church in Scotland a few centuries later, living in monasteries set apart by earthworks among a primitive population. The suggestion that the flat-based Grooved ware found in the giant henges means these sites were equipped with wooden furniture would, if correct, tell the same story.

SOCIAL DEVELOPMENT IN NEOLITHIC BRITAIN

The use of reliable radiocarbon dates in providing an accurate *relative* as well as an absolute chronology for important sites and events in prehistoric contexts has already been described, and the importance of exploiting the new information thus obtained can hardly be over-emphasised. Hitherto it has hardly seemed realistic to hope to trace the geographical extent of individual developments on prehistoric sites, or to link them together in time on separate sites, since there were always too many uncertainties about the absolute methods of dating available. Without an exact chronology detailed pictures of the development of a prehistoric culture as shown in alterations to its domestic, ceremonial and funerary sites cannot be built up, either across the country at particular points in time or in depth over several centuries. For many years after the arrival of radiocarbon dating this still remained true simply because it was normal, owing to the expense and difficulty of obtaining good organic samples, to obtain at best only one or two dates for each phase in the development of a site, and often only one date for a site as a whole. Thus there always remained a strong possibility that a single C-14 date was in fact far away from the true age, and the maxim 'one date is no date' became rightly accepted.

In recent years, however, it has become more usual to obtain several C-14 dates for a given archaeological horizon when this is well defined and when suitable organic material (and money) is available. At the same time the tree-ring calibration of radiocarbon dates has given them real meaning in terms of calendar years. In such cases the reliability of the date of the horizon concerned is enormously increased, and it becomes feasible to maintain, for example, that the main enclosure at Durrington Walls and the second southern roundhouse there were built at the same time in the 26th century BC and that considerable activity at the Grimes Graves flint mines was occurring at the same time. Sites as far away as Skara Brae in Orkney can be tied confidently to the same narrow chronological horizon for the same reasons. Thus we have an entirely new situation in prehistoric archaeology in which significant events at widely separated sites, in this case already linked by their possession of the same characteristic pottery, can reasonably be inferred to have happened together and *as part of the same sequence of social events.*

In this way we have been able to see strong hints that some novel social processes were beginning in Wessex in about the 29th century BC when two sites were built — Stonehenge I and Silbury Hill — of a quality and size respectively which seem to imply that a hierarchical stratified society had emerged among, or been imposed upon, the Neolithic rural population of the area. The size of Silbury Hill surely indicates a centralised social organisation capable of directing a large body of men in a sustained effort, while Stonehenge I in its turn implies that a professional class of wise men using Grooved ware had emerged which was able to command similar resources to construct an elaborate and expensive observatory. It is hard not to conclude that the same ruling group was at work in each case. These two sites might not be sufficient evidence on their own to justify putting forward such a theory with real confidence, particularly as they have but

	archaeological period	phase	sites	suggested events
1500 B.C. (1200 b.c.)	EARLY BRONZE AGE	BARROW-BUILDING II	Bush barrow	Wessex culture
				warrior aristocracy of hybrid Beaker people
			Normanton barrow	
				widespread trade in metal
			Cairnpapple III	
			·	decline in power of Neolithic theocracy
		BARROW-BUILDING I	Beaker barrows	development of fortified sites as at Mount Pleasant III
2000 B.C. (1700 b.c.)	LATE NEOLITHIC or CHALCOLITHIC	TEMPLE BUILDING II	Stonehenge III	gradual transfer of power to hybrid Beaker people
			Cairnpapple II	many stone circles built all over the highland zone
			Woodhenge	
			Stonehenge II Ballochroy	construction of final Stonehenge
			Kintraw	
			Cultoon	Grooved ware people to Orkney
			Durrington Walls (main site)	Beaker people arrive
			Marden	upsurge in astronomical activity
			Skara Brae	building of large ceremonial centres in Wessex
2500 B.C. (2000 b.c.)			Ring of Brodgar	
	MIDDLE NEOLITHIC	TEMPLE BUILDING I	Avebury	steady separation out of élite groups of specialists
			Dorset Cursus	
			Cairnpapple I	beginning of systematic astronomy
			Durrington Walls I	
			The Sanctuary	
			Stonehenge I	increasingly centralised theocracy in Wessex
			Silbury Hill	
3000 B.C. (2300 b.c.)		MONUMENT BUILDING		larger megalithic monuments
			Quanterness Midhowe	steady development in religion architecture with outstanding achievements in a few centres Wessex, the Boyne valley and Orkney and Caithness
			Maes Howe	
			New Grange Knowth	prototype ceremonial centres in Wessex
3500 B.C. (2800 b.c.)			causewayed camps	larger megaliths
	EARLY NEOLITHIC	FORMATIVE	early horned long cairns	many separate stratified societies loosely linked by their related theocracies, all practising collective burial
				small megaliths built
			early passage graves	arrival or emergence of ruling theocratic groups practising collective burial
4000 B.C. (3400 b.c.)			earthen long barrows	colonisation of Britain by Neolithic peasant farmers
	MESOLITHIC		none	scattered bands of hunters and food gatherers

Fig. 36. Suggested chronological chart of major cultural developments among the ruling and specialist classes of southern England, c. 4500-1500 BC

one reliable C-14 date each (a number of other dates done on the turf buried under Silbury Hill were widely scattered). However the hypothesis of a stratified, possibly theocratic society which they suggest does seem to be abundantly supported by the much more copious and solid evidence from the Late Neolithic period.

From about the 26th/25th century BC onwards we can clearly see that the pace of development was accelerating. The modest round wooden buildings which are detectable in Middle Neolithic times, for example in the early phase at the Sanctuary, in the first southern house at Durrington Walls and probably in the structure at Croft Moraig in Perthshire, are now being built in larger numbers and on a grander scale, being either surrounded by their own ditches as at Woodhenge and Mount Pleasant or set within a special large enclosure defined by a huge earthwork. Roundhouses on their own like that at Mount Pleasant were likely to be incorporated in a large henge site at a later date. What is remarkable is the clear evidence from numerous C-14 dates that there was a sudden increase of this activity at a number of sites more or less simultaneously. One might suspect that in the 26th century BC (about 2000 bc) some kind of crisis arose which required a vast outlay of effort in constructing these huge wooden buildings. It must also have involved a systematic search of the forested regions of the country for thousands of deer antlers, the stepping up of flint-mining activity to produce vast numbers of flint axes and an extensive campaign of tree-felling and carpentry. Moreover these great henges seem to have pre-dated by only a short time the building of the series of stone temples at Stonehenge and of large numbers of stone circles and standing stones all over the country. If these activities also were part of the same crisis then it must have been something that affected the whole country in a fundamental way. It is clear, moreover, that the crisis in the 26th century had nothing to do with the arrival of the Beaker people invaders from the continent of Europe: the radiocarbon dates show that these came slightly later.

However, it is the nature of the society rather than that of the crisis — if there was one — with which we are primarily concerned here. A discussion of why there was this tremendous outburst of henge-building and astronomical and ceremonial activity of all kinds in the Late Neolithic and Early Bronze Ages is better postponed until more evidence is available, even though the question is clearly at the root of the whole extraordinary phenomenon. We have seen that the large henge sites can plausibly be interpreted in their own right as the permanently inhabited settlements of a special class of priests and wise men on the Maya pattern, a class moreover with considerable prestige and authority judging by its works. The contrast between this élite and the ordinary rural population is seen very strikingly in the contemporary domestic deposits at Windmill Hill and its neighbour Durrington Walls. We have inferred that this class had arrived or emerged earlier, probably in the 29th century, and by the 26th century had so consolidated its position that it was able greatly to increase the size and splendour of its ceremonial centres (temple precincts, cathedral closes, monasteries, or whatever the best term is). The same process has been observed for the Classical Maya. At the beginning of the first millennium AD there were relatively few and small ceremonial centres in the jungles of the Petén district of Guatemala; the buildings on these sites were relatively modest structures of wood mounted on stone platforms. As the centuries passed the power and prestige of the theocratic élite evidently grew steadily and they were able to command more and more resources to build larger and larger ceremonial centres with bigger and bigger vaulted stone buildings and support ever greater numbers of full-time specialists and retainers to staff the centres. The number of ceremonial centres also grew steadily with the passing of time until in the ninth century AD — just before the abrupt collapse of this remarkable civilisation in the southern part of its area — there were something like 10 major centres (with very many more minor ones) scattered over an area of about 95,000 square miles.[34]

Could the stone circles and standing stones scattered throughout highland Britain be the temples of this Wessex-based Late Neolithic élite group, built in steadily larger numbers over an increasing area as its religion, influence and members spread across the country? It certainly seems a possibility, although careful excavations on sites like Cairnpaple Hill in West Lothian[35] and Croft Moraig in Perthshire[36] have shown that these two stone circles were added to already existing Middle Neolithic sites. If the stone circles do represent the expansion of a new religion and its acolytes—with the origin of both in Wessex and ultimately in Ireland— then in many cases the new temple-observatories would probably have been built on older sacred sites. However the absence of Grooved ware from most of the stone circles which have been excavated implies that this may be an over-simple interpretation and that, in spite of the country-wide connections implied by their standardised metrology and geometry (and demonstrated by the Grooved ware sites in Orkney), more than one 'sect' of these circle builders may have existed, albeit with some common traditions. This certainly seems to be suggested by the separate Irish connections of the structurally distinct recumbent stone circles of northeast Scotland (chapter 2). However this is clearly a problem which requires much more thought and research, and its solution may need to await the discovery of more inhabited ceremonial centres in the regions now lacking them but which have many stone circles.

ASTRONOMER-PRIESTS IN IRON AGE BRITAIN

The Druids

One of the most convincing pieces of evidence that a stratified, theocratic society existed in Britain at about 2500 BC — and one not mentioned hitherto — is that we have good evidence that a class or caste of learned priests and wise men with considerable prestige existed in Iron Age Britain and Gaul. These people are of course the Druids and were described in some detail by Julius Caesar. A study of the Druids not only suggests that they could be the descendants of the Neolithic learned orders which have been inferred in this work but also sheds some light on what kind of presumably non-literate society it was in Late Neolithic times that could have produced and supported the specialists needed to do all the work postulated by Thom, and could have accumulated, stored and passed on to new recruits the mass of detailed knowledge which must thus have been acquired. Indeed intellectual classes of astronomers, wise men, priests and bards are not uncommon among barbarian non-literate societies, as the studies by Lewis of the Polynesian navigators have shown in striking manner.[37] Piggott[38] and Burn[39] have recently reviewed the evidence for the nature of the Druids and analogous holy men of late prehistoric times, the latter concluding for example that 'Celtic Christian monasticism, with its frequent choice of islands for settlement . . . was continuing a practice well known to holy men of pre-Christian times.' Although the term Druid has acquired many fanciful connotations since Caesar's time — so much so that its use can inhibit rational discussion in some quarters — according to Burn, the name may simply mean 'wise': it would in this case be derived from the root 'id' or 'wid' with the intensifying prefix 'dri' added to mean 'thrice wise'. The alternative suggested derivation from the 'Drus' or oak tree root is, he thinks, probably a Graeco-Roman guess with little to recommend it.

Several other Classical authors beside Caesar mentioned the Druids. Strabo wrote that they were well versed in astronomy and calendrical computation and he called this learning *physiologia* or natural science. Hippolytus attributed the status of the Druids as prophets to the fact that 'they can foretell certain events by the Pythagorean reckoning and calculations' while Caesar said that they have 'much knowledge of the stars and their motion, of the size of the world and the earth, of natural philosophy.' There is also the famous passage from the lost *History of the Hyperboreans* by Hecataeus of Abdera (c. 300 BC) which survives as a quotation in the writings of Diodorus Siculus. This describes a spherical temple and a sacred enclosure dedicated to Apollo (the sun) in the island of the Hyperboreans, which is probably though not certainly Britain. If it is Britain the temple and the enclosure might be Stonehenge and Avebury respectively. Diodorus also retails the legend that Apollo visited the island every 19 years, a circumstance which is usually taken to be a reference to the Metonic cycle of the same length of time, at the end of which the lunar and solar calendars coincide (235 lunar months of 29.531 days = 6939.785 days whereas 19 tropical years of 365.242 days = 6939.598 days, or about 4½ hours less). If this story really refers to Britain it implies that people with fairly advanced astronomical skills were already present at about 300 BC.

Julius Caesar provides us with more information about the Druids in *de bello Gallico*, which, as Burn points out, is probably very accurate as he had a first class source to hand in the person of Divitiācus the great druid and chief of the Aedui tribe. Of the Druidical learning or *disciplina* he says that 'it is believed to have been developed first in Britain, and thence introduced to Gaul; and to this day those who wish to pursue their studies of it more deeply usually go to Britain for the purpose.' This is a particularly interesting comment in view of the usually accepted view that the Druids acquired their expertise in *physiologia* from the Greeks, most probably by way of the Greek trading colony of Massilia, founded at Marseilles on the Mediterranean coast of France at about 600 BC. The origin of the Druidical learning would be expected in Gaul if that was the case, but if it was inherited from our hypothetical Late Neolithic learned order of stone circle builders a British origin for the *disciplina*, far older than Pythagoras, would be easily explained.

Druidical practices as well as those of other comparable non-literate learned orders also help us to understand how a relatively sophisticated astronomical and geometrical knowledge could be acquired, or at least transmitted, without the use of writing. Verses and ballads are an obvious medium for storing and learning information, and Caesar also mentions that 'Many are sent to join it [the learned order of Druids] by their parents and families. In it they are said to learn by heart huge quantities of verse. Some spend twenty years in this *disciplina*. They consider it impious to commit this matter to writing.' No doubt this verse contained all the Druids' accumulated wisdom, including data on astronomy and cosmology; similar oral transmissions of practical astronomical data (for navigation) have been observed among the Polynesian hereditary class of navigators.[40] As for mathematical calculations, these too can be done up to quite a sophisticated level without writing. Neugebauer described the Tamil calendar makers of southern India of the last century who calculated the dates and times of eclipses without either any complex apparatus or the writing down of figures, but by mental arithmetic with the aid of pebbles which were arranged on the ground to recall to the mind the steps already performed and those still to go through. One man 'who did not understand a word of the theories of Hindu mathematics, but was endowed with a retentive memory which enabled him to arrange very distinctly his operations in his mind and on the ground' was able by such methods to predict a lunar eclipse in 1825 to within four minutes of its actual time.[41] It is easy to see how the presence of an intellectual class in Late Neolithic Britain having such abilities — which were doubtless encouraged genetically by selective breeding and culturally by the appropriately favourable social environment — could have led to most of the achievements that Thom has inferred.

The broch builders

A considerable span of time, probably more than 2,000 years, lies between these Iron Age astronomer-priests and wise men and the comparable class of people which we are suggesting existed in southern England and elsewhere in Late Neolithic times. Yet it would be wrong to assume that there could be no continuity of learning between even such chronologically widely separated and culturally distinct epochs, and indeed we have already seen that a study of the Iron Age brochs of Scotland has revealed some dramatic and striking direct evidence that the Neolithic learning was handed down over all these centuries to Iron Age times (chapter 3). Not only has an independent mathematical analysis of the internal dimensions of the brochs revealed that a unit of length almost identical to the megalithic yard was used to set out their circular plans on the ground, but it is also clear that a few brochs were built around more complex geometrical figures also seen in the stone circles. Unless broch metrology was an Iron Age invention which by chance is identical to that of the Late Neolithic period — surely a far-fetched notion — this would seem to be a decisive demonstration that the learning of the stone circle builders was handed down intact across two millennia to the time of the Druids. There is not much reason to doubt now that the non-literate learned order of Iron Age Britain and Gaul had at least part of its origins in the wise men who inhabited the giant henges and who built the stone circles and Stonehenge.

EPILOGUE

I have tried to show that a radically different interpretation of part of the Late Neolithic archaeological record in Britain — and one based loosely on analogy with the Classic Maya society — is not only possible but may in fact be said to accommodate much of what has hitherto seemed a diverse and unconnected collection of evidence in one highly satisfactory scheme. This is done, moreover, without the need to rule out whole segments of that evidence as invalid, such as that of Thom. The nature of this attempt — to replace long held traditional views not only of what prehistoric Britons were like but also of what sort of explanations we ought to be thinking about — suggested at the outset that it would be better to concentrate on a few important sites of the period and try to decide whether it was feasible to see in them the inhabited 'ceremonial centres' of the élite class which appeared to be demanded by Thom's discoveries. Unless it was possible to find such evidence, and of a·sufficient quality to pass standard archaeological tests, there would be little point in pursuing the idea further. Not the least of the encouraging aspects of this essay in re-interpretation has been the way that more and more details of the evidence found at these sites seemed to fall neatly into place in the new scheme as the work progressed, particularly the superficially unexciting data obtained from animal bone refuse.

However, this type of approach, concentrated on a relatively narrow front, does mean that several potentially important aspects of the problem, and many potentially important sites, have had to be omitted from the discussion and held over for consideration at another time. These include the problem of the social context of the megalithic 'tombs' of the Early Neolithic period, the whole phenomenon of which must surely be highly relevant to any theory involving theocratic élites. Then there is the problem of the role of the Beaker invaders of the Early Bronze Age of about 2300 BC onwards, a topic hardly touched on here in spite of the many examples of associations of this new pottery with late megalithic tombs, stone circles and with the Grooved ware settlements in Wessex and Orkney. Again we have the problem of the links, if any, between the Late Neolithic giant henge sites and the superficially similar earthwork enclosures of the latter part of the Bronze Age and the Iron Age which are known as hill-forts; this needs to be examined in detail because the possibility that the Neolithic enclosures were ancestral to the latter is the obvious alternative explanation to their being ceremonial centres for a theocracy.

Various other specific lines of research to test the hypothesis favoured here — of a stratified theocratic society — suggest themselves in addition to the numerous opportunities which exist for following up and testing the work and ideas of Professor Thom. For example the concept that Grooved ware was specially made for a distinct class of people could be tested, both with experiments to decide if it was made and traded by professional potters and also by examining in detail the possible links between its decoration and the art of the Irish passage graves. The possibilities of detecting élite groups by the differences between their diets and culinary habits and those of the rural farming population seem very promising, and more ordinary Late Neolithic settlements need to be found, especially in Orkney, and compared with the supposed theocratic residences in this way. There are other implications of the theory which can be defined and tested and it is essential to do this by fieldwork and excavation.

A final point to make — perhaps unnecessarily — is that the new interpretations presented in this book should not be rejected simply because they offer a picture of Late Neolithic Britain which is unfamiliar and somewhat different from those hitherto considered likely. One of the great benefits of the existence of a rival basic theory is that it forces one to re-examine existing ideas and to take a fresh look at familiar evidence. It can also suggest numerous new avenues of research to follow up, and if this happens as a result of this essay in re-interpretation I shall be more than satisfied.

Notes

CHAPTER 1. NEW ASPECTS OF PREHISTORIC BRITAIN

1 Childe 1957, chap. 12; Daniel 1958; Case 1969; Fleming 1972.
2 MacKie 1976.
3 Renfrew 1974.
4 Hawkes 1967.
5 Cunliffe 1974; Harding 1974.
6 Childe 1935, 1940, 1946.
7 Renfrew 1970, 1973.
8 Clarke 1968, 13.
9 Clarke 1970, 276.
10 Hoyle 1972.
11 Rivet 1971.
12 Hawkes 1954; Dymond 1974, 24 ff.
13 Atkinson 1953; Coles 1972; Hole and Heizer 1973.
14 Moroney 1956, 2-3.
15 Bass 1974; Dingle 1972, 121 ff.
16 Doran and Hodson 1975.
17 Dingle 1972, 32-3, 125.
18 Bibby 1972.
19 Bibby 1972, 49-51; Huxley 1869, p.i.
20 Thom 1967, chap. 5.
21 Renfrew 1973, 255 ff.
22 Suess 1965, 1970; Ralph and Michael 1967.
23 McKerrell 1971; Ralph, Michael and Han 1973.
24 Renfrew 1968, 1970, 1973.
25 Childe 1938, 1957, chap. 19.
26 Darlington 1968, 88 ff.
27 Clarke 1968, 12.
28 Renfrew 1973, chaps. 3 and 4.
29 Lewis 1974.

CHAPTER 2. PREHISTORIC METROLOGY AND GEOMETRY

1 Thom 1967, chaps. 5-7.
2 Broadbent 1955.
3 Kendall 1974.
4 Thom 1968, 1969.
5 Thom 1967, 35.
6 Thom 1967, 43.
7 Renfrew 1973, 237 ff.
8 Thomas 1971.
9 Thom 1967, 42-3, tables 5.4 and 5.5.

10 Thom and Thom 1973.
11 Thom 1967, fig. 5.1.
12 Thom 1967, 47.
13 Thom 1967, table 5.1.
14 I am indebted to Dr G. I. Crawford for suggesting this explanation to me.
15 Thom 1967, 47-8.
16 An Interim report will be offered to *Current Archaeology*.
17 Thom 1967, chap. 6.
18 Wainwright 1975, 66-7.
19 Thom 1967, 150.
20 Hutchinson 1973, 28.
21 Hutchinson 1973, table 1.
22 Roy 1963.
23 MacKie 1975, 85 ff.
24 Thom 1967, 123.
25 Thom 1967, chap. 7.
26 Selkirk, Burl and MacKie 1969.
27 Burl 1973, 1976.
28 O'Kelly 1972.
29 Burl 1973, fig. 3.
30 Burl 1972, fig. 3.
31 Burl 1973, 171.
32 Burl 1970, 8. Mr Burl tells me that 14% of all henge monuments contain stone circles.
33 Wainwright 1975, 67.
34 M. J. O'Kelly 1970; C. O'Kelly 1973; Hadingham 1974, section 1.
35 Burl 1973a; Hadingham 1974, fig. 67; Burl 1976, chap. 6.
36 Thom 1968, 1969.
37 Morris and Bailey 1966; Morris 1968.
38 MacKie 1975a, fig. 8; Burl 1972, 31.
39 Hadingham 1974, fig. 76.
40 Hadingham 1974, 76 ff.

CHAPTER 3. THE ORIGINS AND AFFINITIES OF THE MEGALITHIC YARD

1 Berriman 1953; Williamson 1974.
2 Renfrew 1973, 237-9.
3 Thom 1967, 34; Szymanski 1956; Britannica 1929, *14*, 142.
4 Berriman 1953, 70; Skinner 1956, 775.
5 Skinner 1956, fig. 566.
6 Petrie 1926.
7 Petrie 1934; Leach 1956, 111.
8 Berriman 1953, 53-4.
9 Piggott 1950; Wheeler 1966.
10 Berriman 1953, 39; Mackay 1938, vol. 1, 404-6; Vol. 2, pls. cvi no. 30, cxxv no. 1.
11 Darlington 1968, 88 ff; Wheeler 1959, 100 ff.
12 Berriman 1953, 40 ff.
13 Ivimy 1974, 133.
14 I am indebted to Mr J. Williamson for pointing this out to me.
15 Fletcher 1968.
16 Berriman 1953, 121.
17 Skinner 1956, 777.

18 Fletcher 1968.
19 Fletcher 1968.
20 Petrie 1934, Skinner 1956, 777.
21 Skinner 1956, 778.
22 Berriman 1954, 1955, 200.
23 Skinner 1956, 778.
24 Michel 1966, 87-8 and pl. 24.
25 Childe 1929, 339-43.
26 Glob 1970, 31; Bøye 1896.
27 Klindt Jensen 1957, 61 ff.
28 Glob 1970, 38.
29 Bøye 1896, 53.
30 Glob 1970, 43.
31 Bøye 1896, 53.
32 Glob 1967, 261; I have to thank Mr Norman Newton for drawing my
    attention to this find.
33 MacKie 1968, 283.
34 MacKie 1975, 85 ff.
35 MacKie 1965, 1971.
36 MacKie 1975, 85 ff.
37 MacKie 1975, 89.
38 Renfrew 1973, 107.

CHAPTER 4. PREHISTORIC ASTRONOMY

 1 J. Hawkes 1967.
 2 Hawkins 1965.
 3 Baity 1973.
 4 Bergamini 1971, 22.
 5 Hawkins 1965, pl. 18.
 6 Thom 1967, 151; 1971, 36; MacKie 1974, 176.
 7 Bailey et al 1975.
 8 MacKie 1974, fig. 2.
 9 Bailey et al 1975.
10 Thom 1971, chap. 4.
11 Thom 1957, 154; 1971, 36.
12 Simpson 1967.
13 Thom 1967, fig. 8.1 and table 8.1.
14 Thom 1967, 155.
15 Thom 1971, 39.
16 Thom 1971, 39.
17 MacKie 1974, 118-85.
18 Ragg and Bibby 1966.
19 Bibby 1974.
20 MacKie 1975a.
21 MacKie 1974, 175.
22 Bailey et al 1975.
23 Burl 1976, chap. 3.
24 Thom 1967, 144 and 151.
25 Thom 1967, fig. 12.11.
26 Thom 1967, 99.
27 Hawkins 1968; 1974, 288.
28 Atkinson 1966.

29 Atkinson 1968.
30 Hawkins 1965, 104.
31 Thom 1967, 25.
32 Thom 1967, 18.
33 Thom 1967, 118; 1971, 45.
34 Thom 1971, 110.
35 Thom and Thom 1971; 1972; 1972a; 1973a; 1974.
36 Thom 1971, 18.
37 Thom 1971, 45-51.
38 Thom 1974a.

CHAPTER 5. STONEHENGE

1 Thom, Thom and Thom 1974.
2 Wernick 1974; Renfrew 1973, 226.
3 Stone 1958, chaps. 7 and 8.
4 Atkinson 1955.
5 Hawley 1924-8.
6 Atkinson 1960.
7 Hawkins 1964; 1965, 110.
8 Atkinson 1960, 25.
9 Thom, Thom and Thom 1974, fig. 9 and p. 84; Atkinson 1960, 69.
10 Atkinson 1960, 90.
11 Jewell and Dimbleby 1966.
12 H. H. Thomas 1923.
13 Atkinson 1960, 49.
14 Kellaway 1971.
15 Atkinson 1974.
16 Atkinson 1960, 105 ff.
17 Piggott 1941.
18 Alcock 1971, 105.
19 Jarman 1960.
20 Atkinson 1960, 204-6.
21 Atkinson 1960, 33 and 77 f.n.
22 Stone 1923, pl. 11.
23 E. H. Stone 1923; Stone 1958, 24; Atkinson 1960, 36; Newall 1959.
24 Stone 1958, chap. 8; Piggott 1964.
25 Atkinson 1960, pl. 23.
26 Atkinson 1960, pl. 18.
27 Thom, Thom and Thom 1974.
28 I have to thank Mr R. S. Newall for this suggestion.
29 Thom, Thom and Thom 1974, fig. 5.
30 Atkinson 1960, 48.
31 Thom, Thom and Thom 1974, fig. 9.
32 Thom 1967, 77.
33 Thom 1968, 1969.
34 Patrick 1974.
35 MacKie 1973a.
36 Hawkins 1965, pl. 9.
37 Hadingham 1975, fig. on p. 84.
38 Hawkins 1965, 110.
39 Hawkins 1965, pl. 18.
40 E. H. Stone 1924, pl. 7.

41 Atkinson 1966.
42 Hoyle 1966, 270; 1972, 38.
43 Hawkins 1964; 1965, 74.
44 Hawkins 1964, fig. 1.
45 Colton and Martin 1969.
46 Newham 1966; 1972, 15.
47 Hawley 1925, 22.
48 Thom, Thom and Thom 1974, 86.
49 Hoyle 1972.
50 Newham 1966.
51 Thom, Thom and Thom 1974, 84 ff.
52 Named 'Peter's Mound' after the late C. A. 'Peter' Newham.
53 I have to thank Professor A. Thom for this suggestion.
54 Newham 1972, 23; Vatcher 1973.
55 Newham 1972, fig. 5.
56 Hawkins 1965, fig. 12.
57 MacKie 1968, 281.
58 Lockyer 1906.
59 E. H. Stone 1924, 24.
60 Atkinson 1969, 95.
61 Atkinson 1960, 86 ff.
62 Atkinson 1969; 1960, 160-7; Piggott 1964.
63 McKerrell 1972.
64 Renfrew 1969; 1973.

CHAPTER 6. THE BEGINNINGS OF THE NEW ORDER

1 Piggott 1954; Stone 1958.
2 Penny and Wood 1973.
3 MacKie 1974.
4 Smith 1974, 101.
5 Piggott 1954, 17.
6 Smith 1974, 124.
7 Ashbee and Cornwall 1961, 131; Jewell and Dimbleby 1966.
8 Smith 1966; Piggott 1954, 18.
9 Smith 1974, 135; CBA 1971.
10 Piggott 1954, fig. 4; Smith 1965, figs. 5 and 6.
11 Atkinson 1961, 295.
12 Stone 1958, 88; Atkinson and Sorrell 1959.
13 Atkinson 1970.
14 Ashbee and Cornwall 1961, 131.
15 Atkinson 1974, 128.
16 Atkinson 1967; 1969; 1970.
17 Atkinson 1974, 128.
18 Thom and Thom 1972a; Thom 1974, 153.
19 I am grateful to Professor R. J. C. Atkinson for this information.
20 Atkinson 1970, 261.
21 Stone 1958, 83-6; Smith 1965.
22 Atkinson 1961, 295.
23 Wainwright 1971, 197.
24 Atkinson 1974, 128.
25 Smith 1965, 176.
26 Thom 1967, frontispiece and 89-91.

27 Thom 1967, 90-1.
28 Smith 1974, 120.
29 Stone 1958, pl. 27.
30 Cunnington 1931.
31 Piggott 1940.
32 Musson 1971, 368-72.
33 Musson 1971, 371, f.n.
34 Smith 1965, 245.
35 Atkinson 1955; 1974, 127; Penny and Wood 1973.
36 Stone 1948.
37 Penny and Wood 1973.
38 Penny and Wood 1973, fig. 14.
39 Atkinson 1974.
40 Mendelssohn 1974, 141.

CHAPTER 7. DURRINGTON WALLS: A LATE NEOLITHIC
CEREMONIAL CENTRE

1 Atkinson 1960.
2 Atkinson, Piggott and Sandars 1951.
3 Smith 1965, 228.
4 Stone 1957, chap. 7.
5 Stone, Piggott and Booth 1954; Wainwright 1971, 9.
6 Piggott 1959.
7 Wainwright 1971, fig. 3.
8 Ralph, Michael and Han 1973.
9 Wainwright 1971, 197.
10 Jewell and Dimbleby 1966, 314.
11 Atkinson 1960, 86.
12 Atkinson 1971, 362.
13 Musson 1971.
14 Musson 1971.
15 Musson 1971.
16 Bersu 1940; Cunliffe 1974, 165.
17 Musson 1971, 364, f.n.
18 Musson 1971, 365, f.n.
19 Zeuner 1963.
20 Harcourt 1971, 349.
21 Burl 1969, 7.
22 Wainwright 1969, 120; 1971, 234.
23 Wainwright 1974.
24 Morley and Brainerd 1956.
25 Wainwright 1971, 217.
26 Wainwright and Longworth 1971, 247.
27 C.B.A. 1971 ff.
28 Musson 1971.
29 Caldwell and McCann 1941.
30 Bartram 1791; Frazer 1922, 484.
31 Wainwright 1971, 233.
32 Piggott 1954, 89.
33 Marwick 1974.
34 Thom 1967, 73-7.
35 Wainwright 1971, 217-19.
36 MacKie 1974a, pl. IX.

CHAPTER 8. OTHER CEREMONIAL CENTRES IN SOUTHERN ENGLAND

1 Cunnington 1929.
2 Burleigh, Longworth and Wainwright 1972, 396.
3 Cunnington 1929, pl. 17.
4 Cunnington 1932, 475-6.
5 Cunnington 1929, 17.
6 Thom 1967, 73-5.
7 Piggott 1940, 207.
8 Musson 1971, 372.
9 Wainwright 1969, 117; 1970, 210.
10 Wainwright 1970a, 1971a.
11 Ralph, Michael and Han 1973.
12 Wainwright 1971a.
13 Thomas 1971, 29.
14 C.B.A. 1971 ff.
15 Piggott 1954, 36 ff; C.B.A. 1971 ff.
16 Piggott 1954, 36 ff and refs.
17 C.B.A. 1971 ff.
18 British Museum 1974.
19 *Radiocarbon 18* (1976), 32-3. The mean standard deviation is obtained thus, $\dfrac{\Sigma\sigma}{n}\bigg/\sqrt{n}.$
20 Piggott 1954, fig. 1.

CHAPTER 9. EXPANSION TO ORKNEY

1 RCAHMS 1946; MacKie 1975, chap. 8; Laing 1975.
2 Warren *et al* 1936.
3 Piggott 1954, 321.
4 Clarke 1970, 268.
5 Childe 1931 and 1950; Piggott 1954, 374; RCAHMS 1946; MacKie 1975, 243; Laing 1974.
6 Petrie 1868; Traill 1868.
7 Childe 1931.
8 Childe and Grant 1939.
9 Clarke 1970, 189.
10 Childe 1931, 179.
11 Wainwright 1956.
12 Marwick 1974.
13 D. V. Clarke 1976. I am very grateful to Dr Clarke for telling me about the radiocarbon dates in advance of his publication of them.
14 Childe 1931, 38.
15 Childe and Grant 1939, 30.
16 Childe 1950, pl. 3; Piggott 1954, pl. xi.
17 Hamilton 1956.
18 Childe 1931, 179.
19 Warren *et al* 1936.
20 Piggott 1954, 321.
21 Childe and Grant 1939, 26.
22 Wainwright and Longworth 1973.
23 Clark 1970, 269.

24 Childe 1931, 179.
25 Childe 1931, 41.
26 Childe 1931, 61 ff.
27 Laing 1868, 76.
28 Childe 1931, 204.
29 Piggott 1954, 324.
30 RCAHMS 1946, 2.
31 MacKie 1961.
32 Marwick 1974.
33 Henshall 1963, 183.
34 MacKie 1965, 143.
35 RCAHMS 1946, 2.
36 MacKie 1974a, 165.
37 MacKie 1972a, 2, 177.
38 Lethbridge 1952, fig. 1.
39 MacKie 1965; Henshall 1972.
40 Childe 1931, pl. LIV, 2; 1950, pl. 6.
41 C.B.A. 1973, 70; Marwick 1974.
42 Childe 1931, 96.
43 MacKie 1974a, 187.
44 Thomas 1890, 414-15.
45 MacKie 1974a, 66.
46 Lysaght 1974, pl. 5.
47 Lysaght 1974.
48 I have to thank Mr Nicholas Hawley for pointing this out to me.
49 Thom and Thom 1973.
50 Thomas 1851.
51 RCAHMS 1946, 2, 299.
52 Lysaght 1974, pl. 8.
53 RCAHMS 1946, ii, fig. 397.
54 Lysaght 1974, pl. 8.
55 Thom and Thom 1972.
56 Thom and Thom 1973.
57 Thom 1971, 19.
58 Thom 1971, 19.
59 Thom 1971, chap. 9.

CHAPTER 10. LATE NEOLITHIC SOCIETY: CRISIS AND RESPONSE

1 Morley and Brainerd 1956; Thompson 1956; Coe 1966.
2 A. L. Smith 1950; Coe 1965, 1965a.
3 MacKie 1961.
4 Coe 1966, 17 ff.
5 Renfrew 1973, chaps 7 and 11; Wainwright 1975.
6 Wainwright 1975, 70.
7 Willey 1956.
8 MacKie 1961, 1977.
9 MacKie 1977.
10 MacKie 1974, 157.
11 MacKie 1974, 160.
12 Wainwright 1971, 409.
13 Peacock 1968, 1969; Cunliffe 1974, 102; Harding 1974, 91-2.
14 Piggott 1954, 328-9; Wainwright and Longworth 1971, 244 ff.

15 Burleigh, Longworth and Wainwright 1972.
16 Wainwright and Longworth 1971, 266.
17 Helbaek 1952.
18 Wainwright 1971, fig. 27.
19 Wainwright 1971, 246 ff., fig. 29.
20 Hadingham 1974, jacket; O'Kelly 1964, 1970, 1973.
21 Piggott 1954, fig. 33.
22 Patrick 1974.
23 Wainwright 1971, fig. 97.
24 Wainwright 1971, 243 ff.
25 Waddell 1974, 33.
26 Ritchie 1974.
27 I am very grateful to Dr Graham Ritchie for allowing me to mention the Stenness discoveries, and the radiocarbon dates (2356 ± 65 bc and 2238 ± 70 bc) in advance of publication.
28 Smith 1965, 141.
29 Smith 1965, 59 ff.
30 Stone and Wallis 1951, 133.
31 Wainwright 1971, fig. 82.
32 Piggott 1954, fig. 13.
33 Klindt-Jensen 1957, 61.
34 Morley and Brainerd 1956, p. 19.
35 Piggott 1948.
36 Piggott and Simpson 1971.
37 Lewis 1974 and references.
38 Piggott 1968.
39 Burn 1969.
40 Lewis 1974.
41 Neugebauer 1952; Piggott 1968, 124-5.

Bibliography

Alcock, Leslie (1971) *Arthur's Britain; history and archaeology AD 367-634*. Allen Lane, Harmondsworth. (1973) Penguin, New York.

Ashbee, Paul and Cornwall, Ian W. (1961) 'An experiment in field archaeology.' *Antiquity 35*, pp. 129-34.

Atkinson, R. J. C. (1953) *Field Archaeology*. Methuen, London.

— (1955) 'The Dorset Cursus.' *Antiquity 29*, pp. 4-9.

— (1960) *Stonehenge*. Penguin Books, Harmondsworth.

— (1966) 'Moonshine on Stonehenge.' *Antiquity 40*, pp. 212-16.

— (1967) 'Silbury Hill.' *Antiquity 41*, pp. 259-62.

— (1967a) 'Further radiocarbon dates for Stonehenge.' *Antiquity 41*, pp. 63-4.

— (1968) Review of A. Thom, *Megalithic sites in Britain* (1967) in *Antiquity 42*, pp. 77-8.

— (1969) 'The date of Silbury Hill.' *Antiquity 43*. p. 216.

— (1970) 'Silbury Hill, 1969-70.' *Antiquity 44*, pp. 313-14.

— (1971) 'The Southern Circle at Durrington Walls: a numerical investigation.' in Wainwright (1971), pp. 355-62.

— (1974) 'Neolithic science and technology.' *Phil. Trans. Roy. Soc. Lond. A, 276*, no. 1257, pp. 123-31.

— (1974a) 'The Stonehenge bluestones.' *Antiquity 48*, pp. 62-3.

— (1975) 'Megalithic astronomy — a prehistorian's comments.' *J. Hist. Astron. 6*, pp. 42-52.

Atkinson, R. J. C., Piggott, S. and Sandars, N. K. (1951) *Excavations at Dorchester, Oxon, part 1*. Ashmolean Museum, Oxford.

Atkinson, R. J. C. and Sorrell, Alan (1959) *Stonehenge and Avebury*. HMSO, London.

Bailey, M. E. *et al*. (1974) 'Survey of three megalithic sites in Argyllshire.' *Nature 253*, pp. 431-3.

Baity, E. C. (1973) 'Archaeoastronomy and Ethnoastronomy so far.' *Curr. Anthrop. 14*, pp. 389-449.

Bartram, W. (1791) *Travels through N and S Carolina, Georgia, E and W Florida . . . and the country of the Choctaws*. James & Johnson, Philadelphia.

Bass, Robert W. (1974) 'Did worlds collide?' *Pensée 4*, no. 3, pp. 9-20.

— (1974a) ' "Proofs" of the stability of the solar system.' *Pensée 4*, no. 3, pp. 21-6.

Bergamini, D. (1971) *The Universe*. Time-Life International (Nederland), N.V.

Berriman, A. E. (1953) *Historical metrology*. J. M. Dent, London.

— (1954) 'Weights and measures through the ages.' *Monthly Review* of the Institute of Weights and Measures Administration, Oct. 1954, 3 pp.

— (1955) 'A new approach to the study of ancient metrology.' *Revue d'Assyriologie et d'Archéologie Orientale 49*, no. 4, pp. 193-201.

Bersu, G. (1940) 'Excavations at Little Woodbury, part 1.' *Proc. Prehist. Soc. 6*, pp. 30-111.

Bibby, Cyril (1972) *Scientist extraordinary — Thomas Henry Huxley*. Pergamon Press, Oxford.

Bibby, J. S. (1974) 'Petrofabric analysis.' Appendix to MacKie (1974), pp. 191-4.

Bøye, Vilhelm (1896) *Fund af Egekister fra Bronzealderen i Danmark*. Copenhagen.

Britannica (1929) *Encyclopaedia Britannica.* 14th ed., 24 vols. London.
British Museum (1974) *Grimes Graves* (exhibition leaflet), The British Museum, London.
Broadbent, S. R. (1955) 'Quantum hypotheses.' *Biometrika 42,* pp. 45-7.
Burl, H. A. W. (1970) 'Henges: internal features and regional groups.' *Arch. Journ. 126,* pp. 1-28.
— (1972) 'Torhouskie stone circle, Wigtownshire.' *Trans. Dumfries & Galloway Nat. Hist. & Ant. Soc.,* 3rd ser., *49,* pp. 24-34.
— (1973) 'Dating the British stone circles.' *Amer. Scientist 61,* pp. 167-74.
— (1973a) 'The recumbent stone circles of north-east Scotland.' *Proc. Soc. Ant. Scot. 102* (1969-70), pp. 56-81.
— (1976) *The stone circles of the British Isles.* Yale University Press, New Haven and London.
Burleigh, R., Longworth, I. H. and Wainwright, G. J. (1972) 'Relative and absolute dating of four late Neolithic enclosures: an exercise in the interpretation of radiocarbon measurements.' *Proc. Prehist. Soc. 38,* pp. 389-407.
Burn, A. R. (1969) 'Holy men on islands in pre-Christian Britain.' *Glasgow Arch. Journ. 1,* pp. 2-6.
Caldwell, J. and McCann, C. (1941) *Irene Mound site, Chatham County, Georgia.* University of Georgia Press, Georgia.
Camden, William (1789) *Britannia.* Retranslated and revised by Richard Gough.
Case, Humphrey (1969) 'Neolithic explanations.' *Antiquity 43,* pp. 176-86.
Childe, V. Gordon (1931) *Skara Brae: a Pictish village in Orkney.* Kegan Paul, London.
— (1935) *The prehistory of Scotland.* Kegan Paul, London.
— (1938) 'The Orient and Europe.' *Adv. of Science,* pp. 181-96 and in *Nature 142,* pp. 557-9 and 600-3.
— (1940) *Prehistoric Communities of the British Isles.* W. & R. Chambers, Edinburgh. Blom, Benjamin, New York.
— (1946) *Scotland before the Scots.* Methuen, London.
— (1947) 'A Stone Age settlement at the Braes of Rinyo, Rousay, Orkney.' *Proc. Soc. Ant. Scot. 81* (1946-7), pp. 16-42.
— (1950) *Ancient dwellings at Skara Brae, Orkney,* HMSO, London.
— (1957) *The dawn of European civilisation,* 6th ed. Routledge & Kegan Paul, London. (1958) Knopf, New York.
Childe, V. G. and Grant, Walter G. (1939) 'A Stone Age settlement at the Braes of Rinyo, Rousay, Orkney (first report).' *Proc. Soc. Ant. Scot. 73* (1938-9), pp. 6-31.
Clark, J. G. D. (1947) 'Sheep and swine in the husbandry of prehistoric Europe.' *Antiquity 21,* pp. 122-36.
Clark, J. G. D. and Godwin, H. (1962) 'The Neolithic in the Cambridgeshire fens.' *Antiquity 36,* pp. 10-23.
Clarke, David L. (1968) *Analytical Archaeology.* Methuen, London. (1971) Barnes & Noble, New York.
— (1970) *Beaker pottery of Great Britain and Ireland.* Cambridge University Press, Cambridge and New York.
Clarke, D. V. (1976) *The Neolithic village at Skara Brae, Orkney: Excavations 1972-1973, an interim report.* Department of the Environment, Edinburgh.
Coe, M. D. (1966) *The Maya.* Thames & Hudson, London. Praeger, New York.
Coe, William R. (1965) 'Tikal: ten years study of a Maya ruin in the lowlands of Guatemala.' *Expedition 8,* no. 1. pp. 5-56, Philadelphia.
— (1965a) 'Tikal, Guatemala, and emergent Maya civilisation' *Science 147,* no. 3664, pp. 1401-19, Washington.
Coles, John R. (1972) *Field Archaeology in Britain.* Methuen, London. Barnes & Noble, New York.

Colton, R. and Martin, R. L. (1967) 'Eclipse cycles and eclipses at Stonehenge.' *Nature 213*, pp. 476-8.

— (1969) 'Eclipse prediction at Stonehenge.' *Nature 221*, pp. 1011-12.

Council for British Archaeology (1971 ff) *Archaeological site index to radio-carbon dates for Great Britain and Ireland*. CBA, London.

Crawford, G. I. and MacKie, E. W. (1977) 'Units of length and geometry in Scottish brochs.' *Proc. Prehist. Soc.*, forthcoming.

Cunliffe, Barry (1974) *Iron Age Communities in Britain*. Routledge & Kegan Paul, London and Boston.

Cunnington, M. E. (1927) *Woodhenge*. George Simpson, Devizes.

— (1931) 'The "Sanctuary" on Overton Hill near Avebury.' *Wilts. Arch. Mag. 45*, no. 154, pp. 300-35.

Daniel, G. E. (1958) *The megalith builders of western Europe*. Hutchinson, London.

Darlington, C. D. (1968) *The evolution of man and society*. George Allen & Unwin, London. (1970) Simon & Schuster, New York.

Dingle, Herbert (1972) *Science at the crossroads*. Martin Brian & O'Keeffe, London. (1974) International Pubns. Service, New York.

Doran, J. E. and Hodson, F. R. (1975) *Mathematics and computers in Archaeology*. Edinburgh University Press, Edinburgh. Harvard University Press, Massachusetts.

Dymond, D. P. (1974) *Archaeology and history: a plea for reconciliation*. Thames & Hudson, London. Transatlantic Arts, Levittown.

Fleming, A. (1972) 'Vision and design: approaches to ceremonial monument typology.' *Man 7*, pp. 57-73.

Fletcher, E. N. R. (1968) 'Ancient metrology.' *Survey Review 19* (1967-8), pp. 270-7.

Frazer, Sir James (1907-15) *The Golden Bough*. 12 vols. Macmillan, London and New York.

— (1922) *The Golden Bough* (abridged edition). Macmillan, London and New York.

Freeman, P. R. (1976) 'A Bayesian analysis of the megalithic yard.' *J. Roy. Statist. Soc. A. 139*, part I, pp. 20-55.

Glob, P. V. (1967) *Danish prehistoric monuments*. Faber & Faber, London.

— (1970) *The Mound People: Danish Bronze Age man preserved*. Faber & Faber, London. (1974) Cornell University Press, Ithaca.

Hadingham, Evan (1974) *Ancient carvings in Britain: a mystery*. Garnstone Press, London.

— (1975) *Circles and standing stones*. Heinemann, London. Walker, New York.

Harcourt, R. A. (1971) 'Animal bones from Durrington Walls' in Wainwright (1971), pp. 334-50.

Harding, D. W. (1974) *The Iron Age in lowland Britain*. Routledge & Kegan Paul, London.

Harris, J. C. (1971) 'Explanations in prehistory.' *Proc. Prehist. Soc. 37*, pp. 38-55.

Hawkes, C. F. C. (1954) 'Archaeological theory and method: some suggestions from the old world.' *Amer. Anthrop. 56*, pp. 155-68.

Hawkes, Jacquetta (1967) 'God in the machine.' *Antiquity 41*, pp. 174-80.

Hawkins, G. S. (1963) 'Stonehenge decoded.' *Nature 200*, pp. 306-8.

— (1964) 'Stonehenge: a Neolithic computer.' *Nature 202*, pp. 1258-61. Also in Hawkins and White (1965), pp. 174-81.

— (1965) 'Callanish, a Scottish Stonehenge.' *Science 147*, no. 3654, pp. 127-30. Also in Hawkins and White (1965), pp. 182-90.

— (1968) 'Astro-archaeology.' *Vistas in Astronomy 10*, pp. 45-88.

— (1971) 'Photogrammetric survey of Stonehenge and Callanish.' *Nat. Geog. Soc. Research Reps: 1965 projects*, pp. 101-8.

— (1974) 'Astronomical alignments in Britain, Egypt and Peru.' *Phil. Trans. Roy. Soc. Lond. A, 276*, pp. 157-67.

Hawkins, G. S. and White, J. B. (1965) *Stonehenge decoded.* Souvenir Press, London. Doubleday, New York.

Hawley, W. (1924; 1925; 1926; 1928) 'Excavations at Stonehenge.' *Ant. Journ. 4,* pp. 30-9; *5,* pp. 21-50; *6,* pp. 1-16; *8,* pp. 149-76.

Heggie, D. C. (1972) 'Megalithic lunar observatories: an astronomer's view.' *Antiquity 46,* pp. 43-8.

Helbaek, H. (1952) 'Early crops in southern England.' *Proc. Prehist. Soc. 18,* pp. 194-233.

Henshall, Audrey S. (1963, 1972) *The chambered tombs of Scotland.* 2 vols. Edinburgh University Press, Edinburgh. Aldine, Chicago.

Hole, Frank and Heizer, Robert F. (1973) *An introduction to prehistoric archaeology.* Holt, Rinehart & Winston, New York.

Hoyle, F. (1966) 'Speculations on Stonehenge.' *Antiquity 40,* pp. 262-76.

— (1966a) 'Stonehenge: an eclipse predictor.' *Nature 211,* no. 5048, pp. 454-6.

— (1972) *From Stonehenge to modern cosmology.* W. H. Freeman, San Francisco.

Hutchinson, G. Evelyn (1972) 'Long Meg reconsidered.' *Amer. Scientist 60,* pp. 24-31.

— (1972a) 'Long Meg reconsidered: part 2.' *Amer. Scientist 60,* pp. 210-19.

Huxley, T. H. (1869) 'Geological reform.' *Q. J. Geol. Soc. 25,* pp. xxviii-liii and in *Collected Essays, 8,* pp. 305-39, (1893-4), Macmillan, London.

Ivimy, John (1974) *The sphinx and the megaliths.* Turnstone Books, London. (1975) Harper & Row, New York.

Jarman, A. O. H. (1960) *The legend of Merlin.* Inaugural lecture. University of Wales Press, Cardiff.

Jewell, P. A. and Dimbleby, G. W. (1966) 'The experimental earthwork on Overton Down, Wiltshire, England: the first four years.' *Proc. Prehist. Soc. 32,* pp. 313-42.

Kellaway, C. A. (1971) 'Glaciation and the stones of Stonehenge.' *Nature 233,* pp. 30-5.

Kendall, David (1971) Review of A. Thom, *Megalithic lunar observatories* in *Antiquity 45,* pp. 310-12.

— (1974) 'Hunting quanta.' *Phil. Trans. Roy. Soc. Lond. A, 276,* no. 1257, pp. 231-66.

Klindt-Jensen, Ole (1957) *Denmark before the Vikings.* Thames & Hudson, London.

Laing, Lloyd R. (1974) *Orkney and Shetland: an archaeological guide.* David & Charles, Newton Abbott and Vermont.

Laing, S. (1868) 'On the use of the burgs or brochs.' *Proc. Soc. Ant. Scot. 7,* (1866-8), pp. 56-79.

Lamb, H. H. (1974) 'Climate, vegetation and forest limits in early civilised times.' *Phil. Trans. Roy. Soc. Lond. A, 276,* no. 1257, pp. 195-230.

Leach, E. R. (1956) 'Primitive time reckoning.' in Singer, Holmyard and Hall, eds., *A history of technology,* vol. 1, pp. 110-127, Clarendon Press, Oxford.

MacKie, Euan W. (1961) 'New light on the end of the Maya Classic culture at Benque Viejo, British Honduras.' *Amer. Antiquity 27,* no. 2, pp. 216-24.

— (1965) 'The origin and development of the broch and wheelhouse building culture of the Scottish Iron Age.' *Proc. Prehist. Soc. 31,* pp. 93-146.

— (1968) 'Stone circles: for savages or savants?' *Curr. Arch.,* no. 11, pp. 279-83.

— (1971) 'English migrants and Scottish brochs.' *Glasgow Arch. Journ. 2,* pp. 39-71.

— (1972) 'Radiocarbon dates for two Mesolithic shell heaps and a Neolithic axe factory in Scotland.' *Proc. Prehist. Soc. 38,* pp. 412-16.

— (1972a) *The origin and development of the broch and wheelhouse building cultures of the Scottish Iron Age,* Ph.D. thesis. University of Glasgow.

— (1973) 'A challenge to the integrity of science?' *New Scientist,* Jan. 11, pp. 76-7.

— (1973a) 'Duntreath.' *Curr. Arch. 4,* no. 1, pp. 6-7.

— (1974) 'Archaeological tests on supposed prehistoric astronomical sites in

Scotland.' *Phil. Trans. Roy. Soc. Lond. A, 276*, no. 1257, pp. 167-93.

— (1974a) *Dun Mor Vaul: an Iron Age broch on Tiree*. University of Glasgow Press, Glasgow.

— (1975) 'The brochs of Scotland.' in P. J. Fowler, ed., *Recent work in rural archaeology*, pp. 72-92, Moonraker Press, Bradford-on-Avon.

— (1975a) *Scotland: an archaeological guide*. Faber & Faber, London.

— (1975b) 'Historical parallels for the megalithic yard.' in Freeman (1976), pp. 47-8.

— (1976) 'The vitrified forts of Scotland.' in D. Harding, ed., *Hillforts*, pp. 205-35, Academic Press, London.

— (1977) *The megalith builders*. Phaidon Press, London, forthcoming.

— (1977a) *Excavations at Xunantunich (Benique Viejo). British Honduras, in 1959-60*, Glasgow University Press, forthcoming.

Marwick, E. W. (1974) 'New light on our ancient monuments.' *The Orcadian*, Nov. 7.

Mendelssohn, Kurt (1974) *The riddle of the pyramids*. Thames & Hudson, London. Praeger, New York.

Michel, Henri (1967) *Scientific instruments in art and history*. Translated by R. E. W. Maddison and Francis R. Maddison, Barrie & Rockliff, London.

Morley, S. G. and Brainerd, G. W. (1956) *The ancient Maya*. Stanford University Press, California.

Moroney, M. J. (1956) *Facts from figures*. Penguin Books, Harmondsworth and New York.

Morris, R. W. B. (1968) 'The cup-and-ring marks and similar sculptures of Scotland.' *Proc. Soc. Ant. Scot. 100* (1967-8), pp. 47-78.

Morris, R. W. B. and Bailey, D. C. (1966) 'The cup-and-ring marks and similar sculptures of south-west Scotland: a survey.' *Proc. Soc. Ant. Scot. 98* (1964-6), pp. 150-72.

Morrison, Ian (1969) 'Some problems in correlating archaeological material and old shore lines.' *Scott. Arch. Forum 1*, pp. 1-7.

Musson, C. R. (1971) 'A study of possible building forms at Durrington Walls, Woodhenge and The Sanctuary.' in Wainwright (1971), pp. 363-77.

Neugebauer, D. (1952) 'Tamil astronomy.' *Osiris 10*, pp. 252-76.

Newall, R. S. (1959) *Stonehenge, Wiltshire*. HMSO, London.

Newham, C. A. (1966) 'Stonehenge — a Neolithic observatory.' *Nature 211*, pp. 456-8.

— (1972) *The astronomical significance of Stonehenge*. John Blackburn, Leeds.

Newton, R. R. and Jenkins, R. E. (1972) 'Possible use of Stonehenge.' *Nature 239*, pp. 511-12.

Noddle, Barbara (1974) 'The animal bones from Dun Mor Vaul.' in MacKie (1974), pp. 187-98.

O'Kelly, Claire (1973) 'Passage grave art in the Boyne valley, Ireland.' *Proc. Prehist. Soc. 39*, pp. 354-82.

O'Kelly, M. J. (1964) 'New Grange, County Meath.' *Antiquity 38*, pp. 288-90.

— (1970) 'New Grange passage grave, Ireland: the mural art.' *Actes du VII* ⁱᵉᵐᵉ *Congrès Int. des Sciences Préhist. et Protohist.*, pp. 534-6, Prague.

— (1972) 'Further radiocarbon dates from New Grange, Co. Meath, Ireland.' *Antiquity 46*, pp. 226-7.

Olsson, I. U., ed. (1970) *Radiocarbon variations and absolute chronology*. Proceedings of the 12th Nobel Symposium, Wiley, London and New York.

Patrick, J. (1974) 'Midwinter sunrise at New Grange.' *Nature 249*, pp. 517-19.

Patrick, J. and Butler, C. J. (1976) 'On the interpretation of the Carnac menhirs and alignments by A. Thom and A. S. Thom.' *Ulster Journ. Arch. 35*, forthcoming.

Penny, A. and Wood, J. E. (1973) 'The Dorset Cursus complex — a Neolithic astronomical observatory?' *Arch. Journ. 130*, pp. 44-76.

Petrie, George (1868) 'Notice of ruins of ancient dwellings at Skara, Bay of Skaill, . . . Orkney . . .' *Proc. Soc. Ant. Scot. 7*, part 1 (1867-8), pp. 201-19.

Petrie, Sir W. M. F. (1929) 'Ancient weights and measures.' *Encyclopaedia Britannica*, 14th edn., *14*, pp. 142-5.

— (1934) *Measures and weights*. Methuen, London.

Piggott, S. (1940) 'Timber circles: a re-examination.' *Arch, Journ. 96*, pp. 193-22.

— (1941) 'The sources of Geoffrey of Monmouth II: the Stonehenge story.' *Antiquity 15*, pp. 305-19.

— (1948) 'The excavations at Cairnpapple Hill, West Lothian, 1947-8.' *Proc. Soc. Ant. Scot. 82* (1947-8), pp. 68-123.

— (1950) *Prehistoric India*. Penguin Books, Harmondsworth.

— (1954) *Neolithic cultures of the British Isles*. Cambridge University Press, Cambridge.

— (1959) 'The radiocarbon dates from Durrington Walls.' *Antiquity 33*, pp. 289-90.

— (1964) 'The mystery of Stonehenge.' *Life International*, July 13, pp. 58-61.

Piggott, S. and Simpson, D. D. A. (1971) 'Excavation of a stone circle at Croft Moraig, Perthshire, Scotland.' *Proc. Prehist. Soc. 37*, pp. 1-15.

Porteous, H. L. (1973) 'Megalithic yard or megalithic myth?' *J. Hist. Astron. 4*, pp. 22-4.

Ragg, J. M. and Bibby, J. S. (1966) 'Frost weathering and solifluction products in southern Scotland.' *Geog. Annlr. 48*, ser. A1, pp. 12-23.

Ralph, E. K. and Michael, H. N. (1967) 'Problems of the radiocarbon calendar.' *Archaeometry 10*, pp. 3-11.

Ralph, E. K., Michael, H. N. and Han, M. C. (1973) 'Radiocarbon dates and reality.' *MASCA Newsletter 9*, No. 1, pp. 1-20. University Museum, Pennsylvania.

Renfrew, Colin (1968) 'Wessex without Mycenae.' *Ann. Brit. Sch. Arch. at Athens 63*, pp. 277-85.

— (1970) 'The tree-ring calibration of radiocarbon: an archaeological evaluation.' *Proc. Prehist. Soc. 36*, pp. 280-311.

— (1973) *Before civilisation*. Jonathan Cape, London. Knopf, New York.

— (1974) 'British prehistory: changing configurations.' in Renfrew, ed. (1974), pp. 1-40.

Renfrew, Colin, ed. (1974) *British prehistory: a new outline*. Duckworth, London. (1975) Noyes Press, Brooklyn.

Ritchie, J. N. G. (1974) 'Excavations at the stone circle at Balbirnie, Fife.' *Arch. Journ. 131*, pp. 1-32.

Rivet, A. L. F. (1971) 'Hillforts in action.' in M. Jesson and D. Hill, eds., *The Iron Age and its hillforts*, pp. 189-202, Southampton University Press.

Rottlander, Rolf C. A. (1973) 'Mathematische Beziehungen einiger antiker Masssysteme zueinander.' *Mitteilungen der Berliner Gesellschaft für Anthropologie, Ethnologie und Urgeschichte, 2*, pp. 168-73.

Roy, A. E. (1963) 'A new survey of the Tormore circles.' *Trans. Glasgow Arch. Soc.* n.s. *15*, part 2, pp. 59-67.

RCAHMS (1946) The Royal Commission on the Ancient and Historical Monuments of Scotland, *Twelfth report with an inventory of the ancient monuments of Orkney and Shetland*. 3 vols. HMSO, Edinburgh.

Selkirk, A., Burl, H. A. W. and MacKie, E. W. (1969) 'Stone circles again.' *Curr. Arch.* no. 12 (Jan.) pp. 27-8.

Simpson, D. D. A. (1967) 'Excavations at Kintraw, Argyll.' *Proc. Soc. Ant. Scot. 99* (1966-7), pp. 54-9.

Skinner, F. G. (1956) 'Measures and weights.' in Singer, Holmyard and Hall, eds., *A history of technology*, vol. 1, pp. 773-84, Clarendon Press, Oxford.

Smith, A. L. (1950) *Uaxactun, Guatemala: excavations of 1931-1937*. Publ. no. 588,

Carnegie Institution of Washington, Washington DC.

Smith, I. F. (1965) *Windmill Hill and Avebury*. Clarendon Press, Oxford.

— (1966) 'Windmill Hill and its implications.' *Palaeohistoria 12*, pp. 469-81.

— (1974) 'The Neolithic.' in Renfrew, ed. (1974), pp. 100-36.

Somerville, B. (1912) 'Astronomical indications in the megalithic monument at Callanish.' *Journ. Brit. Astron. Assoc. 23*, pp. 83 ff.

— (1923) 'Instances of orientation in prehistoric monuments of the British Isles.' *Archaeologia 73*, pp. 193-224.

Stone, E. H. (1924) *The stones of Stonehenge*. Robert Scott, London.

Stone, J. F. S. (1948) 'The Stonehenge Cursus and its affinities.' *Arch. Journ. 104*, pp. 7-19.

— (1958) *Wessex before the Celts*. Thames & Hudson, London.

Stone, J. F. S., Piggott, S. and Booth, A. (1954) 'Durrington Walls, Wiltshire: recent excavations at a ceremonial site of the early second millennium B.C.' *Ant. Journ. 34*, pp. 155-77.

Stone, J. F. S. and Wallis, F. S. (1951) 'Third report . . . on the petrological identification of stone axes.' *Proc. Prehist. Soc. 17*, pp. 99-158.

Suess, H. E. (1965) 'Secular variations of the cosmic ray-produced Carbon 14 in the atmosphere and their interpretations.' *Journ. Geophys. Res. 70*, pp. 5937-52.

— (1970) 'Bristlecone pine calibration of the radiocarbon time-scale 5200 B.C. to the present.' in I. U. Olsson, ed. (1970), pp. 303-12.

Szymanski, H. (1956) *Jednostki Miar*. Panstwowe Wydawnictwa Techniczne, Warsaw.

Thom, A. (1954) 'The solar observatories of megalithic man.' *Journ. Brit. Astron. Assoc. 64*, pp. 396-404.

— (1955) 'A statistical examination of the megalithic sites in Britain.' *Journ. Roy. Statist. Soc. A, 118*, pp. 275-91.

— (1961) 'The geometry of megalithic man.' *Math. Gaz. 45*, pp. 93 ff.

— (1961a) 'The egg-shaped standing stone rings of Britain.' *Archs. Int. d'Hist. des Sciences 14*, pp. 291-303.

— (1962) 'The megalithic unit of length.' *Journ. Roy. Statist. Soc. A, 125*, pp. 243-51.

— (1964) 'The larger units of length of megalithic man.' *Journ. Roy. Statist. Soc. A, 127*, pp. 527-33.

— (1966) 'Megaliths and mathematics.' *Antiquity 40*, pp. 121-8.

— (1967) *Megalithic sites in Britain*. Oxford University Press, Oxford and New York.

— (1968) 'The metrology and geometry of cup-and-ring marks.' *Systematics 6*, no. 3 (Dec.), pp. 173-89.

— (1969) 'The geometry of cup-and-ring marks.' *Trans. Ancient Mon. Soc. 16* (1968-9), pp. 77-87.

— (1974) 'Astronomical significance of prehistoric monuments in western Europe.' *Phil. Trans. Roy. Soc. Lond. A, 276*, no 1257, pp. 149-56.

— (1974a) 'A megalithic lunar observatory on Islay.' *J. Hist. Astron. 5*, pp. 50-1.

Thom, A. and Thom. A. S. (1971) 'The astronomical significance of the large Carnac menhirs.' *J. Hist. Astron. 2*, pp. 147-60.

— (1972) 'The Carnac alignments.' *Journ. Hist. Astron. 3*, pp. 11-26.

— (1972a) 'The uses of the alignments at Le Menec, Carnac.' *Journ. Hist. Astron. 3*, pp. 151-64.

— (1973) 'A megalithic observatory in Orkney: the Ring of Brodgar and its cairns.' *J. Hist. Astron. 4*, pp. 11-23.

— (1973a) 'The Kerlescan cromlechs.' *J. Hist. Astron. 4*, pp. 168-73.

— (1974) 'The Kermario alignments.' *J. Hist. Astron. 5*, pp. 30-47.

— (1975) 'Further work on the Brodgar lunar observatory.' *Journ. Hist. Astron. 6*, pp. 100-14.

Thom, A., Thom, A. S. and Thom, A. S. (1974) 'Stonehenge.' *J. Hist. Astron.* 5, pp. 71-90.
— (1975) 'Stonehenge as a possible lunar observatory.' *J. Hist. Astron.* 6, pp. 19-30.
Thomas, Charles (1971) *The early Christian archaeology of north Britain.* Oxford University Press, Oxford and New York.
Thomas, F. W. L. (1851) 'Account of some of the Celtic antiquities of Orkney.' *Archaeologia 34*, pp. 88-136.
— (1890) 'On the duns of the Outer Hebrides.' *Arch. Scot.* 5, pp. 365-415.
Thomas, H. H. (1923) 'The source of the stones of Stonehenge.' *Ant. Journ. 111*, pp. 239-60.
Thompson, J. Eric S. (1956) *The rise and fall of Maya civilisation.* Gollancz, London. (1973) University of Oklahoma Press, Norman.
Traill, William (1868) 'General remarks on the dwellings of pre-historic races in Orkney . . .' *Proc. Soc. Ant. Scot.* 7 (1867-8), part 2, pp. 426-39.
Vatcher, Lance and Faith (1973) 'Excavation of three post-holes in the Stonehenge car park.' *Wilts. Arch & Nat. Hist. Mag. 68*, pp. 57-63.
Waddell, John (1974) 'On some aspects of the late Neolithic and early Bronze Age in Ireland.' *Irish Arch. Res. Forum 1* (1974), pp. 32-8.
Wainwright, F. T., ed. (1955) *The problem of the Picts.* Nelson, London. Greenwood Press, Westport.
Wainwright, G. J. (1969) 'A review of henge monuments in the light of recent research.' *Proc. Prehist. Soc. 35*, pp. 112-33.
— (1970) 'Excavations at Marden, Wiltshire, 1969.' *Antiquity 44*, pp. 56-7.
— (1970a) 'Mount Pleasant.' *Curr. Arch.* no. 23 (Nov.), pp. 320-3.
— (1971) *Durrington Walls: excavations 1966-68.* Reports of the Research Committee of the Society of Antiquaries of London, no. 29, London.
— (1971a) 'The excavation of a Late Neolithic enclosure at Marden, Wiltshire.' *Ant. Journ. 51*, pp. 177-239.
— (1974) 'Religion and settlement in Essex 3000-1700 B.C.' in P. J. Fowler, ed., *Recent work in rural archaeology*, Moonraker Press, Bradford on Avon.
Wainwright, G. J. and Longworth, I. H. (1971) 'The Rinyo-Clacton culture reconsidered,' in Wainwright (1971), pp. 235-306.
Wernick, Robert (1974) *The monument builders.* Time Life Books (Nederland) B.V.
Wheeler, Fred (1966) 'Stonehenge: further software.' *New Scientist 31*, no. 507 (Aug. 1) pp. 251-3.
Wheeler, Sir R. E. M. (1966) *Civilisations of the Indus valley and beyond.* Thames & Hudson, London.
Willey, Gordon R. (1956) 'The structure of ancient Maya society: evidence from the southern lowlands.' *Amer. Anthrop. 58*, no. 5, pp. 777-82.
Williamson, J. B. (1974) 'Megalithic units of length.' *Journ. Arch. Sci. 1*, pp. 381-2.
Zeuner, F. E. (1963) *A history of domesticated animals.* Hutchinson, London. (1964) Harper & Row, New York.

Index